North Korea and Myanmar

North Korea and Myanmar

Divergent Paths

ANDRAY ABRAHAMIAN

McFarland & Company, Inc., Publishers
Jefferson, North Carolina

LIBRARY OF CONGRESS CATALOGUING-IN-PUBLICATION DATA

Names: Abrahamian, Andray, author.
Title: North Korea and Myanmar : divergent paths / Andray Abrahamian.
Description: Jefferson, North Carolina : McFarland & Company, Inc., Publishers, 2018. | Includes bibliographical references and index.
Identifiers: LCCN 2017053914 | ISBN 9781476673707 (softcover : acid free paper) ∞
Subjects: LCSH: Korea (North)—Foreign relations. | Economic sanctions—Korea (North) | Korea (North)—Politics and government. | Burma—Foreign relations. | Economic sanctions—Burma. | Burma—Politics and government.
Classification: LCC DS935.65 .A27 2018 | DDC 951.93—dc23
LC record available at https://lccn.loc.gov/2017053914

BRITISH LIBRARY CATALOGUING DATA ARE AVAILABLE

ISBN (print) 978-1-4766-7370-7
ISBN (ebook) 978-1-4766-3200-1

© 2018 Andray Abrahamian. All rights reserved

No part of this book may be reproduced or transmitted in any form or by any means, electronic or mechanical, including photocopying or recording, or by any information storage and retrieval system, without permission in writing from the publisher.

Front cover image of signpost © 2018 HstrongART/iStock

Printed in the United States of America

McFarland & Company, Inc., Publishers
  Box 611, Jefferson, North Carolina 28640
  www.mcfarlandpub.com

Acknowledgments

First, my parents, Henry and Barbara, who made everything in my life possible, and my sister Aleena, for always looking out for me. Most of all I must thank my wife, Victoria, without whom this book would not have been conceivable.

I'd also like to thank in no particular order the following people for discussing, debating and enriching my understanding of North Korea or Myanmar: Geoffrey K. See, Jenny Town, Simon Cockerell, Bernard Seliger, James Pearson, Lee Yejung, Chad O'Carroll, Jean Lee, Sokeel Park, Anna Fifield, Curtis Melvin, Carla Vitantonio, Chris Green, Jacco Zwetsloot, Ryu Jong Sun, Hyonsuk and Myongfa Kim, Kirt Mausert, Nay Yan Oo, Ralph Cossa, Taehyun Kim, Vicky Bowman, Wai Moe, Susanne Kempel, Kevin Shepard and my students at the Myanmar-Korea Center for International Studies at the University of Yangon. Apologies for forgetting others. Sorry.

Thanks also to all the people who agreed to do interviews with me in Myanmar and to many people in Korea who I hope someday will be able to read this book.

I'd also like to thank the University of Southern California Korean Heritage Library for offering me an OKSHF Research Grant as well as the Jeju Peace Institute and Pacific Forum CSIS for resident fellowships during the writing period.

Table of Contents

Acknowledgments	v
Preface	ix
Introduction: Why These Countries	1
1. Cobbled and Cut	11
2. Militaries First, Economies Second	30
3. Becoming Pariah States	58
4. Ideologies	87
5. Propagation and Control	107
6. Sanctions	138
7. Why Myanmar and Not North Korea?	168
Conclusion: What Now?	185
Chapter Notes	197
Bibliography	217
Index	235

Preface

This is an historical account of how Myanmar and North Korea became pariah states and why Myanmar has been able to find its way out of isolation, while North Korea has not. It charts how the traumas of colonialism and decolonization created Asia's most militarized and isolated societies. Self-isolation and unfinished wars fed into decisions to suppress democratic aspirations in Myanmar and to develop nuclear weapons in North Korea, inviting condemnation and sanction by much of the international community. By the 2000s, however, one of these countries, Myanmar, was able to sufficiently win its unfinished wars to begin a cautious exploration of democratic reform and opening. North Korea, by contrast, remains locked in a conflict with the United States and South Korea and its responses to its security threat have become the very reason for its pariah status. The book also explores how North Korea's systems of ideology and control have insulated it from pressure in a way that Myanmar never achieved.

The author has visited North Korea multiple times as well as lived in Myanmar. In Myanmar, dozens of formal and informal interviews were conducted. Some interviewees requested anonymity or the use of pseudonyms; most did not. Formal interviews with North Koreans related to this research project were not (and could not have been) conducted; any quotations from years of formal and informal discussions with North Koreans have been anonymized. The book also relies on a comprehensive review of academic literature on both Myanmar and North Korea, as well as a variety of journalistic reportage and reports by activists, NGOs and international organizations.

Introduction
Why These Countries?

> "In our world there remain outposts of tyranny—and America stands with oppressed people on every continent ... in Cuba, and Burma, and North Korea, and Iran, and Belarus, and Zimbabwe ... we cannot rest until every person living in a 'fear society' has finally won their freedom ... but there are hopeful signs that freedom is on the march."
> —Statement by Dr. Condoleezza Rice, U.S. Secretary of State Designate, to the Senate Foreign Relations Committee on January 18, 2005

In 2010, one of Asia's most intractable and frustrating dictatorships, Myanmar, held elections for the time since 1990. The main opposition party—Aung San Suu Kyi's National League for Democracy (NLD)—chose not to compete, but following that contest, ex-military President Thein Sein continued to push for democratic reform. What followed was a remarkable transition to a more democratic society, one more integrated with the outside world. The NLD participated in by-elections in 2012, international sanctions were rolled back, social and political freedoms improved, and in 2015 the NLD swept to power in a general election that was an important moment in a remarkable transition.

In the meantime, Asia's other intractable and frustrating dictatorship, North Korea, saw the death of its leader Kim Jong Il in 2011 and his son Kim Jong Un consolidate power, an altogether different kind of transition. Under Kim Jong Un, North Korea has increased the pace of its nuclear and missile development and engages in less dialogue with the United States than it has in years. It has experimented with some economic reforms, allowing for more de facto private ownership, but it has stopped short of sacrificing its incredible system of censorship and information control.

Its people remain more cut off from the outside world than any other citizenry.

Despite the shocking treatment of the Rohingya during 2016 and 2017, Myanmar has been able to make a remarkable transition to a more open and globally integrated society, while North Korea remains an outlier, unable to come in from the cold. This book asks why.

But is this comparison worthwhile? Why compare The Democratic People's Republic of Korea (DPRK, or North Korea) and the amazingly awkwardly named The Republic of the Union of Myanmar (Burma, called Myanmar since 1989)? Why lump these very different societies together? Simply, others have done so. And they did share much in common, these Asian pariahs.

Most notoriously, in 2005 and echoing her boss U.S. President George W. Bush's Axis of Evil speech, soon-to-be Secretary of State Condoleezza Rice coined the term "Outposts of Tyranny." These outposts were "fear societies," she argued, and it was America's duty to help them transform into "free societies." Her speech gamely pointed to Afghanistan and Iraq as examples of hope, citing elections and democracy building in both, following U.S.-led wars to topple their governments.

Myanmar had been somewhat off the radar since the war on terror began. North Korea, by contrast, shared with Iran the dubious honor of being the only entries on both the "Axis of Evil" and the "Outposts of Tyranny" lists.

"Outposts of Tyranny" was a catchy turn of phrase, though like most sequels was not quite as inspired as the original. But what did it mean? Did the United States have the appetite for more war? Was it going to topple all these governments, stretching across three continents? Was it going to try other means to undermine them? It may not have reflected much in the way of concrete policy ideas, though all the countries on Rice's list faced U.S. sanctions either before or after her speech. It certainly reflected the Bush worldview: there is good, there is evil, good must triumph over evil. The term reinforced the degree to which Myanmar and North Korea were outliers in 21st century Asia.

Indeed, intuitively they do fit together, these two difficult states bracketing the mass of mainland China. All around them, there have been historic levels of economic growth and wealth creation, from Japan to Singapore, touching almost every state in between. Millions of people across the region have been lifted out of poverty, reshaping the world's political and economic landscapes. This only serves to highlight just how unique and frustrating were these two countries' continued poverty and protracted reluctance to join in Asia's rise.

They are both highly martial states, both with unresolved military conflicts. Myanmar's conflicts have been and are with a variety of internal insurgents. North Korea's is with a state competing for legitimacy—South Korea—and its superpower ally, the United States. This difference has been hugely important for Myanmar's transition, as we will see.

Myanmar's military has been fighting some form of separatist movement since independence in 1948. Fighting continues to this day, even if separatism as such has disappeared, replaced instead by demands for autonomy, federalism, resource-sharing and other things. The DPRK signed an armistice with the United States in 1953, following a brutal three-year war. That war was simultaneously a civil war and the Cold War's first international conflict. The armistice is not a full peace treaty; it was supposed to lead to a "peaceful settlement," but it never has. Both countries remain technically at war, year after year, decade after decade.

Burma and North Korea were both isolationist states, relatively content to turn inward and limit exposure to outside influences. Burma limited U.S. influence in the 1950s, hoping to avoid choosing sides in the Cold War, then cut most ties with India by nationalizing Indian-Burmese owned businesses and expelling much of the Indian population in the 1960s. Conflicts with China further isolated Burma in the 1960s, and in 1974 a new constitution committed it to autarky. The shocking massacres of demonstrators in 1988, even as Burma was trying to reopen its economy, led to further isolation and the beginning of its status as a pariah.

North Korea was also officially committed to autarky, as spelled out in its national ideology, *Juche*, but depended greatly on Soviet and Chinese goodwill and strategic support to prosper. It also cultivated strong relationships with not only friendly socialist states but other countries associated with the non-aligned movement in the 1970s and 1980s. Post–Cold War North Korea has found itself largely without support. Even the relationship with its current largest trading partner and source of aid, China, is tense. China recognized South Korea in 1992 and has opposed the DPRK's nuclear program, supporting several rounds of UN sanctions in the 2000s, even though it has refused to choke off trade to the point where it would destabilize its neighbor.

Pyongyang's economic dependence on China makes its leaders uneasy, a position in which Myanmar has also found itself. Between 1988 and 2013, China accounted for over 42 percent of official investment into

Myanmar.¹ Sanctions and a generally poor investment environment turned off Western investors. North Korea puts up some stiff competition in creating a poor investment environment and also suffers under sanctions, inhibiting interest from a diverse investment community. The DPRK stopped publishing economic data in 1967, leaving much guesswork among economists studying the country. It is known that China is the preponderant provider of investment and represented over 60 percent of North Korea's trade volume through 2015.² With Seoul's closure of Kaesong, the inter-Korean industrial park, after Pyongyang's fourth nuclear test in January 2016, China now represents over 90 percent of North Korean trade.³

Finally, and perhaps most obviously, both countries were also both oppressive dictatorships, without political participation, free speech or freedom of association and communication. They had arbitrary justice systems and widespread, inhumane incarceration facilities. They both employed huge state surveillance apparatuses to control their citizens.

Myanmar's status as a tyrannical state emerged from long-running civil wars, ethnic conflicts, oppression of minorities, a vibrant drug trade and, of course, the massacre of protestors on more than one occasion. Its repression of democracy is the primary reason and has been symbolized and embodied by the extended house arrest of the iconic Aung San Suu Kyi, who spent most of 1989 to 2010 incarcerated. In 2009, pre-transition Myanmar had up to 2,100 political prisoners behind bars.⁴ North Korea, meanwhile, has an estimated 80,000 to 120,000 people in political prison camps.⁵

Despite this, human rights have been less of a concern with North Korea, even if the issues are well known. George W. Bush once stated in a conversation with journalist Bob Woodward that he loathed Kim Jong Il, saying, "I've got a visceral reaction to this guy, because he is starving his people."⁶ Since the early 1990s, the United States has been primarily concerned with North Korea's nuclear program. Insofar as human rights has been an issue, it has been secondary—a point on which to pressure a country with advanced nuclear, biological and ballistic weapons programs. The majority of unilateral and UN sanctions on North Korea have been related to weapons programs, not human rights. Myanmar has not suffered UN sanctions, only unilateral sanctions by the United States, European Union and others.

This book is not going to attempt to answer if these two countries deserved to be the solitary pariahs among Asian states. It *is* going to show that these two countries are vastly different: scratch the surface and the similarities flake away. They are two countries that are very divergent in cultures, strategic concerns and political contexts. These crucial differences are what have allowed Myanmar to make a transition to a more open model.

The dissimilarities we'll explore are varied but are grouped around some major and crucial factors. The first and most important is the nature of the strategic threats that the central authorities face. In Myanmar, the military are preoccupied with maintaining the unity of the state in the face of highly skeptical minority groups. This is partly to do with control over a wealth of natural resources, but it is also connected to the self-perceived historical dominance of the Burman/Bamar people in the area. It's the reason the country is so awkwardly named (the Republic of the Union of Myanmar) and *Tatmadaw* (the military) slogans proclaim things like "The *Tatmadaw* and people, cooperate and crush all those harming the union."

But unity has been a tough sell among a heterogeneous population with centuries of conflict, stretching back from ancient kingdoms through World War II, in which different groups choose to support Japan or Britain. Today's wars are over not only identity but also control over jade, teak, drugs or other resources. To many minorities, "union" just means domination by the Burman majority. Even though it hasn't been able to fully defeat some of these insurgencies, the Myanmar military has been able to contain them. Using an often-harsh "four-cuts" strategy, the military imposed key victories on the Karen and others, while also and major ceasefires with Kachin, Shan and other ethnic armies.

The four-cuts strategy, developed in the 1960s, sought to deny insurgent groups access to food, money, intelligence, and recruits; by the mid–1970s most groups had been pushed back and by the turn of the century were confined to very limited areas and faced a growing and better-trained *Tatmadaw*.[7] This increase in security for the state is the primary reason that the military was comfortable in conceiving of and moving forward with a democratic experiment to end the country's isolation. It had the space to focus on its primary strategic threat before turning to deal with the reasons for its pariah status: the suppression of democracy and the repression of Aung San Suu Kyi and other activists.

North Korea, by contrast, perceives a far different core security threat: that of a hostile superpower on its doorstep; indeed a North Korean might say the United States is "occupying half of our country." A second full-scale war has been avoided since 1953, though should either side err in its deterrence strategy, Pyongyang knows that it would be crushed by American military might. North Korea has always counted on the fact that it could inflict more damage than the United States and its allies care to tolerate to prevent this outcome: The DPRK has 13,000 pieces of artillery and short-range rockets mostly within range of Seoul among its weapons systems.[8] The mutually assured destruction of Seoul and Pyongyang has kept the balance.

Seoul is the capital of a separate Korean state that claims the constitutional right to control the North's territory.[9] That other Korea—the Republic of Korea (South Korea)—is a U.S. ally and is by almost any conceivable measurement a greater success as a state, threatening Pyongyang's legitimacy. How can North Korea claim to its people that it represents their interests better than the manufacturing, trading, tech and cultural powerhouse that is South Korea?

One way has been through a compelling state ideology. North Korea's is a mix of socialism, race-based nationalism and isolationist corporatism packaged in the world's most intense cult of personality. The leader-cult portrays the Kims as the fathers to the nation-family, protecting their children from a hostile world.[10] As North Koreans have gotten more information in recent years, this narrative has frayed at the edges a bit, but it still contains enough salient parts that many people buy into at least elements of it. This provides a significant cushion or resistance to outside influences. Where it fails, the leadership can rely on an incredible apparatus of control to keep its citizens in line.

Burma/Myanmar never managed to find a state ideology as compelling or as inclusive as North Korea's. This was a weakness that made it more likely to eventually bend towards the prevailing system of the era, democratic capitalism. Moreover, the system of repression is far less extensive than that which the North Koreans built. This sets North Korea apart, helping it isolate and insulate itself from outside ideas and pressures that might pose a threat. The kind of cautious grumbling in Yangon tea shops before the reforms of 2010 remains nearly unthinkable in the DPRK, as we shall explore. Nor are there the myriad of civil society or religious organizations you could find in pre-reform Myanmar: the state controls almost all organizational life. The restrictions on almost everything remain more severe than in Myanmar's versions of authoritarianism.

Though we may (and should) argue about the extent to which political and social change has taken place in Myanmar, especially given the ethnic cleansing that has taken place in Rakhine since 2016, Aung San Su Kyi's party's huge victory in a very smooth election in November 2015 seems to suggest the fully authoritarian junta days are over. Myanmar's political isolation has been greatly reduced. Visits by U.S. President Barack Obama (in 2012 and 2014) and his two secretaries of state, Hillary Clinton (2011) and John Kerry (2016), emphasize this fact. Sanctions have been almost entirely lifted as of 2016. Investors are back and numbers of foreign visitors have shot up, from fewer than 800,000 in 2010 to over 3 million in 2014 (though these numbers are contested).[11] People share political opinions (mostly) freely in taxis, on satellite TV channels, on Facebook and in fancy new coffee shops in Yangon. Much of the country remains mired in poverty, conflict still exists and Aung San Suu Kyi's government has been a little too keen to use anti-defamation laws. Nonetheless, the social changes have been rapid and dramatic, especially in urban areas.

This book asks "Why was Myanmar able to embark on a program of dramatic political and social change while North Korea is not? And why now?" Through asking why one country is engaging in broad reforms while the other has doubled down on isolationism and antagonism, we will see that the primary difference between the two is that the reasons for Myanmar's pariah status—human rights violations and oppression of democracy—were disconnected from their primary strategic concerns of the union fragmenting.

For Pyongyang, their pariah status is driven by their nuclear weapons, the development of which is directly aligned with their primary security concern of their half of the peninsula being taken over by the United States and/or South Korea. They cannot "take care of" their strategic threat and then turn to the reasons for their isolation, as the Burmese generals could, because they are one and the same. By the 2000s, the military elites in Myanmar felt they had room to maneuver and the strategic and economic incentives to experiment cautiously with political and economic change.

There is a risk in international relations of overusing a security-based analysis to explain complex social and political interplay. We will have to understand how these countries viewed threats, their positions in the international community and sanctions they face. But we will also need to look at the ideologies and tools of repression and the sui generis historical conditions that the two countries find themselves in.

We will see that if sanctions contributed in a limited way to Myanmar's transformation, they haven't and probably won't contribute at all to fostering change in North Korea. Indeed, the leadership in the DPRK now sees nuclear weapons as absolutely central to the defense of the state—so central that it will endure more economic pain than the United States or the United Nations can impose on it.

This book will not explore the complex interplay between the military, its preferred civilian political part, the opposition led by Aung San Suu Kyi and the international community that led to the transition process from 2010 to 2015; that is another story. Rather, this book will focus on the conditions leading up to that process. We will explain how Burma/Myanmar became a pariah and how it came to decide it could escape that status through the plan its generals announced in 2003, the "Roadmap to Discipline-flourishing Democracy."

Nor will this book devote much time to defining "transition" or "openness" itself. Rather, it assumes that a more open model includes aspects of civilian rule, democratic participation, recognition of human rights, economic integration into global trade and investment flows, and active, positive participation in transnational civil society.

It is important to note that the transition to an open, democratic society is incomplete in Myanmar. Under the 2008 constitution, the military retains control over three important ministries (Home Affairs, Border Affairs and Defence) and 25 percent of parliament. There have been several ongoing conflicts with groups in Shan, Kachin and Kayah States. Most depressingly, there has been repugnant persecution of the Muslim Rohingya population in Rakhine state. In 2017, some 600,000 were forced to flee into Bangladesh to escape violence and destruction. The military's obstructionism and the tepid response from the civilian government has cast a shadow over Myanmar's reintegration into international society.

There is also much work to be done in terms of institutionalizing democratic norms: even under the democratically elected government of 2016, libel laws and other pressure tactics have been used to silence journalists and hush individual critics of the government for posting on their Facebook pages. Nonetheless, it is now undeniably a partial democracy, with a degree of freedom of speech and of information and association that simply did not exist a few years ago.

Some might say it is unfair to state that North Korea is *not* changing. Indeed, an influential academic blog on the country is called "Witness to Transformation."[12] The increased marketization of the economy has had a profound impact on the way people think and their daily lives. This gradual move away from state ownership and state planning of everything was a response to the famine of the mid-nineties. That marketization has also brought an increase in illicitly imported media content from outside and the state has lost its monopoly over information; a recent study found that half of respondents had seen foreign DVDs.[13] More North Koreans than ever now go abroad, though the numbers are in the low hundreds of thousands at best.

Still, the ideology of the state remains largely unchanged, even as it has adapted itself to the breach of its information cordon. It binds people together in a socialist and ethno-nationalist commitment to the Kim family in a struggle against the United States. State controlled social organization and the lack of civil society remain the same. The surveillance and capricious justice system remain largely the same. The isolationist mentality and policies remain largely the same.

We can and should be extremely pleased for the people of Myanmar, while recognizing that the hard work there is just beginning and that ethno-nationalism still represents a considerable threat to their turn towards democracy as well as their legitimate integration into the world. Nonetheless, the progress made in the last five years is heartening and praiseworthy. For now, Rice and Bush's speeches, failed attempts at cooperation, as well as the toppling of Iraq and the overthrow of Ghaddafi have added to a legacy of mutual mistrust that will convince Pyongyang to stay its current course. It is difficult to foresee in the near future, but someday brave leaders in the United States, North and South Korea will hopefully find the right moment to take a chance on changing the strategic and economic incentives facing North Korea's elites. When that happens, we may see an escape path for the situation in which the DPRK finds itself.

Until then, one pariah remains.

A Note on Transliteration

Burmese/Myanmar transliterations are problematic, as there are multiple official and vernacular systems in use. Generally, this book will follow the naming and spelling conventions used during the period under description. Many place names in Myanmar were altered in 1989 by the ruling State Law and Order Restoration Council to rid the country of colonial names or to reflect a more Burmese—and often a less local or minority language—pronunciation. Hence, for example, pre-1989, the country's major city will be written as "Rangoon." Post-1989 it will be "Yangon." The same date will divide the use of "Burma" or "Myanmar" as the country's name.

Korean, as one might expect, is also problematic. Generally, Revised Romanization of Korean (promulgated in the South since 2000) will be used for describing Southern places and names, while the North Korean national system, adopted in 1992, will be used for Northern ones. The McCune–Reischauer system, long favored by academics reluctant to embrace change or use-value, will not be used.

1

Cobbled and Cut

A healthy nation is as unconscious of its nationality as a healthy man of his bones. But if you break a nation's nationality it will think of nothing else but getting it set again.
—George Bernard Shaw

Your first day wandering the streets of downtown Yangon, you quickly realize you've stumbled into a city that is an Instagrammer's no-filter dream. The colonial-era buildings that persist throughout downtown are bursting with texture and color: the baked brick and desert-sunset yellow of the imposing High Court; the brooding teak walls of the old officers' club, musty and silent; the gridded streets, efficiently linking the river port with the railway. Everything seems layered. So often you see a crust of yet bright, but faded paint on the wall of a grand, multi-story building. Pieces are chipped away, revealing a different undercoating; mold on mold in purples and blacks; lush green moss; sometimes creepers or other plants dripping out of cracks and corners. The rich sun beats down on it all as human life clatters around below, swimming through a sea of humidity.

Within minutes, these buildings have told you this was an important colonial port. They also tell you that the stewards of the city haven't been able or haven't seen fit to take care of this legacy. Buildings in shambolic states are still used by minor government ministries or small businesses. Human and vehicular traffic bump up against each other on roadways designed for the transportation needs of a century ago. The chaos of street vending has eliminated the original utility of sidewalks.

By contrast, driving into the city center from Pyongyang's Sunan Airport, you notice that things are unusually tidy. Switzerland or Singapore tidy. You may catch someone hand-sweeping the road if you arrive in the morning. Not the sidewalk or pavement. The road.[1]

The buildings are simple concrete structures, often tired looking, but nicely painted and well attended to, with made-in-China plastic flowers brightening balconies. Then as you approach Victory Road, magnificence begins to greet you. First the April 25 Performance Hall and the 40-meter tall Immortality Tower boldly proclaiming that "Comrades Kim Il Sung and Kim Jong Il will live with us forever," then the winged-horse Chollima monument. Then rise the famous, 20-meter high bronze statues of the leaders at Mansudae, forever surveying their domain. A couple minutes past them you reach Kim Il Sung Square, a place already etched in your memory from countless news broadcasts of soldiers goose-stepping in a perfection of purpose. The city clearly has Soviet or Chinese influences in design, but there is nothing else like it. It is mid-twentieth century. It is organized. Old buildings cannot be spotted; it has been planned and built from scratch. It is unmistakably North Korean.

Like Yangon, Pyongyang was an important colonial city, though for a shorter period. Japan's occupation of Korea lasted from just 1910 to 1945. Pyongyang was a distant second to Seoul under the Japanese and for hundreds of years before, but by the time of independence it was cosmopolitan and very Christianized: in Northern Korea altogether there were about 3,000 churches and 300,000 Christians.[2] It was connected to an industrial belt built by the Japanese, squeezing modernity into and resources out from the North of the peninsula and Manchuria.

We have to understand the colonial legacies of Myanmar and North Korea because the colonial experiences and decolonization of both countries directly led to the tortured late-20th century histories that their peoples have endured. Both countries became militarized, repressive and economically backward because the security concerns that developed in the immediate aftermath of the post-colonial period persisted so long. The somewhat justified paranoia—if such a term makes sense—of the leadership in both countries created a situation in which security and strategic concerns subjugated all other goals, bending and distorting all social needs and desires.

Burma was cobbled together under the British as a mix of ethnic groups with divergent interests and goals. Upon independence, Burmese elites saw these groups as a separatist security threat with the potential to tear the country apart. Those elites saw their primary responsibility as holding the country together and preventing its fracture. They also sought to prevent communists from taking over during a period when the state was weak and besieged.

North Korea's leaders saw their near-holy mandate as unification of the country, also. The Japanese Empire's sudden collapse under the combination of 14 grinding years of war and then split-second atomic explosions left a vacuum in Korea. The country was quickly divided into U.S. and Soviet areas of control, which calcified into permanence through a subsequent war for reunification. An armistice was signed in July 1953 but not a peace treaty. North Korea still lives a daily struggle against the combined might of South Korea and the United States. The quest for unification dominates official North Korean discourse.

When the Union Jack was lowered in Rangoon for the last time in 1948, the British may have felt pleased at some of their legacy. They left behind the most highly renowned university in Southeast Asia. They had also left road and rail infrastructure as well as the region's most important airport. (This may be hard to believe now, when one compares Singapore's gleaming and sprawling Changi Airport with Yangon's dim and grimy Mingaladon Airport, which suffers an alarming number of power cuts.[3]) The British also left behind a clear legal code, which could have been useful for attracting foreign investors. Burma had abundant natural resources such as oil, natural gas, teak and minerals, as well—the Brits couldn't take all of it. Agricultural output was high: the British had helped irrigate the lowlands to create more farmland and by 1910 had nearly tripled the amount of land used for rice in 1885.[4] Consequently, Burma was known as the rice bowl of the world.

However, the British also left behind a brewing ethnic problem as they had amalgamated a number of ethnic groups under colonial rule, focusing little on racial harmony as they went about extracting wealth from Burma for the benefit of the British economy and its companies.

In Korea, the Japanese similarly bequeathed quality infrastructure and industrial capacity, leaving, for example, the most developed rail network in Asia other than in Japan itself.[5] The sudden end to World War II also meant there was no transition period or grooming of a class of native successors to Japanese governance. Japan's capitulation in August 1945 created a power vacuum, with competing exiles scrambling to take the reins of power. The USSR, which had declared war on Japan just a week before the nuclear bombings of Hiroshima and Nagasaki, and the United States agreed to temporarily divide the Korean peninsula into zones of control. The Soviets took the North, the Americans took the South—they both installed leaders they thought they could control. In retrospect, of course, it is difficult to see how a peaceful reunification of this temporary division would have ever been possible in the ideologically charged atmosphere of the early Cold War.

Taking and Making Burma

The British Empire took Burma in three stages, through three wars against the overmatched Burmese monarchy. The first of these was in 1824, when Burmese encroachment on British-held Northeastern Indian territories inspired a naval incursion that took Rangoon. This war dragged on for two years, costing a great deal of materiel and men on both sides—over 15,000 on the Indian/British side of the conflict.[6]

The subsequent peace held for just 25 years, when the Second Anglo-Burmese War broke out over trade conditions. The British quickly captured the ports of Lower Burma, marched on the capital and forced the submission of the king. All of Lower Burma was annexed in 1852.

A generation later, the Third Anglo-Burmese War saw Upper Burma (Mandalay and Northern areas) annexed. The Burmese were in a perilous position leading up to the war: do nothing and British economic might would gradually overwhelm them—resistance to it through tariffs or sanctions could lead to another military intervention, similar to 1852; reaching out to another great power to form an alliance could help improve the kingdom's security, but it could also give the British the pretext it needed to take over completely. The Burmese tried the latter, assiduously working to cultivate a closer relationship with the French. London, already concerned about French control over Indochina, used this (and another trade dispute) as a pretext to move against Mandalay—then the capital—and quickly emerged victorious in 1886.[7] Thibaw, the last king of Burma, was taken into exile in India. He never saw Burma again. (In a dismal imperial symmetry, the last Indian emperor was exiled to Burma in 1858 and died there.)

Myanmar can still roughly be described as lowland plains, which are largely populated by Burmans, more recently called Bamar (the name Burma being derived from the name of the major ethnicity). These lowlands are surrounded by a horseshoe of higher-elevation, minority controlled or influenced areas. Upper Burma included ethnic minority areas, such as the Shan States and modern Kachin State. These highland minority groups had been for varying periods and degrees subject to Burman hegemony, at times dominated and subjugated, but at other times cooperative, peaceful and autonomous. One influential scholar argues that the very essence of such highland Asian societies has been the resistance to control by lowland-based states.[8]

During the pre–British semi-feudal system, as with feudalisms anywhere, however, control bled outward from the metropolitan center. The feudal system could deal with ambiguity and semi-autonomy on the fringes. There were ebbs and flows. There was no such thing as citizenship, just relations between neighboring groups, so identity politics as such were largely non-existent.

By contrast, the modern nation-state system into which Burma's people were pulled, first as imperial subjects and then citizens of an independent state, is much more rigid in its dealings with peripheries. Laws and rights are supposed to be uniform across the entire territory—all the way until you cross a border checkpoint. The British disruption of feudal life altered Burmese society through immigration, internal migration, changes in class and religion. But, perhaps above all, it *made* Burma. Britain literally drew its borders and categorized its people.

Categorizing things, as Britain and other colonizing Europeans were wont to do, often reified them. Categorizing "the races of Burma" helped solidify in the imagination the differences between ethnic groups.[9] The British classification and administration of their newly acquired territory into lowlands and highlands, Burma Proper and Frontier Areas, help emphasize these differences. This would come into play after independence.

Also, for many minorities, things were not necessarily worse under the British. The colonial economy was fundamentally exploitative and discriminatory, but often too was life under Burman hegemony. With the British came new opportunities for social and individual development. And as the groundswell for independence grew in the 1920s and '30s, many minority leaders feared that they would be trapped in a state controlled by a majority with whom tensions had risen.

The Karen people, for example, mostly in the southern Irrawaddy (now officially styled "Ayeyarwady") River Delta and along the border with Thailand, feared the worst. Their subordinate status for hundreds of years had led to a "mutual hatred of the races," according to one British anthropologist.[10] The Karen, with a mix of animist and Buddhist faiths, had had contact with American missionaries before the arrival of the British, though converts were sternly persecuted. After the British took control of Lower Burma in 1853, however, missionaries became free to operate and evangelize, converting a great many Karen to Christianity.[11] Today, about 20 percent of the 8 million Karen are Christian. (Missionaries did even better with the Chin and Kachin minorities, who now are about 90 percent and 80 percent to 90 percent Christian, respectively.[12])

Even before gaining enough control to allow missionary work, the

British recruited Karen to act as expeditionary guides for the first two Anglo-Burmese wars. One account of the 1826 campaign by a British general praised our "Carian friends" for having helped "inviolably kept secret" their knowledge of British maneuvers against the Burmese, even though so many must have known about them.[13] This, of course, exacerbated any discord that existed. "The Burmese knew the Karen regarded the English as their deliverers and took vengeance on them accordingly."[14]

A hundred years after this British-Karen collusion, a prominent Karen leader and intellectual, San C. Po, bluntly argued for the need for the Empire to remain, writing, "It is the unanimous opinion of the Karens that Burma is not yet fit for Home Rule." He continues: "Home Rule today would be a curse rather than a blessing, just as the affairs in a family could not be safely entrusted to a *pater familias* who is apparently incompetent!"[15] No guesses as to which ethnic group Po was calling a bad father in this passage.

Po acknowledges that some form of federation may someday work, but Great Britain must continue its "arduous, unpleasant and thankless" duty to rule "until such a day as every country and every nation which has looked up to her as its savior and protector is made happy with every prospect of a future of contentment."[16]

The Karen may have been the group most at odds with the Burman majority, but they were by no means the only highland people to suffer tensions with their neighbors that were exacerbated by the codifying British. The Kachin, in the far north of the country, were also heavily recruited into the colonial military. Indeed, the British believed the highland folks to be "martial races," another concept borrowed from their occupation of India.

This dubious idea was essentially that some races were good at fighting while others "didn't have it in them." In the 21st century this reads like an absurdity, but in the 18th and 19th centuries the concept was literally used to organize the lives of hundreds of thousands of men. In India, this meant Punjabis and Nepalis were turned into fighting forces and for much of British rule in Burma, Indians were imported to make up a large percentage of the military. Among the local population, along with the Karen, the Kachin, Chin and Shan were heavily recruited.[17]

This was particularly evident when the colonial administration decided more troops were needed as war began to cast its shadow over Europe. From 1939 to 1941, the Burma army was made up of 2,578 Indians, 1,893 Burmans, 2,797 Karens, 1,258 Chins, 852 Kachins and a few hundred others.[18]

Even the term "Kachin" suggests the complexity of modern and historical Burma: Kachin is not universally accepted, as it appears to be an exonym, or term from the outside. "Jinghpaw Wunpawng" is a preferred endonym for some, and that term is reflected in the names used in India and China for the branches of Kachins in their territories: Singpho and Jinpo in India and China, respectively. Like the Karen, missionaries found these tribes receptive to Christianity.

It helped, again as with the Karen, that the missionaries came bearing the tools of modern education. This group of tribes had no writing system of their own prior to Western intervention, with an orally transmitted culture and value system. In an example of what Edward Said would later call Orientalism, a 19th century Swedish-American missionary devised a writing system on their behalf, which then came into widespread use among the Kachin tribes.[19]

There was a high degree of fluidity in ethnic identity among these groups, something that the British, with their very European either/or categorizing approach, found hard to capture. Harder, perhaps, than capturing ports and cities. In a way, the traditional anthropology and knowledge-building that came with the colonials may have advanced disciplinary thinking, but also "it can produce intellectual lockdown."[20]

The Shan, for example, treated as distinct by both the British and the successor state of Burma, had a great deal of interaction and intermixing with the Kachin. Families might identify both as Kachin and Shan in custom and lineage.[21] This isn't the only example of hybridity: the non-static nature of ethnicity also meant people could, for example, consider themselves both Mon—early settlers of Southeast Asia—and Burmese, even if at times those groups were in military or cultural conflict.[22] The Mon are also an interesting case in that a common conception of them by others is that they are civilized and refined. They also experience discrimination by the Burmese, but perhaps less from simple condescension and more from a mild resentment: the Mon built great kingdoms early in the region's history, some early Burmese kings were actually Mon, and various scholars claim the Mon language is a precursor to Burmese.[23]

The Shan had also built a great Kingdom, Ava, in the 14th century and sometimes identify with the Thais, their ethnic and cultural cousins. After the 16th century fall of Ava to a Burmese king, the Shan had been organized as a series of principalities. As if to illustrate the complexity and fluidity of inter-ethnic relations, one 20th-century Shan memoir opined: "They resisted all Burmese moves to subjugate them. At times they submitted to strong or wise monarchs, but they rebelled whenever they could." The memoir also notes that the Shan experienced "some peace during the British period, since there was no Burmese center of power."[24]

It is important—though difficult—not to oversimplify the different identities and cultures that were to feed into post-colonial civil wars. Furthermore, even though there were periods of domination and tension between different groups and between the center and the periphery, there were periods of fruitful cultural and economic exchange. There were also ideological and social shifts and the motivations and boundaries of inclusion and exclusion were not fixed. But although it was "a very complex, extremely heterogeneous political and social landscape, those who lived within it were perfectly capable of dealing with that complexity and developing their own methods for handling different ideological pretentions."[25]

It is an understatement to say that the territory now known as Myanmar was an extremely complex milieu. As of 2017, the state recognizes eight main ethnic groups, most of which have sub-groups with distinct languages that make up a staggering 135 ethnic groups. A 2014 census should provide strong data on ethnic populations, but, given the sensitivity of such information, the results have not been released as of 2017. (Data on religion was finally released in June 2016.) The eight main ethnicities are estimated to make up 80 percent to 90 percent of the population.[26] This group of eight does not include Chinese-Burmese or Indian-Burmese.

This is despite the fact that Chinese people have been migrating to Burma since at least the 10th century and have played significant roles in its society, as they have throughout Southeast Asia. The British altered the major pattern of migration by providing a maritime route via Malaya; previously, people tended to come overland via Yunnan province.[27]

It was through Indian immigration patterns that the British made one final dubious contribution to Burma's ethnic milieu. Indian immigrants had made their way to Burma before, but something was new about the Indian migration that occurred in the mid to late 19th century.[28] India had already been under British rule for decades. Indians had been exposed to modern capitalism and government administration since the mid–17th century as well as direct imperial administration under the Raj since 1858. Because Burma was tacked on as a province of British India, it was more expedient to populate the civil service with Indians, who already knew what they were expected to do, rather than train Burmese. As such, the business of government became an Indian business.

Coolies, farmers, laborers and artisans followed the opening of Burma, too, squeezing the labor pool from the bottom and competing with locals for manual work. Rangoon's Indian population swelled from just 16 percent of the population in 1872 to 56 percent in 1911 and remained over 50 percent until the Japanese invaded in 1942.

Filling precious labor and government roles was one thing, but it was the Indian accumulated experience in finance that really caused intercommunal strife. Some of the immigrant populations were already successful in their home states and their savings "actually paved the way for the building of Rangoon. Yet, Indian capital acquired a bad if not poisonous reputation. By the beginning of the new century many Burmans, who had initially benefitted from the economic activity which occurred after the country was united under British rule, found themselves in significant debt."[29]

Burmese nationalism developed in this context, indignant at being grafted on to India and then indebted and subordinated to not only the British, but the Indians themselves. This led to a series of anti–Indian riots in the 1930s and a great deal of tension in the urban centers by the time the Japanese arrived.

And when they did, they shattered both the myth of European superiority and whatever ethnic harmony was imposed by British rule of law. The Japanese invasion unleashed tensions that had been coiled tightly. The energies released still affect Burma, which has been at war with itself ever since.

Japan Takes Korea

A generation before the Japanese invasion of Burma, the island nation entered the imperial club by snatching up first Taiwan, then Korea, through a combination of crafty politicking and military might. Japan was a latecomer to colonialism and towards the end of the 19th century set its gaze upon its neighbor and began exerting greater influence in trade and political relations. Korea clung to a policy of isolationism, rather than trying to balance this influence. This was to prove disastrous.

In 1876, Japan forced a treaty on Korea that began to wrest it away from the Chinese, of whom Korea had long been a tributary. Korea was proclaimed a "sovereign nation," though one without the resources or political wherewithal to resist Japanese dominance.[30] The Chinese recognized that this was happening and eventually went to war with Japan in 1894, largely over the fate of Korea. China, in the midst of its humiliating century, was trounced.

Meanwhile, the Western powers were pleased to see the rise of Japan. Great Britain was keen on it so Japan could check the expansion of the Russian Empire in the Far East. Japan and Britain formalized this anti–Russian front through an alliance in 1902.[31] United States President Theodore Roosevelt summed up the American position as simply as this: "I should like to see Japan have Korea."[32]

He was to see his wish come true soon thereafter: in 1905, Korea became a protectorate of Japan following Japan's defeat of Russia in a war; the first-ever defeat of a European power by an Asian country. Japan annexed Korea completely in 1910.

Japan thrust modernity upon Korea, as did Britain upon Burma, uprooting social and economic structures along the way. There had been feudal and inflexible structures, whereby an elite class, called *Yangban*, monopolized scholarship, wealth and political power in a conservative embrace of Confucianism.[33] This Confucianism elevated the value of scholarship and study to tremendous levels and the *Yangban* controlled access to the examination system that was perhaps the only (and very narrow) means of social mobility. Your social status was set at birth. Certainly, the elites weren't interested in supporting a merchant class or expanding economic opportunity.

Upon the arrival of the Japanese, the *Yangban* were suddenly subordinate. Lower down the social ladder, also, people were suddenly faced with not only a foreign occupier, but also the upheaval of capitalism. The Japanese created new industries to feed the economy of the homeland and infrastructure to link their territories together. They moved a labor force around the region, greatly stimulating a nascent Korean diaspora. They also created incredible tension between "resisters" and "collaborators" that endures in the Korean psyche a century later.

In many ways, this experience of Japanese colonialism is still raw, over 70 years after it ended. To quote historian Bruce Cumings:

> Korea was Japan's most important colony, and also its most recalcitrant colony. Among Koreans, North and South, the mere mention of the idea that Japan somehow modernized Korea calls forth indignant denials, raw emotions, and the imminent sense of mayhem having just been, or just about to be, committed. For the foreigner, I know from my own work, even the most extensive cataloguing of Japanese atrocities will pale beside the bare mention of anything positive and lasting that might have emerged from the colonial period.[34]

This is surprising, perhaps, in South Korea, where Japan is every year a top five export and import partner.[35] It is less surprising in the North, where propaganda constantly emphasizes Japan's evil and there is now minimal economic interaction.

In the Korean collective memory, the often-harsh Japanese occupation is universally decried and the positive, proactive resistance movements are emphasized—sometimes overemphasized. In North Korean historiography, the most meaningful resistance originated with the patriotic theories and revolutionary activities of Kim Il Sung.

Perhaps more complicated than the simple subjugation and economic exploitation of their country, Japanese attempts to assimilate and "Japanify" their colony remain the most troubling for Koreans, who see it still as a form of cultural obliteration. Japan's policies included subordination of the Korean language, Japanification of Korean names and eventually, during Japan's war years, even the proclaimed idea that Korea was not a colony but part of Japan itself.[36]

Losing Burma

Eventually, the erstwhile allies and island empires of Britain and Japan came to conflict in Southeast Asia, first on the Malay Peninsula and then in Burma. One British officer recalled his grim task as it became clear Rangoon was going to fall in early 1942: "Every Japanese air raid increased the steady stream northwards of the city (Rangoon) population, and more and more institutions ground to a standstill. One afternoon, I joined in a bizarre and melancholy foray to shoot all dangerous animals in the zoo, as all their keepers had decamped. Tigers, panthers and poisonous snakes were killed and the deer released in the park, except for one which we shot for fresh meat. When we had gutted the poor beast, we threw its entrails into the lake and great fish thrashed and swirled in the course of their unusual meal."[37]

As British power was overwhelmed by the Japanese military machine, Burma's ethnic schism deepened even further. The Karen, by and large, took up arms alongside their colonial masters. Many Kachin also fought for the allies, having been organized into the Kachin Rangers and the Northern Kachin Levies, a special jungle fighting force under the command of British officers.

As some argue, certain groups fought less out of love for their colonial overlords than for "autonomy from both Burmese and Japanese nationalist incorporation."[38] But there could also be intense bonds between the British and ethnic soldiers; indeed, perhaps the kind that only comes with taking up arms together.

During VJ Day in 2015, one aged Karen combatant spoke glowingly of his British commander: "He loved the Karen people. He gave his life (for us)." He was speaking of Maj. Hugh Paul Seagrim, who the Karen called "Grandfather Longlegs" and who "wore their native dress, shared their food and helped till their fields." He gave himself up to be executed with seven of his Karen comrades in order to prevent reprisals against non-combatants by the Japanese.[39]

Shan princes also chipped in, despite having their aspirations for more autonomy ignored by the British for several decades. They collected some £57,000 to £60,000 to support the war effort.[40] Far from following their princes' lead, however, many younger, educated Shan were persuaded by and attracted to the Burmese nationalists led by Aung San, who had a brief but remarkable career as a student activist in the 1930s, as a general during World War II, and finally as the politician who won independence from the British and negotiated the formation of the Union of Burma.[41]

Most of the world will have heard of Aung San Suu Kyi, Nobel laureate, democracy activist, and, well, the most famous Burmese person of all time. Her role in modern Myanmar, her fame and by her own account the reason she was under house arrest rather than in jail is due to the fact she is the daughter of Aung San.[42]

Aung San and an important, educated clique sided and fought with the Japanese. He and a now heavily mythologized "Thirty Comrades" traveled to Imperial Japan for military training. They formed the nucleus of the newly formed Burma Independence Army (BIA), which they grew to 3,500 volunteers. They were armed by the Japanese and integrated into invasion plans. These Burmese thought Japan would liberate them from the yolk of colonial control and followed the Japanese Imperial Army into Burma in 1942 in high spirits. The BIA ranks swelled to as many as 25,000 to 30,000 men and they began to fill the vacuum left by the retreating British.[43]

The boisterous and fervent nature of this force spelled trouble for some of the minority groups, especially the Karen. "The close association of the Karen with the British and their role in sustaining the colonial regime made them a primary target of Burman nationalists."[44] Without a leviathan to keep these two armed groups pacified, mistrust in several regions—particularly linked to Burmese demands that the Karen give up their weapons—turned bloody.

The worst example of the downward cycle of reprisals and revenge was in in March 1942. Up to 2,000 Karen were killed in Myaungmya when leaders on both sides allowed passions to spiral out of control. For many Karen, this was a turning point from which their imagined place in a future independent Burma could never be the same. Other groups of Karen further north and further west managed to avoid the worst of the strife, as did most of the Chin, Kachin and Shan.[45] Still, the resurgent and potent Burmese nationalism was cause for concern among minorities throughout the country.

Aung San was hardly an ideologue. His paramount concern was Burmese independence. In the mid–1930s as a student, he considered isolationist nationalism as a movement, as well as internationalism and communism. He actually helped found a communist party in 1939, though his dedication to its ideals faded away fairly quickly.[46] He may have accepted any foreign patron who might assist with his goals. As it happened, on a trip to Amoy, China, to explore communist support in 1940, he managed to get the attention of the Japanese. (He also managed to get severe dysentery on the trip.[47] One wonders how different modern Burmese history would look had he not recovered.)

The Japanese sent Aung San back to Burma with a disguise that seems to have mainly consisted of false teeth, truly Clark Kent-esqe in its casualness.[48] His mission was to sneak his cohorts—the "Thirty Comrades"—out of Burma. They were to be taken first to Japan and then on to Japanese occupied Hainan for guerrilla training. After training they would be sent back to Burma to sabotage British control and fight alongside the Japanese. Let's ponder for a moment how detailed people-smuggling, guerrilla training and invasion plans relied on such a poor disguise, when Aung San snuck back into Burma after his first interlocution with the Japanese.

This was essentially the process of setting up the BIA, of which he became head. He's still remembered as the founding father of the Burmese army, something Aung San Suu Kyi would later reference as she became a public figure locked in a struggle with that very military.

Aung San, along with his cohorts, were present on August 1, 1943, when "with great pomp and solemnity," Burma was granted independence.[49] By that point, however, Aung San and the Burmese could already see that

Japan's "Asian co-prosperity sphere" was little more than a euphemism for a new colonialism and that "independence" meant new subjugation. His inner circle was already considering an underground resistance to the Japanese occupation and by the end of the year Aung San himself was openly giving speeches criticizing the state of so-called independence under the Japanese.[50]

The following year, Aung San led the BIA into an agreement with the Communist Party of Burma to form an anti-fascist organization and, as when the British scored a major victory against the Japanese at Imphal, the resistance movement was put into action.[51] By March 1945, the BIA was actively cooperating with the British. The end of Japanese control over Burma was in sight.

Sudden Vacuum in Korea

Of course, by mid–1945, the Japanese Empire was being rolled back in several theaters. Still, its position in its first and most important colony appeared secure. The end of Japanese rule was going to come quickly and unexpectedly.

It is important to try to imagine just how shocking the atomic blasts in Hiroshima and then Nagasaki were to the world. Nobody knew about this terrifying technology. Japan was steeled to endure a great deal of pain yet: they were prepared for an invasion of their home islands and perhaps the death and immiseration of much of its population. The morality of the Fat Man and Little Boy bombs is less than clear; what was instantly clear to Tokyo was that it could not endure any more. On August 5, the whole world was expecting the war to drag on for months, perhaps years, even. On August 15, Japan surrendered unconditionally.

In one of many twists of fate that would define Korea's future, the USSR declared war on Japan on August 8, two days after the first atomic bomb was dropped on Hiroshima and just hours before the second bomb obliterated Nagasaki. This fateful timing was to have a lasting affect on Korea. The Red Army, after all, moved into Manchuria, in China's Northeast, on August 9. Suddenly, the previously neglected issue of what would happen to Korea became of piercing concern to the Americans.

The nearest U.S. forces were in Okinawa—what if Stalin's army just swept south and took all of Korea, perhaps even parts of Southern Japan? On August 10, as the White House pondered the implications of the imminent peace, two lieutenant-colonels (one of whom, Dean Rusk, would go on to be Secretary of State) were sent into an adjacent room to find a solution to administering the peninsula. Neither had any Korea-experience and they were under immense pressure. There was no time to consult a Korea expert, apparently. They chose the 38th parallel as a dividing line, largely because it put the capital, Seoul, in the American zone.[52] In another mystery, given Stalin's preoccupation with power and power projection, the Soviets accepted the proposal.

The Americans took charge of their section of the "temporarily divided" country, the Soviets theirs, and they set about setting up two exiled leaders to run their respective portions. Both leaders, Sungman Rhee in the South and Kim Il Sung in the North, sought to unify the country on their terms. They could not agree on terms for joint North-South elections or any other mechanism to bring the two sides together. In the end, South Korea held separate elections in 1948. North Korea followed suit in 1949.

Crucially, both the Republic of Korea in the south and the Democratic People's Republic of Korea in the north claimed the right to control the entire peninsula. It is impossible to understand this fact's importance, even today: neither side views the other as legitimate. Indeed, it has proved very difficult for one to deal with the other in good faith when both are still *constitutionally dedicated to the elimination of the other.*

Kim Il Sung, whom the Russians thought would be a pliable leader for the DPRK, proved to be a dynamic and ruthless politician. He set about eliminating rivals, cultivating a mythological public image and planning for unification. His plan for the latter, long resisted by his patron Stalin, was to attack the South, foment an uprising and take over the country. By 1950, with a successful Chinese communist revolution and a Soviet nuclear bomb test completed the previous year, Stalin was ready to give Kim the green light.

The Korean War

North Korean troops poured over the temporary border on June 25, 1950. The South Korean army disintegrated like ash before them and within two months the (North) Korean People's Army had swept down nearly the whole peninsula. The U.S. rallied the United Nations to provide a legal fig leaf for American intervention and joined just in time to protect the southern port of Pusan. In September, the United States caught the North Koreans off-guard by landing at Incheon, behind their lines, severing their supply lines and causing mayhem in the Korean People's Army ranks. The North Koreans retreated in disarray and the UN forces pushed forward all the way to the border with China. The year-old People's Republic of China decided this was too close for comfort and sent soldiers pouring into Korea, pushing UN forces back to the 38th parallel—basically where the war began.

For two and half years, the war ground on, both sides competing for a matter of kilometers here and there around that 38th parallel. During that time, the U.S. prosecuted an air war that has left a deep scar in the North Korean psyche. The country was flattened. Napalm, made famous in Vietnam, was used for the first time in Korea but hardly on a trial basis: Napalm burned and choked perhaps hundreds of thousands of people to death: 33,000 tons of it was used.[53]

It is also worth noting that General MacArthur—hero of World War II and architect of the Incheon landings—made plans to use nuclear weapons in the Korean theater.[54] This never came to fruition, but the North Koreans have felt the threat of nuclear warfare since this time. The Koreans, both North and South, used shifting fortunes to purge and avenge opponents, real and imagined, in an often gruesome and extrajudicial bloodletting. In the end, a staggering 3 million to 4 million civilians and well over a million combatants died between 1950 and 1953.[55]

Why did all this happen? To quote Cumings again, at length:

> [There is] blame enough to go around for everyone—and blame enough to include Americans who thoughtlessly divided Korea and then reestablished the colonial government machinery and the Koreans who served it. How many Koreans might still be alive had not that happened? Blame enough to include a Soviet Union likewise unconcerned with Korea's ancient integrity and determined to "build socialism" whether Koreans wanted their kind of system or not. How many Koreans might still be alive had that not happened? And then, as we peer inside Korea to inquire about Korean actions that might have avoided national division and fratricidal conflict, we get a long list indeed.[56]

Cumings is often labeled a revisionist or anti–American historian. While not perfect, his main argument is that both international and local forces combined to cause this devastating war. Most importantly, those dynamics—domestic and foreign—were ossified by the conflict, creating a rigidity that has lasted beyond all expectation into the 21st century. It also contributed to the militarization-in-perpetuity of North Korea.

Rangoon Striving for Unity Among the Ethnic Groups?

After the defeat of Japan, Aung San was faced with two related tasks: to get the British to accede to independence and to build a pan-ethnic coalition. London proposed a three-year period of British rule, leading to dominion status, and then, perhaps, to a republic.[57] This was totally unacceptable to Aung San and his now-broadened Anti-Fascist People's Freedom League (AFPFL), a significant political front.

Fortunately for him, as he locked horns in a battle of wills with London and the British Governor in Rangoon, he found himself consistently negotiating from a position of strength: his popularity throughout the country was immense—incomparable, really. His charisma, intellect and, above all, his honest and scrupulous nature won hearts all over Burma. One of his Japanese interlocutors once noted that Aung San's "political thinking (is) not so mature."[58] However, the flipside of naivety is, perhaps, forthrightness.

So after signing an agreement with British Prime Minister Clement Attlee in January 1947 that promised Burma independence within a year, he drew on this well of trust to finalize negotiations for a federated union with the ethnic minorities. Or, more accurately, some of the ethnic minorities.

What emerged, in February, was called the Panglong Agreement, signed by representatives of the Chin, Kachin and Shan. The Kachin and Shan were to get autonomous states in the union, with the right to secede after a ten-year period. The right of secession was hugely significant: it meant the Burmese majority was to be forced into governing well and allowing sufficient autonomy in local affairs.

The Chin sought only a special administrative division, which they were duly granted after their representative had just one meeting with Aung San, so impressed was he by Aung San's character and promises of development assistance.[59] All this helped dispel British doubts about whether Aung San could manage relations with the ethnic leaders.[60] Clearly, however, some people were missing. Where were the Karen? The Mon? The others? They did not participate.

It is unclear if Panglong was a good start by Aung San: potentially it was a document he could show other groups as a working model. We'll never know if he would have been able to keep his promises or forge lasting agreements with other ethnic groups. Aung San was assassinated by a rival during a cabinet meeting in July 1947. Untainted by future failures and disappointments, he departed this world a legend who had navigated his country to independence as both a military and political leader.

His successor, U Nu, soon faced a communist split from his coalition as well as an insurgency. He relied in large part on Kachin and Karen troops to quell it, even while Karen desires for independence were being ignored. Inter-communal tensions and violent incidents grew in intensity and number, and finally the Karen rose up in arms in 1949, with other groups to follow. They have been fighting ever since.

20th Century Patterns Set

By 1953 the formations of division (in Korea) and fracture (in Burma) had been set. In the early 1950s Rangoon was dealing with insurgencies backed by foreign groups, including the CIA, who supported remnants of the Kuomintang Chinese forces, who in turn cooperated with Shan insurgents.[61] The Thais were also supporting the Karen, Karreni and Mon in an effort to weaken Burma.[62]

In July of 1953, a weary America and battered North Korea signed an armistice to end the fighting, though they couldn't reach a full peace treaty. This left U.S. troops in South Korea and North Koreans with an acute sense of victimhood: first the Japanese had abused them, then their country was divided and occupied by a hostile superpower, preventing them from taking rightful control over their land. Their victimhood is enhanced by their historiography, which claims that the United States invaded the North on June 25, 1950; Soviet documents show otherwise.[63] (Besides, to believe this you'd have to accept that the world's most powerful military meticulously planned an invasion but were somehow in full retreat within a few hours.)

With the two states turning to rebuild after the devastation of war, the contest for both legitimacy—hearts and minds—and economic prowess between North and South Korea began in earnest.

Everything that Pyongyang did in the coming decades was framed by its victimhood complex, competition with Seoul, and the external security threat posed by the United States. Rangoon, too, was driven by the desperation to hold onto Aung San's vision of a union that would keep Burma strong in the era of independent nations. Along with managing military threats, the challenge for both leaderships became the need to justify their visions of a national future to secure their respective positions. Towards the end of the century, the Burmese military would gradually succeed regarding the former, having failed at the latter. For the North Koreans, it was almost the opposite.

2

Militaries First, Economies Second

If there is one brute fact of both Burmese and North Korean life, it is a militarization of society to a degree that is unprecedented in the rest of Asia, except in wartime. Of course, this was not some abstract choice on the part of ruling elites: both states are engaged in unfinished wars. Both states were in very real ways birthed through these unfinished wars. These states-of-war have created an over-reliance on the military and on militarization to organize the two societies. Eventually, it also led to the reasons both states became pariahs: the Burmese military suppressed democracy and Aung San Suu Kyi because they believed only the military could keep the country together; Pyongyang pushed forward with nuclear weapons and missile programs, coming to believe that only they could provide it security against the United States and South Korea.

The man who navigated the transition to Burma's independence was Aung San, the father of Aung San Suu Kyi. One can't help feel a little humbled by the list of Aung San's achievements by the time of his death at age 32 in 1947. He'd started a student movement, founded an army, fought against two imperialisms, negotiated independence for his country, and helped forge a tenuous union. Even if some of his life recedes into the mists of hagiography and myth, his story is a compelling one. The abrupt end to it may have cost his country dearly, but at least he didn't have to witness the political meltdown, enduring conflict, and economic failures of the following years and decades. Almost immediately following the independence he'd negotiated, several rebellions broke out; the perceived incompetence of the civilian leaders in the face of such pressures led the military to take over twice—once temporarily in 1958 and then in perpetuity four years later.

2. Militaries First, Economies Second

Born three years before Aung San, Kim Il Sung, by contrast, lived long enough to preside over both expectation-obliterating growth and unity *and then* economic stagnation. He returned from exile and guerrilla war at age 33, in 1945, following the Soviet Union's Red Army as it rolled down the Korean peninsula to meet the Americans at the 38th parallel—though to believe North Korean hagiography he was basically on his own. The early years of the DPRK saw fantastic growth, war, and the twin pillars of ideology and ethnic unity as the foundations that helped uphold the state while frenetic reconstruction took place in the late 1950s. The economy slowed in the 1960s, however, and an inflation of martial values and military spending cemented North Korea's status as a garrison state.

Both countries were in desperate straits in their early years, literally fighting for survival. Understanding how these military conflicts shaped elite thinking and hampered economic growth is key to understanding why Burma and North Korea focused on their security concerns at the expense of wealth creation and integration into international society. In both cases, the leadership in the 1960s decided that a military-first approach was the only way to protect their states against their perceived threats.

Moreover, it calls into relief the improvements in strategic/military changes that took place in Myanmar in the 1990s and 2000s, which allowed for a movement towards increased civilian rule. This can then be compared with the relative rigidity to the DPRK's strategic vulnerabilities over a similar time period. Their inability to resolve their security dilemma drives North Korea's nuclear program, which drives their pariah status.

Burma

Within months of independence, a coalition government was facing the utter collapse of the country: there was a communist insurgency, a series of ethnic uprisings, and then Chinese nationalist incursions all within the first two years. The salient fact is not only that the *Tatmadaw* (Burmese military) was an unlikely winner against post-independence insurgents: it was that it "could barely be distinguished from the dizzying array of other quasi-state and private armies circulating throughout the country."[1] The chaos of this period "left physical and psychological scars from which Burma has never recovered."[2]

When Ne Win—Burma's future long-term dictator—took over the

Army in February 1949 he had fewer than 2,000 troops at his disposal. Most major cities were not in the central government's hands; even a major Rangoon suburb, Insein, was not.

The Karen had taken many of these cities, including Insein. An irony, perhaps, considering that just a few months earlier the Rangoon government was relying on the Karen, Chin and Kachin soldiers to defend against the communists, so useless were the government forces. The irony is an especially bitter one for those ethnic groups. Their loyalty in 1948 hurt them doubly: first, they battled ethnic Burman communists on Rangoon's orders in areas where the communists were popular, increasing racial tensions; second, they bought Rangoon time to stabilize and build up its military, which was then to prosecute decades-long wars against ethnic armies, as we will see.[3]

It is impossible here to provide a comprehensive survey of all the insurgent groups that took up arms against Burma, whether in the early years of independence or later. Indeed, such a project would likely be doomed to some sort of failure—amalgamations, splinter groups, factionalisms and shifting allegiances make the landscape of conflict a messy one indeed. It is important to understand the major threats to the state, however. It was these challenges—and their eventual resolutions—that first inspired dictatorship in Rangoon and then opened the door to prospective democratization.

The initial threat to the new state was from Communists, though the Communist Party of Burma (CPB) was experiencing factional strife even before independence. One wing, led by Thakin Soe, had advocated for armed struggle against imperialism. When it became clear that the Anti-Fascist People's Freedom League (AFPFL) as going to negotiate independence and other Communist leaders wanted to work within that framework, he took a significant minority of cadres underground in March 1946, leaving urban politics for the jungle.[4] They became known as the Red Flag Communists.

Thakin Than Tun, Aung San's brother-in-law, led those that remained, becoming known as the White Flag Communists.[5] Than Tun at that point may have been second in prestige only to Aung San himself.[6] They had made up an influential element of the AFPFL, Aung San's political front that included a wide range of political actors. They were "outmaneuvered by non–Communist elements," as a 1950 CIA report put it, and kicked out of the league in November 1946. This was in part possible due to the Communists' vocal opposition to Buddhism.[7] In the following months, the CPB drifted away from advocating cooperation towards a more

2. Militaries First, Economies Second

revolutionary line.[8] And the appeal of Marxism in Burmese politics meant that they could continue to "exert an influence far out of proportion to their actual numbers."[9]

This influence meant that the White Flags continued to organize strikes and opposition to the coalition government until March 1948. That month, the government broke the strikes and arrested several communist leaders. Not the right ones, however: "All important BCP leaders escaped … and a full-fledged Communist-led insurrection soon commenced under their direction."[10] Their tactics were guerrilla in nature, drawing on a reserve of popularity generated not only from their leadership but also from sound organizational practices (they were Burma's first political party, after all) and an accessible, compelling message.

The Karen National Union (KNU) had been advocating for Karen independence before the end of the colonial period, while other Karen leaders were lobbying for genuine autonomy, though not making much headway. The Karen did not participate in the 1946 Panglong conference as the Chin, Shan and Kachin did: those three ethnic groups, along with the majority Bamar, signed the Panglong Agreement on February 12, 1947, forming the Union of Burma. By that time, Karen leaders were losing faith in the independence experiment and created Karen fighting units, known as the Karen National Defence Organisation.

Ba U Gyi, a former official under the British and first President of the KNU, defined their four core principles thus: surrender is out of the question; the recognition of the Karen State must be completed; we shall retain our arms; we shall decide our own political destiny.[11] Those guiding principles are still on their website as of 2017.[12]

The Karen were forced out of Insein later in 1949 but set up headquarters in Taungoo, a major town in between Rangoon and Mandalay and former seat of the 1st Karen Rifles under the British. This effectively cut the country in half and saw them controlling a key stretch of railway, for which they sold tickets and collected taxes from passing trains. The *Tatmadaw* was able to regroup and re-arm by March 1950, when they marched on Taungoo and forced the rebellion out of the city and into the uplands and jungle.[13]

Tensions had also flared up in the postwar years between the Muslim and Buddhist populations in Arakan (later called Rakhine), rooted in unequal treatment under the British and what the Buddhists believed was Islamic encroachment on their lands. These tensions were exacerbated during the war as the Muslim population, like the Karen, were generally loyal to the British, while the Buddhist Arakanese worked more closely with the Japanese. Both groups carried out attacks and reprisals against one another during and after the war.[14]

Though they had had far less communication than the Karen with the British, many Muslims in that region were under the impression that they'd earned some kind of autonomy in an independence scenario through their loyalty. They didn't want to live in a Buddhist Arakanese state and were making such demands by mid–1947. The central government had very few troops in the region and after violence between police and participants in a Muslim rally supporting *jihad* erupted in April 1948, an organized rebellion kicked off.[15]

Fortunes ebbed and flowed for the Islamists in the early 1950s, but in 1954 they went on the offensive and gained territory. This, combined with Arakan Buddhist lobbying in Rangoon, compelled the government to devote more resources to this rebellion, largely defeating it by the end of the year. The insurgency, though greatly diminished, dragged on until July 4, 1961, when *Tatmadaw* General Aung Gyi (who would later become Ne Win's no. 2 man) accepted the surrender of the remaining fighters.[16]

In 1947, Arakan Buddhist troops had also gone underground to struggle for independence. They surrendered in 1958, though other Arakan groups would later pop up in the 1960s, as would other small Muslim groups in the region.[17]

Meanwhile, soon after they went underground, the main group of Communists had set up guerrilla bases in the Pegu hills just 90 to 100 miles north of Rangoon, as well as in swathes of territory in northern Shan State. They came to be extremely well equipped, with China supplying everything from pots and pans to anti-aircraft guns.[18]

The U Nu government offered several amnesties to try to end the insurgency in 1948, 1949, 1950 and 1955, the last one even extending to all the leadership, but to no avail. U Nu took to exhorting villagers not to support Communists in a propaganda war against the insurgents. Using religion was a key element, helping frame the Communists as in opposition to key cultural traditions: "Nu's speeches, and his personal conduct as he toured the country—visiting pagodas, offering almsfood to the monks, and propitiating the *nats*—also played an important role in opposing the Communists."[19] "Nats" are localized supernatural beings, like ghosts or sprites, which feature in Burmese superstition.[20]

Militarily, the White Flag Communists were failing to capitalize on a chaotic situation. By 1955, they held no towns, were scattered through various mountain ranges and had been reduced, essentially, to carrying out minor raids and ambushes, sometimes fairly indiscriminately. Defections and desertions plagued the CPB as it became clear that they had no chance of taking Rangoon.[21]

Meanwhile, the Red Flag faction, always smaller, more extreme and less willing to broach compromise positions, was becoming increasingly irrelevant as the 1950s dragged on. The People's Volunteer Organization, another left-leaning armed group, surrendered and became legalized in 1958.[22] Other ethnic-based communist parties popped up in the 1950s but remained small.

By 1955, the greater concern may have been, ironically, the Chinese Nationalists. In 1949, after Mao has already declared the People's Republic of China a political fact on October 1, Kuomintang (KMT) troops were still holding out in remote areas of China, including Yunnan Province. In need of an operational base from which they optimistically planned to retake China, they made for Laos, hoping the colonial authorities in Indochina would be willing to support their plans.[23]

The Chinese People's Liberation Army (PLA) cut that route off, however, and the KMT stragglers found themselves along the Thai-Burma border in Shan State. There they made a base out of the town of Monghsat. By 1951 the United States was supplying these troops, whose numbers were being reinforced from Taiwan, with airdrops; by 1953, they had built an airstrip.[24] Plans to retake Yunnan in the early 1950s failed, with at least two "invasions" turned back. PLA troops also crossed into Shan State in pursuit of the KMT.

The threat of the KMT was not a direct one. The KMT had no designs on Rangoon the way Burmese Communists did. Their presence did open up several potential risks, however. First, it offered Communist China a pretext to invade and perhaps occupy Shan State: the border was not a clear, indelible one, particularly since the colonial period. China may or may not have wanted to expand Yunnan's amorphous borders, but Rangoon could easily envision parts of Shan State being turned into independent republics or fiefdoms with Chinese backing. (A version of this was to happen in the Wa regions, ironically only after the Burmese Communists gave up their ideological struggle, as we will see later.)

The other risk was that the KMT themselves would ally with ethnic militias for the same reason: creating a hospitable state from which to base operations in the struggle against Beijing. For that reason, Rangoon took the issue of KMT troops on its soil to the United Nations in 1953 and the following year the United States and Taiwan did diminish their presence by helping to evacuate half the troops.[25]

U Nu also went to Beijing in 1954 and was effusive in his thanks that China had "never taken advantage" of the fact that KMT troops were in Burma. Beijing-Rangoon relations progressed relatively smoothly and in October 1960, the two countries signed a treaty that included demarcation of the Yunnan-Shan border. Meanwhile, the KMT were building up forces again, with the aim of taking advantage of China's economic failures, and had by then reached about 6,000 troops. The treaty had made Rangoon comfortable enough to cooperate with China sending PLA troops into Shan in order to eliminate the KMT.[26] This they duly did, putting enough military pressure on KMT forces that by March 1961 almost all of them had to be evacuated to Taiwan or face being routed.

Chinese support for the CPB, meanwhile, had been equally restrained. The People's Republic of China had remained dispassionate and cautious vis-à-vis Burma throughout the 1950s, attempting to keep friendly relations with neutral countries, especially those nearby.[27] The decade-long Cultural Revolution beginning in 1966 was to shatter that policy, however, as an ideologically reinvigorated China sought to export revolution and upend class relations beyond its borders.

Unfortunately for Chinese-Burmese people, this ideological tension quickly turned into racial tension. Mao badges worn by Chinese students in a Chinese school became a media issue and were banned by Rangoon, leading to protests by ethnic Chinese students. These protests escalated into anti–Chinese riots. Individuals, Chinese shops, and the embassy were attacked by mobs.[28] From this point, covert Chinese support for the CPB became overt.[29] Within a year, 300 re-armed and well-prepared CPB troops crossed from China over a small river into Möng Ko, overwhelmed the local Burmese garrison, and began an insurgency anew.[30]

The Karen, meanwhile, found themselves from the early 1950s fighting a "protracted rearguard action."[31] In 1952, the government in Rangoon created a new Karen state, which didn't include Karenni areas, separating the lowlands from the highlands.[32] As well as encouraging gaps between different sub-groups or factions of Karen, this also emphasized that during these years the main insurgency was militarily losing control of lowland areas. By the late 1960s, the Karen were largely forced eastward into highland areas.[33]

The Karenni were another group that rose up in arms in the 1950s. The Karenni, or Kayah, are a grouping of nine or more ethnic groups who lived in the highlands East of Rangoon, largely autonomously under both Burman kings and the British. The Karenni were not Panglong Agreement signatories and after independence the Rangoon government moved on the Karenni National Organization (KNO) headquarters in Myat Leh village. The Karenni leader, U Bee Htu Re, was captured and killed. The Karenni now sometimes call the date of that operation, August 9, the "Day of Resistance."[34]

Fighting was largely scattered and disorganized until 1957, when the Karenni National Progressive Party (KNPP) was formed. Despite this newfound unity, the KNPP struggled to become a major force and remained under frequent pressure from the *Tatmadaw*, however.

Another relatively small revolt grew into a bigger threat in the early 1960s. The Mon People's Front, which had initially fought alongside the Karen, gave up their arms when U Nu promised an ethnic state to the Mon. This inspired the formation of the New Mon State Party (NMSP) in July 1958, which eventually grew disillusioned with Rangoon and formed the Mon National Liberation Army (MNLA) in 1971 to struggle for genuine Mon autonomy and the right to secession.[35]

A number of small Chin rebellions sprung up in the 1950s, also. As if to highlight the overwhelmingly complex nature of ethnic politics in Burma, most of these uprisings "were rooted in local ethnic sub-groups," somewhat opposed to what majority Chin leaders were pursuing; they couldn't sustain momentum autonomously and "after the 1962 coup, they were largely subsumed by communist groups or driven out from the Chin hills to the Thai and Indian borders where they linked up with other ethnic nationalist fronts."[36]

Another rebellion was launched by the Pa-O, who are ethnically related to the Karen and usually thought of as a sub-group. They also took up arms in the early 1950s. Initially, they were most concerned about oppression by the Shan princes, or *Sabhwa*. It is even alleged that they may have received *Tatmadaw* support in the early 1950s.[37] By 1955, however, the Pa-O saw the Rangoon government as the greater threat and began fighting against them.

In 1958, convinced to give up armed struggle, 2,000 Pa-O men handed in weapons, along with some fighters from other armed groups.[38] Some remained armed, but in the 1970s the remaining Pa-O fighters split into red and white factions. The Red faction harassed the nearby Karenni, who had not been swayed by communist ideology, and by the end of the decade the Pa-O Nationalist Organization and Red Faction fought each other, a state of affairs that continued well into the 1980s.[39] The Karen also struggled with factionalism in this period. Such have been the vicissitudes and vagaries of the politics of identity and liberation in Burma.

Not only were there conflicts in the field between minority groups and the central authorities, however, but such rivalries also occurred in the corridors of power in Rangoon. The political coalition that governed the country, the Anti-Fascist People's Freedom League was under considerable strain in the mid–1950s. The AFPFL, as a political front, brought together diverse actors with diverse views. It was formed in 1945 with the goal of freeing Burma from Japanese control and then gaining independence. Pro-communist elements split from the AFPFL in 1948, some turning to armed struggle. Other leftists withdrew or were kicked out in 1951 over the government's support for the United Nations in the Korean War. This group formed the Burma Workers and Peasants Party.

As for the larger AFPFL, with independence accomplished and firmly in the rear-view mirror, disagreements among the coalition continued to intensify, particularly over who should rule and how. As one contemporaneous account put it:

> The main cause of the rift that rent asunder the AFPFL was personal feuds as a result of rivalry, jealousies, and distrust among the colleagues who, after long years of power, became intoxicated and succumbed to blind conceit and power corruption.[40]

The AFPFL was descending into dysfunctional factionalism, with one group led by Prime Minister U Nu and Thakin Tin and another led by Ba Swe and U Kyaw Nyein.

U Nu's faction, dubbed the "Clean AFPFL," only managed to stay in power because the left-wing National United Front (NUF)—previously the opposition party—supported him. This new coalition gave them greater influence over the cabinet and caused some consternation that the farther left or even pro-communist elements in the NUF could be working towards installing a communist regime in the country. To the *Tatmadaw*, it appeared as if the leftist rebels they were fighting in the jungles now had representation in the government. And "after more than ten years fighting the communists," as one scholar puts it, "senior officers were in no mood to see them take power."[41]

Whether or not such an outcome was really at hand, General Ne Win and his colleagues had come to believe that the politicians were incapable of running the country. In the words of one of the protagonists, Colonel

2. Militaries First, Economies Second

Chit Myaing, "We in the military felt that most of the political leaders were more interested in their positions and power than keeping the country united. They just could not agree on how to solve the nation's problems."[42]

Broadly, there had also been a growing personal tension between the politicians and the military men. Once cohorts in the independence movement, those who remained in the military found themselves under the civilian control of men who, instead of "sticking it out," had left for the rather less honorable field of politics. And now they were messing that up.

Finally, while the military had been fighting insurgencies in the jungles, the politicians had *not* been delivering economic growth. By 1958, a full decade after independence, the economy was underperforming and not yet at pre–World War II levels, with a two- and then eight-year plan failing to deliver results.[43]

Given the paralysis in government, with the (probably reluctant) consent of Prime Minister U Nu, the army took control of the country and formed a "caretaker government" in September 1958. (Chit Myaing was given charge of the Ministry of Immigration, National Registration and Census in that government. After the military coup d'état in 1962 he was made a member of the ruling Revolutionary Council.)

The military had the functional capacity to do this because in 1951 the leadership had recognized that they suffered from institutional weaknesses and lack of expertise in several fields. They had set up a "Military Planning Staff" (MPS) under Lieutenant Colonels Aung Gyi and Maung Maung and tasked them with researching and planning in a variety of fields, including economic policy and social policy. The MPS created educational and training institutions; they set up the tools of the post–1962 military regime, including psyops and counterintelligence agencies; they set up the Defence Services Institute, which came to control huge swathes of the economy through its companies.[44]

The civilian government also created a National Defence Committee (NDC) under the Ministry of Defence. The NDC was comprised of key cabinet officials and could form policy. The military also created autonomy for itself through the Defence Services Council, staffed only with military men, to oversee internal armed-forces affairs.[45] These reorganizations helped create an empowered, bureaucratically sound military.

The army instituted discipline and better administration in many sectors after its 1958 takeover. "They were not corrupt and forced lower prices in the bazaars.... They instituted law and order, cleaned the cities and forced squatters to the outskirts of Rangoon."[46]

However, they also found that governance was turning them into what they'd originally sought to eliminate. Divisions and policy fractures were forming within the military itself, with junior officers criticizing their seniors for becoming "just like the politicians."[47] The prospect of intra-military conflict had potentially destabilizing consequences. This, combined with the fact that if they gave up power the military could maintain the moral high ground, convinced the generals to keep their promise of temporary governance. Thus, somewhat gracefully, the Army retreated from politics, allowing free and fair elections in February 1960.

U Nu's party won a resounding victory in these elections and took office again. But dissatisfaction among the minorities over control from the Burman-dominated center remained the single most important political problem of the 22 months of U Nu's second premiership. Some of his policies upset the tenuous balance of relations with minority groups and quickly reconfirmed for the military that he would be unable to preserve the union.

First, he made Buddhism the state religion in August 1961 through the State Religion Act. Prior, there had been no state religion. This immediately inflamed ethnic tensions. In response, a small group of non–Buddhist Kachins formed the Kachin Independence Organization (KIO) in October 1960. A council was soon formed with the Kachin Independence Army (KIA) as its military wing. The Kachin staged a "small revolt" in 1961, deeply worrying Ne Win and the military.[48] The Kachin leadership had been convinced by at least 1954 that the agreement they had signed at Panglong was insufficient and that a new constitution was needed.[49]

Simultaneously, U Nu was allowing a much broader range of discussions with minority groups on topics of federalism and separatism.[50] There had already been a smattering of Shan rebellions in 1958, a "spontaneous uprising without any centralized, proper leadership."[51] The chieftains of Shan State had long been suspicious that Rangoon wanted to revoke their status of an autonomous state. They also had the constitutional right to secede, which the military felt was being used as a threat, politically.[52]

In 1961, Shan delegates, led by Sao Shwe Thaik, who was also Burma's first president, began talks with the government over greater autonomy and a weaker federal system. The combination of alienating non–Buddhists while empowering a political debate that could allow for secession was perceived by the military to be an unacceptable risk to the integrity of the state.

At the same time, according to diplomats stationed in Rangoon, several months after the election the government was still not settling down to business; it was suffering a paralysis of "indecision and procrastination" that had bedeviled previous U Nu administrations.[53]

The military decided to step in again, though this time without the pretense of being a "caretaker government." On March 2, 1962, tanks and personnel carriers blocked key streets and the army seized control of important buildings, including the Secretariat, Government House and the High Court. A meeting about federalism between Prime Minister U Nu and minority leaders was taking place at the time. He and thirty other ethnic leaders were arrested. Although the coup is generally called bloodless, one person, Sao Mye Thaik, was shot dead while trying to defend his father, the Shan leader Sao Shwe Thaik.[54] Sao Shwe Thaik died in prison later that year. "Both deaths have never been forgotten by the Shan and other minority peoples."[55]

A revolutionary council was set up and would rule until 1974, when a new constitution was passed creating a national assembly and restoring some form of constitutional governance. The council's early decisions portended the isolationist path that Burma would chart. Foreign influence was reduced right away: "two American philanthropic organizations—the Ford and Asia Foundations ... were ordered to leave Burma within six months."[56] The Fulbright and British Council programs, which provided training and exchanges for both students and teachers, were also discontinued.

Foreign cultural influences were also pushed away. As one student who had joined St. Philo's Convent School lamented, they'd dreamed of improving their English, since most of their teachers would be Irish nuns, of rich extracurricular activities and of free use of the school's library but "those dreams never came true. Instead we found all our classes except English taught in Burmese ... with the library closed to borrowers, I could only gaze at the books inside locked cases." Foreign stories and ideas disappeared from curricula.[57]

Older students conducted a protest a few months after the coup at Rangoon University, the heart of a Burmese tradition of student activism. They were met first with tear gas, then beatings and then gunfire. In an act meant to symbolize the commitment and power of the new regime, the military dynamited the Student Union building.[58] The intellectual heart of the independence movement was destroyed.

New Insurgencies

The Karen and Communist insurgencies still raged after the coup, though General Min Maung, commander of the Karen rebels, had been killed by government troops on April 13, 1961. The Revolutionary Council and most of the Karen rebels agreed to a ceasefire in 1964, which held for a decade, until fighting resumed in 1975.[59]

Ironically, after 1962, the *Tatmadaw*'s restraints on the rights of minorities greatly retarded the prospects of running a unified, inclusive state, driving even more groups into open rebellion. Nothing epitomized the grievances of the non–Bamar like the banning of minority languages from state schools.[60] Majority-minority relations had been turned into a zero-sum game.

Two smaller Shan organizations merged to form the Shan State Army (SSA) in 1964. They launched a rebellion following the Revolutionary Council's declaration that the constitutional right to secede was now null and void.[61] The widow of Sao Shwe Thaik and another of his sons led the SSA. In 1971, the Shan State Progress Party (SSPP) was established and its first congress was held, giving the insurgency a political wing.

Another ethnic group, the Palaung, in cooperation with Shan groups and in Shan State, took up arms on January 12, 1963, forming the Palaung National Force. This group underwent a number of permutations and names in the subsequent decades.

"Losing" Shan State to insurgency was to have global consequences. It was already an opium-producing region, even if use of opium had been banned by British-governed India in 1885. It was simply too easy to produce and transport the opium, and in much of remote Shan it was too hard to enforce prohibition. This had led the British to accept its prevalence.[62]

The anarchy caused by having the area at the mercy of multiple rebellions and without genuine governance meant that individual farmers had to rely on opium to survive: there was logistically no market for anything else.[63] The SSA was mildly opposed to using drugs to fund their rebellion, and SSA-controlled areas were less opium-dependent, but other groups were not.

Moreover, the KMT, who had controlled Burma's major opium growing regions until forced to flee in 1961, took their drug-production expertise across to Northern Thailand and Laos with them. They came not only to oversee tribes in those regions growing poppies but also to expand production and create a distribution network for moving Burmese-grown opium to external markets. By the mid–1970s, the Golden Triangle of Northeast Burma, Northern Thailand and Northern Laos was supplying 70 percent of the world's illicit opium.[64]

The Kachin Independence Army (KIA), meanwhile, was turning "into one of the most successful and best organized" of the various fighting forces.[65] As one contemporary observer put it in an annual report, by 1968 the Communists were mostly nuisances not dangers to the state: the one group that was a danger was the KIA.[66] Disciplined, based in areas that the *Tatmadaw* struggled to reach, and with support from China, the Kachin came to be at the vanguard of armed struggle against the state as other groups suffered setbacks.

Still, as the same author noted in his report from the year prior, "each day the Burmese press published some item of rebel activity, as it has for almost twenty years. A day's news in 1967 was like that of 1957."[67] He summed up the disarray thus:

> Burma's chronic insurrectionary activity continued in 1967 as it has since 1948. As in the past, it stemmed from two major sources: first, assorted varieties of Communists, now predominantly pro–Maoist, and their "fronts," such as the National Democratic United Front (NDUF) which includes pro–Communist Karens (who refused to accept the peace negotiated by General Ne Win and Saw Hunter Tha Hmwe in 1963); and second, dissident groups among the ethnic minorities. The latter include the Kachins of the Kachin Independence Army, some of whose leaders are also involved in the NDUF; the anti–Communist Karens who still pine for a Karenistan outside of the Union of Burma and who today are being wooed by a small group of former military associates of Ne Win, known as the National Liberation Army; and several insurgent factions of Shans, the chief one of which is composed of the followers of the late Sao Shwe Thaike and his wife, the Mahadevi, now reportedly living in Thailand and supporting a Shan secessionist move of some kind through the traditional opium trade.[68]

It remained a profoundly complicated and unruly set of shifting fortunes for dozens of armies or factions fighting over ethnic identity, political ideals or control over resources. Major and small groups alike vied for influence as priorities and power relations shifted.

One latecomer to the insurgency chessboard, the Mon, Buddhist cousins of the Khmer, had maintained an uneasy alliance with the Karen insurgency and fairly moderate demands: They wanted their own state, which they were given in 1974, though not to the extent they'd hoped for. As their president put it in 1981, Mon State was just "two former districts of Tenasserim; Moulmein and Thaton ... there are four million of us in Burma, how can we jam together in the small area we have been allotted by Ne Win. We demand the rest of Tenasserim as well, T'avoy and Mergui."[69] They moderated these claims in the 1980s.

Smaller challenges to the state by other groups in rural areas would pop up from time to time in the years after the coup. For example, Arakan nationalists formed the Arakan Liberation Army in 1968 with the help of the Karen National Union. The leadership was quickly imprisoned though were able to revive a small force of 300 men in the mid–1970s. They were eventually crushed in 1977.[70]

Another example was when the Lahu minority rose up in 1972, following a call to arms by a spiritual leader.[71] Again, by way of illustration of the complexities of ethnic identity and conflict in the region, the Lahu are spread across Yunnan, Shan, and Northern Thailand and have multiple languages and subdivisions. There is considerable debate among scholars and some confusion among the tribes themselves as to which constitute Lahu and which are distinct.[72] Who is rebelling against whom and for what purpose can often be difficult to tell when identity and economic interests overlap.

Over the years, the fortunes of various groups would ebb and flow, ceasefires would be negotiated and fail, alliances form and come undone, fronts between groups built and then have to be reconstituted. The most significant might have been the National Democratic Front (NDF) in May 1976, borne out of the Federal National Democratic Front of 1975. The former was exclusively a minority grouping, calling for a federal union.

For someone first reading about the insurgencies that have bedeviled Burma since independence, this may seem like an impossibly complex web of conflict. Imagine for a second how difficult it must have been trying to craft and execute strategic goals in this environment.

As soon as Burma was independent, the state faced threats almost literally from all sides. Some were very real existential threats. Others were threats that sought to dismember the union and slice away at Bamar hegemony. Others had vague, amorphous goals but drained the state's resources away.

It was in this context that the military, which saw themselves as the guardians of the very idea of an independent Burma, took power and kept it for so long. In their view, only they could keep the country together from military and social forces seeking to tear it apart. Only they could prevent the chaos caused by venal politicians. Only they could create a successful, modern, disciplined Burma.

And in the end, only keeping the military at the forefront of society and politics could save the country. Democracy, in this view, was not the answer to any of the problems plaguing the young state. It could, and would, wait.

Burmese Military Men Running the Economy

Ne Win, while fighting to keep the union together, formed the Burma Socialist Programme Party (BSPP) as the state's sole party and ruled through the Revolutionary Council. The military leaders were never willing or able to focus on the economy. The Revolutionary Council initially seemed pro-business and private enterprise, but these ideas had essentially died within a couple years as Ne Win decided to embark on the "Burmese Way to Socialism."[73]

Almost all-private businesses of any size were nationalized and handed over to military-run, state-owned enterprises. Sometimes, even small mercantilists and entrepreneurs weren't spared. Even tiny shops in downtown Rangoon were taken over, with little or no compensation. Small business families went from being part of a market-distribution of goods to having to wait in queues before dawn to get basic necessities once the government distribution came into effect.[74] Within two years, over 100,000 Indians had left Burma, squeezed out economically.[75]

As part of its goal to control prices, Rangoon forced farmers to sell rice to the state (and theoretically no one else) at artificially low prices. They would then compensate for this by subsidizing farmer's inputs, but this system "provided the peasant with few incentives for investment, and until the state began making significant investment in agricultural technology in the mid–1970s, rice production stagnated. In the mid–1960s, Burma ceased to be one of the world's major rice exporting nations, and even faced rice shortages."[76] Recall that under British development of transportation and irrigation infrastructure, Burma had gone from producing rice just for domestic consumption to exporting more rice than any other country in the world by World War II. It retained that status into the early 1960s, but by 1967 it is said that Ne Win would privately admit the country could no longer feed itself.[77]

The Revolutionary Council chose also in the 1960s to shun foreign corporate investment and foreign aid, relying on domestic sources of investment. However, with an expansion of an increasingly inefficient state sector and without an effective taxation system for non-state economic actors, the government struggled to raise capital and invest it into productive growth. In a bitter irony, the decline in rice production meant that income from agricultural surpluses that could also drive modernization and growth was also non-existent.[78]

A culture of bureaucratic paralysis developed, which still persists and is summed up by the phrase *ma lok, ma shot, ma pyot*—"don't do any work, don't get implicated, and don't get fired." Lower level officials simply would not make decisions due to the associated risks. Moreover, further up the chain, a practice called "triple-grazing" became common, wherein a military man would attempt to leverage additional positions in the civilian government and a state-owned enterprise (SOE).[79] With three incomes, his family could do quite well. Without the requisite expertise to handle three divergent positions, his institutions would also suffer, however.

For most of the 1960s, foreign experts were shunned, also. Chinese shoe factory staff members were sent away as soon as locals could manage operations, for example.[80] More importantly, in terms of export earning potential, the mining industry was crippled as local staff with less training replaced foreign experts.[81] Exploration and capital heavy equipment investment also didn't take place in the 1960s.

By the mid–1970s, Burma was facing difficulties in paying back its debts from international agencies and development banks. Despite this, it was taking on more debt yet failing to introduce greater efficiencies into its industries: major extractives such as coal, tin and zinc were still below prewar production levels.[82] Much of Burma's loans came from Germany and Japan, and in the mid–1980s, as the Yen and Deutschmark appreciated while the price of rice, lentils and teak declined, Burma found itself unable to handle its debt service obligations.[83]

By 1987, the situation was in rapid decline. The socialist government had had a state procurement system for rice, which purchased the grain at a deflated price and depressed production and earnings for farmers. Under pressure from farmers, however, in 1987 they liberalized agricultural markets, leading to a surge in prices and a deep strain on the pockets of ordinary citizens.[84] Inflation rose to 26 percent.[85]

The same week it announced the relaxation of controls on the agricultural sector (in September 1987), Rangoon suddenly announced its three biggest bills would become worthless. They had used this trick in 1985, also, attempting to crack down on black marketeering and inflation. Both attempts failed. From the 1987 currency reform, one can draw a fairly straight line between the upheaval and economic pressure put on the population to the uprising and crackdown the following year. It was that crackdown and the events that followed that drove the country into its pariah status.

North Korea

North and South Korea got less than five years of peace between the end of World War II and the Korean War. This period was marred by purges and dislocations in both states, but it could be called "peace" insofar as there was not a total mobilization for war. When all-out war came in June 1950 and ended in 1953, it left two shattered, broken and still unified states. South Korea's response (eventually) was to become an economic powerhouse and to gain relevance and security through its importance in the global economy. North Korea's response was to turn itself into a fortress society, one that any enemy would be fearful of.

It did this to fend off the military threat of a superpower adversary, the United States, and to compete with South Korea, its rival for political legitimacy, economic success and military power. Through its first couple decades, the DPRK appeared to have the upper hand in this conflict: its military and strategic strengths—as well as economic prowess—were capable of threatening and undermining its competitor to the south. As the Cold War dragged on, however, Pyongyang had failed to rid its peninsula of the Americans and was watching South Korea transform into an economic powerhouse. Its reliance on a militarized society couldn't change these facts.

Songun means "military first." It emerged as a term in the 1990s as the economy crumbled and Kim Jong Il essentially abandoned the economy as a priority, with disastrous results. In practical terms, this meant prioritizing military companies for concessions and personnel for rations as famine swept in during the mid–1990s. Politically, it meant the Korean Workers Party became partially subordinated to the military as Kim Jong Il ruled primarily from the National Defence Commission. In ideological terms, Songun is viewed as an extension of the country's *Juche Ideology*, which emphasizes national independence among a mishmash of leader-centric socialist and race-nationalist ideals.

If you can't independently protect your country, none of the other tenets of Juche are achievable. In practical terms, during the collapse of global socialism and the famine, Songun meant protecting the state through the survival of the military taking precedence over survival of individuals.

Interestingly, North Koreans today will tell you that Songun emerged in the 1960s. The country has a penchant for backdating or adjusting historical records, such as when they remove disgraced cadres from pictures, but in this case there is perhaps a logic to it. DPRK military spending shot up in the 1960s. By some accounts, military spending went from 2.6 percent of GDP per year to around 30 percent in just a few years as Kim Il Sung and Khrushchev's relationship deteriorated and Kim felt the Russians could not be trusted to protect Korea.[86] In a 1963 speech, Kim Il Sung said the buildup had the goal of "turning the whole country into a fortress and thus preventing our enemies from venturing to provoke us."[87]

The year before, the Korean Workers' Party had held a plenum that established four fundamental military policies: first, arming the entire population; adding training for existing soldiers; turning the whole country into a fortress; and modernizing the armed forces.[88] A country and culture welded together in the inferno of the Korean War was on the way to ceaselessly reproducing the conflict as a means of perpetuating state survival.

Kim Il Sung did at one point seem to recognize that quality of life was being subordinated to militarization. After all, Kim had called for an important shift at the fourth Korean Worker's Party Congress in 1961: he introduced a seven-year economic plan that emphasized light industry and the production of consumer goods to improve quality of life in the DPRK. The first years of the plan were to make sure that heavy industry was able to supply the inputs necessary for light manufacturing to take off and supply more and better daily-life products. This seven-year plan came after two extremely successful economic plans of three years (1954–1956) and five years (1957–1961) focused on heavy industry that reported hitting their targets ahead of schedule. Now it was time to improve the lives of average citizens, both for the sake of it and also to demonstrate to South Koreans how good things were in the North.

In the face of the ballooning military expenditures, however, the seven-year plan lost steam. It had to be extended to 1970, when at the next Workers' Party Congress Kim himself admitted the price had been high in terms of quality of life. The cultural and economic ramifications persist to this day.

Why did it turn out this way? A North Korean text explains it like this:

> The United States precipitated the "missile crisis" against the Republic of Cuba, escalated its war of aggression against Vietnam and in south Korea, stepped up its aggressive provocations against the northern part of Korea, making frenzied preparations for a new war.
> In order to cope with this situation, the Fifth Plenary Meeting of the Fourth Party Central Committee of the WPK (December 1962) set forth the line of simultaneously carrying out economic construction and defence building.[89]

The text continues to state that in order to accomplish this "every sector had to greatly increase its output." As if to illustrate how impossible this would be, it cites a slogan of the time: "A Gun in One Hand and a Sickle and Hammer in the Other!"[90] How does one work effectively when trying to hold a sickle *and* a hammer in one hand?

Some argue that North Korea has always been dedicated to the military takeover of the South, even when it has seemed far out of their reach. As Kim Il Sung said in December 1954, "the future duty of our army is the liberation of the southern part of the peninsula. Therefore it won't do to impatiently rush in to liberating the south right now, tomorrow or the day after."[91] Part of that statement may have been Kim managing his people and institutions, but given the subsequent focus on re-militarization, it is unlikely to only have been empty rhetoric.

After all, "the Kimist ethos was a military ethos," writes Adrian Buzo. Its founders saw life as "an unremitting struggle, its world-view was one of near-victory, followed by the bitter humiliation of defeat amid catastrophic material destruction ... the Kimists reconstituted the DPRK as a militarist society under the leadership of former guerillas whose major objective was the reversal of the verdict of the Korean War and who made an astounding material commitment to military production to achieve this."[92]

That ethos may have provided the background, but actual conditions internationally and on the peninsula certainly affected Pyongyang's decision to invest so much in its military in the early 1960s. Part of it may be explicable by the politics of South Korea. Throughout the 1950s, South Korea's dictator Sungman Rhee was willing to fight for "unification by any means," including war. Prior to the Korean War, the United States had even held off supplying him with offensive weapons for fear he would start a war with the North.[93] Rhee was swept out of power in a student movement in April 1960, and the two short-lived presidencies that followed both signaled a softer line on unification.

This attitude may have been perceived of as weakness in Pyongyang, but it wouldn't last long. Park Chung-hee's coup in May 1961 was accompanied by a staunch anti-communist focus and an overt call for economic growth as a prelude to unification.⁹⁴ In the zero-sum world of inter-Korean politics, the opportunity to project strength against conciliation and political uncertainty (during the place-holding presidencies) was quickly replaced by the need to match Park's toughness with toughness. Kim certainly hoped for an eventual revolution in the South as a means for unifying Korea and significant numbers of South Koreans were attracted to Juche, Kim's patriotism and the promises of socialism. A collected volume of his speeches and tracts from 1948 to 1968 was indeed titled "On South Korea's Revolution and Unification of the Fatherland."

However, he also saw that struggle for unification under his control as part of an international conflict against "American Imperialism." Kim noticed that in the early 1960s the United States was demonstrating a willingness to go to war in another divided Asian country, Vietnam. Or as he put it, "the American Imperialists are dragging South Vietnam into a blind abyss. Those bastards will not only stop there, but on the contrary are threatening to expand the war to Northern Vietnam." His view was that South Korea held the same function for the Americans, who while suppressing socialism in the South "plot to use Korea as a bridge to invade China or the USSR."⁹⁵ Kim's DPRK remained therefore on the frontline of a global struggle long after the hot war had ended. Re-ignition of the war was always possible.

To that end, while another all-out war was avoided, there was an intensification of North Korean incursions and attacks on the South in the late 1960s: some call this period "the second Korean War." In 1966, there were 42 American and South Korean casualties along the DMZ. In the first nine months of 1967, the number had jumped to perhaps 300.⁹⁶ North Korean Special Forces would typically clandestinely insert themselves behind enemy lines and wreak havoc on infrastructure and conduct harassing, sometimes deadly small attacks before fleeing. They were extremely well trained, with one military analyst stating: "Man for man, the DPRK special forces soldiers of 1966–69 might have been the toughest opponents ever to face American soldiers."⁹⁷ According to one author, the 1960s saw the most violations of the armistice—82 times, out of a total of 219 (or 37.44 percent) between 1953 and 2009.⁹⁸

In January 1968, two audacious military actions had the United States and South Korea on their heels. The first was a thwarted commando raid on the Blue House, Seoul's presidential residence and office. The second was the capture of the U.S. naval spy ship, the *Pueblo*, which sparked a yearlong crisis while the crew was held captive. The ship itself remains the prize possession of the DPRK's war museum in Pyongyang.

Editorials in the main North Korean newspaper, *Rodong Sinmun*, also changed in tone. In the early 1960s, the Worker's Party and its goals and policies were the dominant theme on the "opinion" pages. But from 1967 to 1969 the content shifted focus in two ways: first, and predominantly, they portrayed Kim Il Sung as the unified and unchallengeable center of a monolith leadership under the Juche idea; second they emphasized the importance of the military. Towards the end of a difficult decade, "North Korea came to advocate for *Juche* and ordered the quickening of the militarization of society to respond to a military-security threat."[99]

Broadly speaking, the necessity of this militarization is justified by North Korea's view of its place in the world and its struggle against the forces of evil. This is expressed in a tract by Kim Jong Il in 2002 called "On the Creative Military Thought of the Great Leader." Kim Jong Il cites his dad's identification that since "imperialism remains in this world, the source of war can not be eliminated, and the danger of war can not be made to disappear."[100]

Interpretations for the timing of Kim's militarization of society and the uptick in military actions are varied but tend to begin with the international context. The same week as the *Pueblo* saga began, so did the Tet Offensive in Vietnam. This would come to consume American attention and also began to seriously erode the American public's belief that Vietnam was a winnable war.

Concurrently, Kim recognized that the United States was increasingly tied down in the growing conflict in Vietnam. American commanders wanted to avoid trouble in Korea so as not to detract from the effort in Vietnam and stretch thin the resources being devoted to that theater.[101] Moreover—though Kim probably couldn't have known this—the Vietnam War meant that the best equipment and best commanders were no longer sent to Korea, making U.S. forces there more vulnerable to insurgent tactics.[102] Finally, Kim Il Sung rightly inferred that he could assist a communist state in North Vietnam by engaging their common enemy in Korea.

This was an idea that Pyongyang began selling to its own citizens by the mid–1960s. For example, a *Rodong Sinmun* editorial from 1966 argues that while Koreans should be focused on self-reliance, they have to strengthen the "communal anti-imperialist struggle." This meant "workers parties and communist parties have to oppose American imperialism and support the Vietnamese people with all possible efforts."[103] In terms of this joint struggle, Kim was only keen enough to send a handful of pilots to directly engage the United States in Vietnam.[104] Rather, he saw his role in the shared fight against American power as opening a second front on the Korean peninsula.

There was also a "threat from the rear" of the DPRK. The years 1966 to 1969 were the peak of China's Great Proletarian Cultural Revolution, which saw China simultaneously turn inward in a destructive purge of bourgeois and foreign elements, while also criticizing neighbors such as Vietnam and North Korea for not supporting the Cultural Revolution. The strain with a major ally was a huge threat to the Kim regime.[105] It also, however, provided a perceived opportunity for Kim to portray himself as being at the vanguard of global revolutionary and anti-imperialist forces, taking over from Mao as both an ideological and revolutionary leader while the PRC turned inward.[106]

The relative economic gains of the DPRK were also under threat by the mid–1960s, as South Korea's development model began to kick into high gear. South Korea's economy was not only surging forward, but also it appeared as if Seoul was becoming a mature state in international politics, earning for itself an air of permanence. In June 1966, President Park hosted the Asian Pacific Council (composed of Taiwan, Japan, Malaysia, the Philippines, South Vietnam, Thailand, Australia and Laos). Countries giving diplomatic recognition to South Korea doubled during 1966 and Seoul also negotiated a Status of Forces Agreement with the United States, implying equal official status as a sovereign partner of the United States, rather than a mere dependent or proxy.[107] The consolidation of political recognition from the outside, non-communist world threatened Kim's vision of a unified Korea under his control.

Kim Il Sung's potential as a successor to Mao as a global leader was also likely linked to the perceived need to foment a revolution in South Korea. Pyongyang couldn't wage a successful war against South Korean and U.S. forces, but it still hoped that the South Korean people might rise up in support of their Communist kin. Kim began arguing for this with the Soviets from the mid–1960s. The failed raid on the Blue House might be read as an attempt to create a power vacuum in which an uprising could develop; after the failure of the raid, grabbing the *Pueblo* was a means of distracting and shifting blame to "U.S. aggression."[108]

By 1970 it was clear that Pyongyang was unlikely to be able to unify the peninsula by force or by fomenting a southern revolution. The battle switched largely to a diplomatic one and a competition for legitimacy in

2. Militaries First, Economies Second 53

the international community. For the first time, however, it included direct, semi-official and official interactions between the two Koreas.

On July 4, 1972, after several rounds of meetings, Seoul and Pyongyang agreed on some basic principles for unification in a Joint Communiqué. The key principles were that unification should be achieved independently, without being subject to external influence or interference (something of a hopeful fantasy), through peaceful means, and transcending differences in ideologies and systems. The agreement also set up a direct phone line for the first time and promised "numerous exchanges in many fields."[109] The concept of a "Federal Republic of Koryo" was revived by Kim Il Sung in 1973; it had first been proposed by Pyongyang when Seoul was in flux in 1960–61. Kim's Federal Republic has been widely seen as an attempt to put pressure on Seoul by making it appear less interested in unification in the face of a proactive Pyongyang. In the zero-sum relations of the two Koreas it was also widely seen as a long-term strategy towards communization of the South.[110] In the medium term it was at least an attempt by the DPRK to get American troops out of the Republic of Korea.

A decade on, South Korean scholar Lee Man-woo wrote that the Joint Communiqué was doomed to fail because President Park Chung-hee of South Korea regarded the July accord as nothing more than a limited undertaking between himself and Kim so that he could manage his own domain unimpeded. North of the DMZ the primary aim was to use the principle of non-interference by foreign powers to see if Seoul would consent to the removal of U.S. forces from South Korea.[111]

Even this shift towards diplomatic competition was fundamentally shaped by the military standoff with South Korea and the United States. The stalemate on the battlefield and the failures to generate an uprising in the South forced Pyongyang to look to other types of competition. This did not mean that Pyongyang appreciably reduced the militarization of its society, nor did incidents and threats disappear, even if they were reduced in frequency. For example, during the rapprochement of the early 1970s, the DPRK appeared to be building its guerrilla-trained forces as subversive campaigns and multiple naval or coastal incidents still took place.[112] "Asymmetric violence" was not off the table, either.

This may have reached its apex in 1983, when the fates of the DPRK and Burma came together in a most dramatic fashion. On October 9, 1983, three North Korean special agents detonated a bomb during the visit of a high-level South Korean delegation to the Aung San Martyr's Mausoleum in Rangoon. The explosion killed four Burmese and 17 senior South

Korean officials, including four cabinet ministers and two senior presidential secretaries. It missed President Chun Doo-hwan only because his motorcade had been delayed.[113] Burmese authorities quickly captured two of the agents and killed one as they tried to exfiltrate. Rangoon severed ties with Pyongyang.

A frontal attack on the ROK was decreasingly viable by the 1980s, so Pyongyang "devised a kind of substitute war": "Given President Chun's unpopularity among dissidents and students in South Korea today," wrote Lee Man-woo in the 1980s, "the North Korean authorities undoubtedly perceived and calculated that the elimination of the Chun government would represent a supreme achievement of national duty and also heighten the sense of urgency regarding the Korean question in the international community."[114] Ironically, the attempt on Chun probably helped generate "popular emotion" that solidified support for his regime among the South Korean public.[115]

Part of Pyongyang's impetus for the attack may have been that Burma and other Asian countries that were part of Chun Doo-hwan's itinerary at the time had been historically more pro–Pyongyang. Many, including Burma, were cohorts in the non-aligned movement. Pyongyang recognized that Seoul was trying to erode support for North Korea among these countries and had vituperated "that this criminal act would neither be attainable nor tolerated."[116]

The same year, 1983, the close relationship between North Korea's military output and its diplomatic efforts was visible elsewhere: reports suggest Pyongyang sold some $800 million worth of weapons to Iran in 1982, delivered $640 million worth of arms to Zimbabwe, and sent military advisors to more than a dozen countries, including Brunei, Grenada, Libya, Seychelles, Somalia, Uganda and Zimbabwe.[117]

Domestically during the late 1970s and 1980s, Kim Jong Il began consolidating his position as successor to his father, Kim Il Sung. In October 1980 he was put on the Party's Military Commission and began to politically and bureaucratically organize the military along lines that would strengthen his rule and created kind of a military-led system.[118] (Having control over military institutions is what later allowed Kim Jong Il to survive the famine of the mid–1990s.)

Regardless, Pyongyang's view of the world remained intensely militarized. Pyongyang has always perceived itself to be under siege. It imbues every individual in society with that mentality. In 2013, for example, there was a period of tensions with the United States and South Korea during which family heads (usually fathers) were told by their work units to ready their family for war at any moment. This perpetual state of anxiety can be exhausting. In April 2016, during another period of heightened tensions, more than one of this author's North Korean interlocutors, from somewhat different social classes, expressed the view that "we should just get it over with and have a war. This is too stressful."

Efforts at dialogue from the United States or South Korea were often seen as covert efforts to destroy the state. Joint U.S.–ROK military drills are still seen as a "rehearsal for invasion." When information emerged about an American war plan drawn up in the 1980s called OPLAN 5027, which included not only counterattack plans but also massive expeditionary forces from the United States, it gave the Kims the opportunity to rail that the destruction of the DPRK was always the goal.[119] In the face of such enemies, they could argue, what choice did they have but to create a garrison state?

On the other hand, the militarization of North Korea has not only been defensive. Throughout the late 1960s, Kim Il Sung hung onto a very real hope that the South Korean populace could be coaxed to overthrow his Southern rivals in Seoul, allowing him to either sweep down the peninsula militarily or politically absorb a new, revolutionary government in Seoul. In this way, too, it was imperative to have a potent fighting force, either to push out the Americans or to ensure political rivals in the South couldn't emerge during an uprising.

The choice in the 1960s to construct a military society has been profound. Even as the prospects for reunification by direct force or subversion of the Republic of Korea have faded, the garrison state, a militarized culture and a deep us-against-the-world mentality has persisted.

Economy Second

Centralized economies always have problems, though throughout the 1980s Pyongyang was able to provide housing, supplies and rations to most of its people through a coupon and work-unit supply system. Kim Il Sung wanted to stamp out the market economy completely but was never quite able to do it. Farmers markets and other small-scale trading always took place, for example.

China's experimentation with SEZs has had a clear impact on Pyongyang's decision-makers, even though Pyongyang's commitment to economic reform has been considerably more reluctant that Beijing's, to say the least. The DPRK simply couldn't afford to open in the same way and maintain its garrison state.

Kim Il Sung visited Deng Xiaoping in 1982 and was taken to see Sichuan Province's economic growth (as well as used to snub Margret Thatcher, with whom negotiations over Hong Kong were going poorly—another story). Kim Jong Il visited China in 1983 and a delegation of some 50 North Koreans toured Shenzhen and Shanghai in 1984. The next year saw not only Kim Il Sung return to China, but also a delegation of 500 North Koreans take a southern tour to Shenzhen.[120] Beijing was eager to show off its results, while at the same time keeping a respectful distance from DPRK internal politics. There were several top-level Chinese visits to Pyongyang in this period, also.[121]

These exchanges contributed to the first DPRK attempt to deal with foreign investment: the passing of the Joint Venture Law (JVL) in September 1984, which was modeled on China's 1979 JVL.[122] Rajin-Sonbong (now commonly referred to as "Rason") Free Economic Trade Zone was set up on the border of Northeast China and Russia in 1991 after a Kim Il Sung visit to China. It was also in some ways a facsimile of China's booming Shenzhen Special Economic Zone: far from the political center, a place to experiment.

It was not accompanied, however, by the commitment to economic reform that Beijing shifted rapidly towards in the early 1980s. This was because, as any North Korean will tell you, the DPRK "faces unique conditions and circumstances."[123] Pyongyang's decision-makers were still consumed with a fortress-nation survival mentality and saw relaxing central control as far too risky to give people running the SEZ real autonomy.

Still, by the late 1980s a nascent consumerism in Pyongyang was also visible, as was a social class with a bit of spending power.[124] By all accounts, this was by DPRK standards a fairly relaxed time socially, evident in the country's music and fashion.

This period was to be obliterated by the economic disaster of the 1990s. Refusing to reform as the Communist world crumbled around them, the Kims lost their economic patron, the Soviet Union, and their other trading and bartering partners. Following the fall of the Soviet Union, Moscow began demanding payment in hard currency, precipitating a crash in the DPRK's trade volume from over $4 billion down to $2.5 billion per year by 1991.[125]

Much of North Korea's imports were cereals and foodstuffs: when

2. Militaries First, Economies Second   57

severe flooding hit in the summer of 1995, destroying crops *and* industrial facilities, the economy went into freefall. Proud, fiercely independent Pyongyang had to request emergency aid on August 19, 1995.[126]

Up until this point the majority of people had depended on the state's public distribution system for all or most of its food. When this collapsed, famine struck, leading to deaths by starvation as well as diseases related to malnutrition. In the end this probably claimed the lives of 600,000 to one million people, though estimates range from 220,000 to 3.5 million.[127]

The economy has recovered somewhat since then, in no small part to the acceptance of marketization in the Kim Jong Un era. North Korea is essentially a market economy now. Kim has accepted that the state does not have the capacity to control everything as it once did. He has ceded management of companies to individuals and allowed entrepreneurship to grow. However, key bottlenecks remain. Pyongyang is reluctant to give up control of its citizens and let them freely communicate with foreigners or have access to the information they need to truly plug into the global economy, issues we will explore later.

The overwhelming perceived need to use extreme methods of social control to provide security against the United States remains strong. Many North Koreans still think that they could be more like China except that a hostile superpower is still occupying half of what is in their minds rightfully the territory of the DPRK.

For both Burma/Myanmar and the DPRK, dramatic political pressures and military conflict defined the early years of independence. In the decades that followed, Myanmar was under constant threat of fracture or dissolution from a myriad of groups that had no wish to be part of the 20th century construct of Burma, many of whom had support from other countries. North Korea also was and remains under threat from a superpower whose goals are diametrically opposed to Pyongyang's. The DPRK also faced and faces a competitor state—one which seemed ripe for revolution for decades, but eventually became a greater success by almost any reasonable metric.

In both cases, this created a class of political and military elites who were defined by conflict and sought political and military control at the expense of all other values, including and especially the human rights and freedoms that most Westerners enjoy. Crucially, the military-first mentality also meant that both countries missed significant opportunities to improve the material quality of life for their citizens. Eventually, this mentality would see the countries become Asia's pariah states.

3

Becoming Pariah States

Seeds of destruction take root in the human heart, and even among those who long for peace, they call to our darker instincts and urge us to violence.[1]
—Victoria Armour-Hileman, *Singing to the Dead*

What does it mean to be a pariah state? To take actions so far outside the norm you suffer near-universal rejection and condemnation? In the context of the Cold War it was a hard thing to achieve. No matter how mismanaged or despicable a government might be, usually one side or the other of the binary world would embrace you, so long as there was an ideological and/or strategic gain to be had. Notable exceptions would include South Africa and Zimbabwe.

Once the Cold War ended, however, U.S. President George H.W. Bush's "New World Order" came into view. Defying that order or violating the norms of the liberal and neoliberal ideas that underpinned it became much harder. In the 1990s, military challenges to the unipolar international system or human rights abuses could be more easily pointed out and pressured. There was no longer an opposing camp to shield such ethical or strategic challenges.

Both the DPRK and Myanmar are by any contemporary definitions, human rights violators. In Myanmar, human rights, particularly the suppression of democracy, drove the country into pariah status. For North Korea, it was its nuclear program that turned it into an outsider. Human rights were secondary, as were military clashes, such as naval skirmishes in 2002 or the sinking of the Cheonan naval corvette in 2010, though certainly such episodes contribute to its "rogue" image.

It is important, though displeasing to some, to recognize that the international politics of pressure and sanctions relate to power relations, also. There is a reason activism on human rights in China and Saudi Arabia is not translated into political action. There is a reason that just two years after sanctions were applied to Russia over the Ukraine crisis, there has been considerable political debate in the West about their removal. By contrast, both Myanmar and North Korea endured multi-decade sanctions regimes in response to their policies.

This is not in any way to suggest that human rights are not a real or valid concept, nor that these two states were not deserving of their pariah status. Rather, that their strategic situations made them vulnerable to reprisals from the international community and from the United States in particular. Essentially, they could not get away with it.

The end of the Cold War was profoundly important. Burma, never the most committed Socialist state, was already walking back from state-ownership and state planning in 1987. North Korea, long used to the leverage it enjoyed by being a crucial strategic piece on a global chessboard found itself isolated and under pressure. Elsewhere, as the end of the 1980s approached, fissures were appearing in the socialist block as people began to find voice in their rejection of communism. The leaders of both countries were faced with stark choices. Ultimately, these choices would earn them their pariah statuses.

North Korea's Deindustrialization

For the North Koreans, this retreat of Communism was "ideological confusion," the result not of a bankrupt ideology or social system but a lack of Juche. As Kim Il Sung is purported to have put it to a European guest: "In the past the East European socialist countries used to do everything the way the Soviet Union did; for example, if the Soviet Union uttered 'A,' they said 'A,' and if the former pronounced 'B,' they said 'B.'" Kim also blamed the bureaucratic mindset—again, leaders and officials failing to mix with their people to understand the problems of their country and instead looking to Moscow for answers.[2]

This attitude spoke to a ferocious self-perception of independence, an idea at the very heart of North Korea's conception of itself. (We will examine this later.) An autarkic economy was always out of reach, however. Already Soviet bloc partners believed the North Korean economy had entered into stagnation and decline by the mid–1980s; Moscow reacted by allowing a large trade imbalance to develop, subsidizing the economy.[3] When the Soviet Union disappeared so did a variety of support, without which the DPRK struggled.

This precipitated what might be the "most arresting tale of economic failure from modern times," as one observer put it.[4] North Korea hasn't published economic data since the 1960s, but it became clear that it was experiencing a catastrophic economic contraction. Floods ravaged the country in 1995 and again in 1996, damaging both industry and its tenuous food production system, which was already not producing enough to feed everyone.[5] A full-blown famine was triggered.

Estimates of the tragedy vary wildly, but sober assessments put the total number of deaths between 600,000 and 1 million people or 3 percent to 5 percent of the population. That basic number doesn't capture the increase in malnourishment, physical underdevelopment, crime, displacement, or other social problems that grew out of that period.[6] In retrospect, the country's unwillingness to dramatically reform its economy and allow a more open system created a social and public health crisis. It was also linked to the strategic and geopolitical crisis of the mid–1990s that most captured the attention of the world.

Nuclear Weapons

It would not be greatly exaggerating to say North Korea's leadership has been obsessed by nuclear weapons since its founding. Despite what their official history emphasizes—a narrative that Kim Il Sung largely drove the Japanese off the peninsula—elites have always known that American nuclear weapons are what brought Japan to its knees. Kim Il Sung also watched as President Truman and his military debated using nuclear weapons again in the Korean War.

The USSR—having helped China develop nuclear capability, then coming to regret it—was more reluctant to help their smaller Korean ally. Nuclear assistance "was transmitted grudgingly and with many strings attached." Despite this, in 1959 Moscow agreed to help establish a nuclear research center in the DPRK.[7] By 1967, a small research reactor was operating in Yongbyon, 90 kilometers north of Pyongyang. The Russians were hesitant to help Pyongyang build a more substantial plant, however, so in the 1960s the North Koreans began asking East Germany and China for the assistance the Russians wouldn't provide. Well into the 1980s they were making requests to other socialist countries for training and equipment that could feed into a nuclear weapons program. They were consistently rebuffed.[8]

The North Koreans spent the 1970s trying to work towards a nuclear program that could be weaponized, a fact that seemed to elude the Kremlin. (North Korea's reputation for opacity has been long earned.) Pyongyang's continued requests for more nuclear cooperation led Moscow to pledge to build four civilian-use reactors from which it would be difficult to extract weapons-use material. In turn, North Korea agreed to join the Non-Proliferation Treaty (NPT), signing on in 1985.[9] The essence of the NPT is that the Nuclear Weapons States agree not to help Non-Nuclear Weapons States develop or acquire nuclear weapons and the Non-Nuclear Weapons States permanently swear off the development of such weapons. In return, the Nuclear Weapons States pledge not to use nuclear weapons against these states and to share the benefits of peaceful nuclear technology.

As Moscow became more cooperative in the mid–1980s, Pyongyang neared completion of its own small light-water reactor, which came online in Yongbyon, North Pyongan Province, in 1986. By 1989, North Korea was suspected of having discharged spent fuel and obtaining about 12 kilograms of weapons-grade plutonium.[10] Let us note here that there are basically two ways to get weapons-grade material. Both start with uranium. Uranium is mined and refined, producing U-235, the isotope necessary for creating energy. A low amount of this, often just 3.5 percent of the uranium, can be used for generating energy. This is called low-enriched uranium. For weapons, you need a much higher percentage: 90 percent. This is called highly enriched uranium or HEU. Uranium can be enriched, or purified, to this level by using centrifuges to spin the fissile material at super-fast speeds to concentrate it.

The other way to get material for weapons is by putting low-enriched uranium into fuel rods, which are then used up by heating water through controlled nuclear reactions, generating steam that produces electricity at nuclear power plants. One of the by-products of this process is plutonium-239. Used, or spent, fuel rods can be taken out and the plutonium extracted. This plutonium is also suitable for weapons use.

Under the NPT, the DPRK had inspection and access obligations towards the International Atomic Energy Agency (IAEA). Pyongyang was greatly suspicious of the IAEA, however: from their perspective, it was an extension of American intelligence. Signatories of the NPT are supposed to submit to a Safeguards Agreement that includes routine inspections within 18 months. By 1991, under various pretexts, Pyongyang had not.

On September 27, 1991, for its part, the United States announced that all land and sea-based U.S. tactical nuclear weapons would be removed from overseas bases. This was to balance Soviet reductions, but it included all U.S. nuclear weapons in South Korea. This paved the way for inter-Korean negotiations on nuclear weapons. On December 31, 1991, Seoul and Pyongyang announced the North-South Denuclearization Declaration, with Washington heavily advising Seoul behind the scenes. Also, in 1992 the United States promised not to hold their annual Team Spirit military drills to encourage Pyongyang to cooperate with the IAEA. (The annual drills, conducted with South Korea, cause much consternation in Pyongyang.)

Washington had leaned on Moscow to apply pressure to Pyongyang to sign the NPT in the mid–1980s. It then paved the way for North Korea's accession to the Safeguards Agreement and inspections in April 1992 by offering concessions to Pyongyang and cooperating with Seoul. When Pyongyang joined, these two successes contributed to the feeling that the situation was under control.[11]

This feeling would end quickly. The contemporary, two-decade North Korean Nuclear Crisis was sparked when the IAEA found evidence that the North Koreans had produced more fissile material than they had acknowledged. Two sites that the Americans suspected held additional plutonium were also not declared on the DPRK's list of facilities declared to the IAEA. The Americans tipped the IAEA off on this and the IAEA demanded to inspect them.[12]

If Pyongyang harbored suspicions about the IAEA being too close with or supported too much by the Americans before the inspectors arrived, the intrusiveness of the inspection regime did nothing to allay this mistrust. The South Koreans were also pushing the IAEA to conduct "challenge inspections," while at the same time, the United States and R.O.K. were dragging their heels on allowing North Korean inspections of former nuclear bases in the South.[13]

Pyongyang dug its heels in and declared the two key sites military facilities and thus off-limits to the IAEA. They also raised the stakes by threatening to leave the NPT, a 90-day procedure. By the end of the year, the United States declared that Team Spirit would go ahead after all. Deft diplomatic maneuvering by the Kim Dae-jung administration in Seoul and Clinton's team in Washington got the North Koreans to pledge not to leave the NPT. This was in June 1993. Within twelve months, however, the same cycle of events would recur.[14]

The situation came down to two core assertions: the United States said if North Korea didn't comply with NPT obligations, sanctions would be imposed. North Korea said sanctions would be treated as an act of war. These positions hardened through the spring of 1994 even as IAEA inspectors were being let back in. Then, in May, Pyongyang crossed one of Washington's red lines: they removed the fuel rods from their 5-megawatt nuclear research reactor, without international monitors present. This not only gave the Koreans fuel that could be used for weapons but, in removing them, Pyongyang also destroyed the historical record of their activities.[15]

At this point, with both sides boxed in by their own rhetoric, U.S. President Bill Clinton was considering not only sanctions but also airstrikes on the facility. Meanwhile, ramen noodles and bottled water were flying off the shelves in South Korea, where some segments of the populace feared the worst given the rhetorical boiling point that had been reached. Airstrikes could have led to all-out war. Sanctions too could have triggered a North Korean military action. Whichever side shot first, it was difficult to know how far things might escalate. Even a limited conflict could leave Seoul devastated, as a North Korean negotiator had all but promised in the now infamous "sea of fire" remark.

It was from this position that a new player stepped onto the stage: former U.S. President Jimmy Carter. Carter was alarmed to see both sides drifting towards a war that neither really wanted. With Clinton's permission, though very much acting on his own, Carter visited Pyongyang. He struck a deal directly with Kim Il Sung, confirming Pyongyang's willingness to "freeze" its nuclear weapons program, keep the inspections regime in place and return to talks with the United States. He also made promises about not imposing sanctions that stretched beyond his remit.[16]

Carter's trip, with 20-years hindsight, remains controversial. Hawks believe he simply bought an untrustworthy regime time to develop into a nuclear power. More dove-ish analysts see him as providing an off-ramp from the road to war, and that it was subsequent trust-building measures from both sides where failures lie.

According to the former view, the North Koreans were hell-bent on acquiring nuclear weapons and saw them as their only guarantee of state survival. They would never negotiate them away. By the accounts of a variety of Kim Il Sung's Western interlocutors in the 1990s, his attitudes towards a number of things seemed to have softened; we didn't get a chance to see how far he would have carried the rapprochement sketched out with Jimmy Carter. Kim died on July 8, less than a month after Carter's visit.

Certainly, both Kim Jong Il and Kim Il Sung rhetorically pushed for normalization of relations with the United States. This carried on throughout the 1990s and it was at North Korea's behest that language about the eventual normalization of relations was included in the text of the 1994 agreement between the two sides.[17]

As such, others have argued that the North Koreans *wanted* the IAEA to find discrepancies and for the Americans to become suspicious. The North Koreans were aware of how U.S. satellites and spy planes were closely scrutinizing their nuclear programs. One can conclude they wanted at least part of their facilities to be seen. If not, "they would have chosen the Israeli option and built everything underground."[18] Certainly, through the mid–1990s it appears as if North Korea was at least interested in bargaining away part of its nuclear program for a package of major concessions, including and especially normalization of relations with their chief antagonist, the USA.

Both perspectives are plausible. The first makes sense in that North Korea's interest in nuclear weapons was long term, but it had intensified after the fall of their major patron, the USSR. More isolated than ever, they needed nuclear weapons to guarantee their security. The second—that the nuclear program was a major bargaining chip—has credence, as it might have been the only thing disruptive enough to convince the Americans to offer a peace treaty and concessions.

A peace treaty wasn't yet on the cards, but what was negotiated out of the 1994 crisis was called "The Agreed Framework between the United States of America and the Democratic People's Republic of Korea." This agreement took four months to negotiate and produced a series of concessions. The United States formed a consortium with several allies and agreed to supply two light water reactors, which are harder to extract weapons-grade fuel from. The United States also agreed to supply 500,000 tons of heavy fuel oil annually until the reactors were completed. Full inspections would resume, North Korea would remain a part of the NPT, and the United States would have greater access and input into the storage and reprocessing of fuel.[19] The United States, North Korea, South Korea, Japan and others formed the Korean Peninsula Energy Development Organization (KEDO) to oversee the program.

It wasn't the end of the back and forth. One early hiccup was that that KEDO selected South Korean designed light water reactors. The North Koreans rejected this—out of pride, presumably—triggering three additional weeks of negotiations between American and DPRK diplomats in Kuala Lumpur, Malaysia. In the end, Pyongyang relented.[20] During this period, normalization of relations between the DPRK and the United States were actively discussed.[21]

But bigger problems were to occur. The Democrats lost control of the House of Representatives and the Senate just two weeks after the Agreed Framework was signed. Republicans in Congress were highly critical of the deal and generally media commentary was also. Congress made it difficult for the administration to secure funding for the heavy-fuel shipments. Then Clinton became embroiled in a sex scandal, draining political capital.[22]

Not only were fuel shipments delayed by a disinterested Congress, the quality of the fuel sent to the DPRK was especially low. It had a high-sulfur content, making it corrosive and ultimately damaging some of the North's power station equipment. The Americans tried to explain this was essentially a bureaucratic error: a non-technical government purchaser just buying the cheapest fuel he or she could.[23] The North Koreans suspected more sinister machinations on the part of their old enemy. It didn't help that much of the academic debate in Washington was about how long the DPRK could survive: the death of its founding leader and its economic collapse seemed to portend a political collapse.

Pyongyang's mistrust led it to hedge its bets, too, in the end. "Hedging" here unfortunately has a synonym: "cheating." A major question, perhaps unresolvable, is whether Pyongyang always intended to cheat or whether it's cheating was in reaction to American prevarications on its commitments under KEDO. As noted, North Korea had been interested in nuclear weapons for nearly its entire existence. A spending spree on components for uranium enrichment doesn't seem to have begun until 1997, however, after Pyongyang had sent several signals that it felt the United States was not living up to its end of the Agreed Framework bargain.[24]

As the century drew to a close, intelligence organizations found a number of clues that the DPRK was secretly pursuing uranium enrichment for weapons. By 1999 the Clinton administration was unable to certify to Congress that North Korea was *not* pursuing a uranium-based weapons program.[25] Pakistan's AQ Khan, the hub of an illicit international nuclear transfer market, began visiting North Korea in the mid–1990s, and while it wasn't yet clear exactly what he was doing, American and other intelligence agencies had evidence that the Pakistanis and Koreans were actively exchanging knowledge and components related to both missile and nuclear weapons development.[26]

It hadn't all been backsliding since 1994, however. Another mini-crisis provided the opportunity for a breakthrough. In 1998, North Korea test-fired a Taepo Dong-1 ballistic missile over Japan. This kicked off several rounds of intense diplomacy between the United States and North Korea.

Meanwhile, a new president in South Korea, Kim Dae-jung, pushed forward a new policy he dubbed "Sunshine," named after one of Aesop's fables in which the wind, for all its bluster and power, cannot force a man to take off his coat while the sun merely shines and the man is compelled to do so. The Sunshine Policy represented a sea change in Seoul's attitude towards Pyongyang. Public opinion followed and the North came to be seen as a wayward family member in a tight spot, an entity to sympathize with rather than fear. This policy ended up being controversial when several years later it was revealed that significant amounts of cash were paid to the DPRK, apparently for access and to ensure joint projects went ahead.[27] Less than two years after taking office, Kim Dae-jung travelled north and met Kim Jong Il in a historic inter-Korean summit.

Kim Dae-jung helped convince the Clinton administration that Kim Jong Il was genuine in his desire for normalization with the United States.[28] Having come close to war in 1994, diplomacy did seem like the only option.

Diplomacy culminated with two high-level meetings in October 2000. First, Vice Marshal Jo Myong Rok, widely seen as second in command to Kim Jong Il, went to Washington, D.C., where he met with President Clinton. The meeting went very well, ending in a statement emphasizing a nuclear-free Korean Peninsula and the need to resolve the ballistic missile issue. Importantly, it made clear that Clinton's Secretary of State Madeline Albright would visit Pyongyang and that a summit could follow. The North Koreans were especially keen on a Clinton visit.[29]

Just a week later, Albright visited Pyongyang to discuss the North Korea missile program and U.S.-DPRK relations. Kim Jong Il again emphasized normalization of relations as a key goal during the Albright visit, telling her there was no significance to weapons if there were no confrontations.[30] She clearly left with the strong impression that his weapons programs were a means towards recognition by and relations with Washington.[31] Pyongyang agreed to a moratorium on missile tests.

A Clinton-Kim summit was by now on the cards when bad luck struck again. Instead of an Al Gore victory in the November 2000 U.S. elections that would have ensured policy continuity, electoral and constitutional deadlock emerged. With political turmoil at home in the wake of the tightest of elections, the time didn't seem right for Clinton to make a risky trip to an enemy capital to broker a deal that had been insufficiently discussed. A sports metaphor is commonly deployed to describe the situation: the administration "ran out of clock." There simply wasn't enough time left in Clinton's tenure to organize a summit.[32] The administration was also preoccupied trying to wrap up and cement legacy peace agreements in the Middle East and another divided country, Ireland.

Second Nuclear Crisis

However one views the Agreed Framework, Carter's intervention in the 1994 crisis or the Framework's breakdown, what is undeniable is that the failures of the Agreed Framework greatly diminished the possibility of a normalization of U.S. relations with North Korea. Despite the mistrust and discouragements on both sides, both Clinton and Kim seemed interested in pursuing diplomacy and leaving options for reconciliation open.

When George W. Bush took office in 2001, having won the swing state of Florida and thus the election by 537 votes, that all changed. Secretary of State Colin Powell was in many ways convinced by the Clinton approach, but hardliners in the administration quickly and effectively sidelined him. They were determined to end what they saw as the hopeless naivety of talks with an untrustworthy and illegitimate regime.

The attacks on September 11 further clarified in the minds of administration hardliners the nature of the world and America's role in it. In January 2002, in President Bush's State of the Union address, he labeled North Korea a "founding member" of the "Axis of Evil." After a year of mixed signals, Pyongyang was starting to sense a particular picture of Bush: he intended to either destroy the country or alter its behavior.[33] This also caused tensions with South Korea, which was still pursuing Kim Daejung's vision of engagement with the North.

Later that year, when the Bush Administration found stronger evidence of Pyongyang's uranium program, based on something of a shopping spree for components, they dispatched Assistant Secretary of State James Kelly to the DPRK to confront the Koreans. To the American delegation's surprise, the Koreans basically acknowledged a uranium program, while attempting to blame the United States for its aggressive posture under Bush. In Kelly's own words:

> Top North Korean officials acknowledged the existence of a covert uranium enrichment program. Ironically, the North Koreans sought to blame their own misbehavior, which constitutes a fundamental violation of the Agreed Framework's goal of a non-nuclear Korean Peninsula, on the alleged "hostility" of the U.S. Government. When I pointed out, however, that we had recently learned that the North Koreans had been pursuing a highly enriched uranium (HEU) program for more than 2 years, even as very senior U.S. officials were holding talks with Kim Jong Il personally, the North Koreans had no response. The North Koreans concluded by telling me that they regarded the Agreed Framework as "nullified."[34]

Some observers felt that despite its rhetoric, Pyongyang was willing to negotiate on the uranium program and it was the Bush administration that was too eager to pull the plug on the Agreed Framework.[35] Regardless, whatever remaining trust earned between Washington and Pyongyang during the Clinton years was now smashed to bits.

The United States stopped fuel shipments in December 2002. Pyongyang kicked out IAEA inspectors the same month and the Agreed Framework was dead. North Korea unsealed its reactor at Yongbyon. The IAEA adopted a resolution on January 6, 2003, deploring Pyongyang's actions and demanding an immediate meeting "as a first step." Pyongyang's response? Just four days later, it declared that it had left the NPT.[36]

This renewed crisis saw China take on a proactive role that it had not a decade earlier. Beijing's involvement was prominent in that it organized and hosted what came to be known as the Six-Party Talks. These multilateral negotiations that took place between the United States, North Korea, South Korea, China, Russia and Japan were supposed to find a way to resolve the nuclear issue. The first round began in August 2003. The group convened again in February 2004. Both these rounds of talks yielded little, except agreements to keep talking.

It was a bumpy road, but the first positive notes were struck in June 2004. At this point, the United States laid out some concessions it was willing to make and the North reciprocated. (One analyst argues that North Korea took a conciliatory approach four times during the second crisis, in March 2003, June 2004, June 2005 and February 2007.)[37]

A high point might have been the agreement of all parties to a statement in September 2005, which affirmed the joint goal of a "verifiable denuclearization of the Korean Peninsula in a peaceful manner." All parties also agreed in principle that light water reactors would have to be provided and other energy assistance would be given.[38] Indeed, all six were "aware that the central issue of the talks is to get North Korea to give up its nuclear weapons programme in return for security guarantees, trade, energy supply and economic aid." They differed over the manner and sequence in which this may and should be done.[39]

A low point may have curiously come concurrently with the relative high point, when the lack of consensus in the Bush administration manifested itself again. In the same month that U.S. State Department diplomats were negotiating their joint statement, the Treasury Department designated Banco Delta Asia as a "Primary Money Laundering Concern," freezing DPRK assets there. This Macau bank was being used by North Koreans for a variety of transactions. The U.S. Treasury has tremendous power over U.S. dollar transactions. As well as freezing some $20 million, what the designation did was suddenly put the world's banks on notice: dealing with North Korean funds was toxic.

It was the perfect example of one branch of the U.S. government, with hardline allies in the administration, undermining another branch. The issue of Banco Delta Asia then logjammed the talks. With no forward progress being made, Pyongyang decided to up the stakes and conducted a nuclear test on October 9, 2006. The U.N. Security Council responded with a sanctions resolution.

The Crisis Drags On

Following Bush's re-election, incidentally, Pyongyang specifically took umbrage with the term "outposts of tyranny," demanding it be renounced before talks could continue.[40] Condoleezza Rice had used the term in her confirmation hearing for the position of Secretary of State in January 2005. The rhetoric may still have been similar, but with two wars underway Bush was far less confrontational over North Korea than in his early administration.

Despite the nuclear test, the United States was still interested in negotiations, but Pyongyang continued to demand a resolution to the Banco Delta Asia issue first.[41] In January 2007, an agreement was reached to return the funds, though this proved difficult as banks around the world were wary of involvement. In return, at least in the short term, Pyongyang agreed to accept IAEA inspectors again. Japan and the United States agreed to pursue normalization as a long-term goal.[42] In October, North Korea agreed to disable its Yongbyon facilities and provide a complete nuclear declaration by the end of the year. However, there was a fairly high degree of vagueness in the October agreement.[43]

Pyongyang missed the deadline for its declaration, but in June 2008 officials delivered a 60-page declaration to China describing three separate efforts to develop plutonium. The documents didn't mention a uranium program. Nor did 18,000 pages of records delivered to the United States in May contain any information about uranium. What the documents *did* contain were actual traces of uranium.[44]

The Bush administration, by now far more flexible than in 2002, decided to at least temporarily turn a blind eye to this so as to push on with other agreements, including energy assistance for a re-freeze of facilities. Bush also announced on June 26 he was removing North Korea from the U.S. list of state sponsors of terrorism and lifting some sanctions under the Trading with the Enemy Act.

The next day, the DPRK destroyed a steel-reinforced concrete cooling tower at the Yongbyon facility, both a tangible and symbolic act. The Americans paid the North Koreans $2.5 million to carry out the demolition. It took place on June 27 and was televised.[45]

The rest of the year proceeded badly, however. Washington slowed down the process of de-listing North Korea as a state sponsor of terrorism (it eventually happened in October 2008). At the same time, Pyongyang was slow to address the issues of verification and of its uranium program. In August, Kim Jong Il was struck by some affliction, likely a stroke. Perhaps absent its leader's input, stalemate on the sensitive issue of verification was inevitable. By the end of the year, talks had broken down again.

Pyongyang welcomed President Obama into office with a series of challenges. On April 5, 2009, North Korea launched the three-stage Unha-2 rocket in violation of previous UN sanctions. Following the UN's response—more sanctions—Pyongyang kicked out IAEA inspectors and declared the six-party talks finished. On May 25 Pyongyang conducted its second nuclear test. More UN sanctions followed.

In November 2010 an American delegation was taken to see, among other things, an "ultra-modern and clean" 2000-centrifuge uranium facility that exceeded most expectations for what the North Koreans might have had. They were also shown a small, experimental light-water reactor.[46]

Pyongyang "spent the better part of 2011 negotiating for food aid, a process that survived the death of Kim Jong Il," which took place in December.[47] This culminated with the "leap-day deal" of 2012, so called as it was announced on February 29. North Korea "agreed to implement a moratorium on long-range missile launches, nuclear tests and nuclear activities

3. Becoming Pariah States

at Yongbyon, including uranium enrichment activities." The United States offered a small food aid program, promising 240,000 metric tons of aid. The Obama administration thought this could be a signal that the new leader, Kim Jong Un, might want to reset relations.[48]

This cautious optimism lasted barely two weeks: On March 16, 2012, Pyongyang announced it would soon launch a satellite to celebrate the centennial birthdate of the country's founder Kim Il Sung. This launch failed, but Pyongyang followed up with a second, more successful attempt in December. In response, the UN Security Council passed a sanctions resolution on January 22; Pyongyang followed up with its third nuclear test on February 12, 2013. More sanctions followed.

The Obama administration began to settle into a policy of "strategic patience." This entailed matching North Korean tests with increasing pressure, coordinating closely with allies, and a willingness to negotiate if denuclearization was on the table.[49] It was, however, also tantamount to admitting: "We don't know what to do." Pyongyang was no longer interested in discussing denuclearization in any meaningful sense. The new Kim's relations with its main ally, China, remained extremely strained. Relations with Japan were virtually non-existent due to the abduction issue, and tensions with Seoul had grown since 2010 with fewer and fewer cooperative projects taking place.

More missile tests of varying types took place in the following years. In Obama's final year in office, as if to underscore not only his failure but also the non-achievements of three two-term American presidents in a row, Pyongyang tested not just one, but two nuclear devices. The first test was in January 2016 and claimed to be a "hydrogen bomb" while the second was in September. UN sanctions followed both.

Korea-watchers are divided on key questions about Pyongyang's intentions. Some believe that North Korea was, throughout the 1990s and 2000s, willing to deal away its nukes and missiles for normalization and other material incentives. Others believe North Korea was never interested in this and only sought to extract concessions and create delays while secretly developing a nuclear arsenal. Some think negotiations could still work now; others that that containment and pressure are the only options.

The failure to resolve these crises could well be defined thus: "Washington's inability, after several years of on-again, off-again negotiations in Beijing, to learn whether North Korea is actually willing to surrender its nuclear weapons program, and if so, at what price."[50] The fact that it can still be debated years after the fact speaks to that failure.

It is this author's opinion that into the early 2000s, denuclearization or a meaningful freeze was possible. The sheer number of times Pyongyang signaled it wanted a peace deal and normalization of relations with the United States suggests a seriousness of purpose. Under the Agreed Framework, Pyongyang extracted clear and not-insignificant material benefits while also vaguely defining a diplomatic path forward. A peace treaty may have put tremendous pressure on the United States to draw down its forces in the South, but it would have had to be matched by reciprocal actions on the North Korean side.

It may, importantly, have allowed for Kim Jong Il to explore different ways of organizing his society and economy, despite the attendant risks. As trust between the United States and the DPRK eroded and Pyongyang's weapons programs grew more advanced, however, the likelihood of Pyongyang giving up its weapons has seemed to decrease. With all the mistrust built up in the post–Cold War period, what could the United States now offer that would be as good a security guarantee as nuclear weapons?

This appears to be even more the case in the Kim Jong Un era. There is no serious messaging about denuclearization emanating from Pyongyang. There is little talk of normalization. Instead, Pyongyang frequently emphasizes its nuclear status, essentially demanding that the United States admit that it has lost the battle to keep North Korea nonnuclear. In 2012 the DPRK even amended its constitution to refer to itself as a "nuclear state" or "a state in possession of nuclear power." Afterwards, North Korean media made sure to link the nuclear state concept with weapons, not power plants.[51] Pyongyang now views the nuclear issue and the issue of normalization as de-linked. For Washington, normalization before denuclearization is a bad deal—and a clear defeat.

Kim Jong Un, needing to consolidate power and earn legitimacy, has perhaps less room to experiment with his foreign policy than his father did. Pushing towards developing a miniaturized nuclear warhead that can sit atop a North Korean ICBM and can reach the mainland United States does two things. It not only improves the DPRK's military position vis-à-vis its external threat, it also satisfies military hardliners in Pyongyang—important to keep onside in the early years of Kim Jong Un's rule.

There is also, as an enemy of the United States, less impetus to experiment with policy. Pyongyang took away a key lesson from Saddam Hussein's downfall: get nuclear weapons before the United States considers invasion. Pyongyang also watched Libya's Ghaddafi with interest: he bargained away his weapons of mass destruction program and was welcomed as a partner by the West. In 2004, he even hosted Tony Blair for a summit meeting. Then in 2011 he was beaten to death and sodomized with a bayonet. Ukraine must also now weigh in the minds of the DPRK's leadership as a country that gave up nuclear weapons in exchange for promises of territorial integrity.

It should be noted that since 1994, North Korea has taken other actions that have earned it disapproval and censure in the international community. Its pariah status has come largely from disrupting nonproliferation regimes, but it has also engaged in deadly skirmishes with South Korea. Examples include 2002 and 2009 in Korea's West Sea and in 2010, when it shelled a South Korean island, killing civilians, and likely sunk a South Korean naval vessel.

In 2002, Kim Jong Il came clean (at least partly, anyway) about the country's extensive kidnapping program in the 1970s and 1980s. Other historical acts of terrorism, such as the 1987 bombing of Korean Air Flight 858 or the 1983 Rangoon bombing may have faded from most memories, but they still contribute to the country's overall record.

The DPRK's human rights record, arguably worse than Myanmar's, also gradually came to light in the post–Cold War period. Earlier reports, through perhaps even the mid–1990s, could possibly be dismissed as exaggerated or under the influence of South Korean propagandists. Over time, however, the sheer number and consistency of reports emerging from the country, particularly on its prison system, placed the country well outside international norms, contributing to its pariah status.

Despite this, it is the issue of nuclear weapons and the attendant ballistic missile program that most animates Washington, D.C. It is this issue that has inspired sanctions through nine UN resolutions since 2006. It is the military threat that North Korea poses to its neighbors and U.S. allies that has led to its pariah status.

Burma and the Infamy of 1988

By contrast, it was the threat that Burma/Myanmar posed largely to its own citizens that led to its condemnation and isolation.

There, the political opposition movement grew out of an economic policy decision. The regime, having always struggled with legitimacy, made the catastrophic decision to demonetize three key banknotes. On

September 5, 1987, the 75, 35, and 25 kyat bills were rendered useless, effective that very day. For almost everyone, there was no chance to exchange bills for the new 45 and 90 kyat notes.

Replacing the larger notes with units divisible by nine—Ne Win's lucky number—was supposed to control inflation by removing currency from circulation and hurt insurgent groups who'd stockpiled cash.[52] What it did was instantly destroy what little wealth had been accumulated by swathes of the poor population, who were suddenly thrown into an extremely vulnerable position. People who lived through it universally describe scenes of panic and chaos among the millions of people who lost their meager cash savings.

Ironically, the month before, Ne Win had announced that the country was going to walk back from its socialist experiment with economic management: the state was going to permit private market activity, allowing the market to set prices. Burma would encourage foreign investment. Then they went and obliterated the cash holdings of its citizens. Some protests and limited violence took place following the currency reform.

This was a country that had humiliatingly just been put on the United Nations' Least Developed Countries list, allowing some debt relief.[53] Burma's foreign debt had risen from $1 billion in 1979 to over $4 billion in 1988. External debt to GDP ratios had grown to 45 percent by 1986.[54] Nearly half of the country's minuscule economic output had to go to servicing debts.

The tumults of 1988 unfolded in this strained context. The events of that year have framed all the (non-ethnic) political trauma that has come since. It was also the point at which the military became inexorably linked with injustice in the eyes of most urban Burmese, rather than being just the agents of economic mismanagement.

Taking to the Streets

On March 13, 1988, an unexceptional fight broke out between Rangoon Institute of Technology students and what Americans might call "townies." It was over what music was being played in a teashop—there has been little said about what the offending tunes were. Police were called in and whether under orders or just unduly aggressive, they ended up killing a student, Phone Maw. The government then attempted to cover up what had happened, even from Phone Maw's family.[55] News spread, however, and in the following days students protested again in several locations.

On March 15, one student recalls being stopped by a police barricade while trying to join a bigger group of protestors.

> The officer waved his pistol and several riot police standing behind him aimed their M16 rifles at us. "Do you want me to order them to shoot you now?" he asked. Then, more than twenty trucks filled with soldiers appeared on the road—a sign that the army had taken over control of the situation from police. The soldiers looked exhausted, having just been recalled from the front lines of the many ethnic conflicts in the border regions in order to reinforce the troops in Rangoon. Young officers no older than me stared at us as the trucks passed by. One of them waved his pistol menacingly.[56]

Then on March 16, students marching north along Pyay Road were stopped at a bridge and cornered by police. The police attacked mercilessly. The location became known as the Red Bridge. "If you were there at the time," one student leader recalls, "you would still be able to hear the sound of crying and could see the blood of the young students who were just trying to bring about change."[57]

The next day, a group gathered to protest at Rangoon University and were met with force by the police, who rounded up over a thousand and hauled them away to prison. Tales of rape and torture soon emerged and spread throughout the city. In one horrifying incident, 41 students were crammed into a police van and suffocated to death. Their bodies were quickly cremated and news of it suppressed.[58] An official inquiry, conducted in April while students had been sent out of the capital, concluded that one student had died. This was insufficient contrition, even if in July the authorities admitted the suffocation incident had taken place.[59]

It certainly wasn't enough for the students, who returned to school in June and began protesting again. Towards the end of the month, more clashes and deaths took place. The students also made the decision around then to leave the university areas and head out into townships to rally other people.

Meanwhile, former Ne Win confidant, Brigadier General Aung Gyi, was writing open letters to the leader, calling for reform. Amid the crisis, Ne Win called an assembly of the BSPP, promised democratic and economic reforms, and then abruptly retired. In an extreme misjudgment of the national mood, he allowed Sein Lwin to assume the positions of party leader and head of state.

Sein Lwin had been in charge of the police. He'd also put down student movements in 1962, 1974 and 1987.[60] People held him most responsible for the violence. The students were outraged at his elevation to maximal leader, so when he declared martial law on August 3, the students responded by calling for a general strike five days later: August 8, 1988, or as it is now known: 8888.

Ne Win, in a speech given on his way out, said: "The army has no tradition of shooting into the air."[61] Sein Lwin made sure that principle was upheld. As thousands took to the streets, a standoff was mounting. It was broken when tanks and personnel carriers rolled into the open area by Sule Pagoda in downtown Rangoon and scattered the crowd with waves of gunfire. This time it wasn't the police but the army, who'd previously been thought of as neutral, if not a force for the people.[62] Several days of urban search-and-destroy missions ensued. "Troops, fully deployed all over the city, fired on unarmed demonstrators at will, chased fleeing civilians and shot at them, and fired indiscriminately into houses."[63]

Zaw Min was one student who was part of the strategy for getting ordinary people on to the street. He organized Ledawkan Street, in Thingangyun township. August 9 saw a large gathering, which moved en masse towards Pyithayan and Wayzayanthar junction. There they were met by Battalion 22 of the army, who announced that the crowd must disperse. The army then shot into the crowd almost immediately—just three minutes passed between the warning and the shots, he recalls.

Zaw Min was shot in the thigh while running. He hit the ground "while all around was running and screaming. At least four died and many were injured." He states: "My friends picked me up and carried me to a clinic. I had been hit by a bullet in my thigh and shotgun pellets in my lower leg ... at the clinic they took out all the fragments from my lower leg."

He continues: "I was very afraid, a lot of tears, shaking. Still, the next day I was marching with pain. The will to protest was stronger than the pain."[64]

Many protests in various townships around Rangoon did not experience violence, but people returning from downtown or other areas soon brought news of what they'd seen. Shocked, people became too terrified to leave their neighborhoods. The city came to a standstill.

In times of upheaval and repression, keeping statistics on violence is impossible. However, "reliable diplomatic observers estimate that over a thousand people were killed and more than two thousand were wounded."[65]

3. Becoming Pariah States

After four days of mayhem, Sein Lwin stepped down. Maung Maung, another of Ne Win's confidants, though not a military man, took over. He pulled the army from the streets and promised reforms. The masses felt they were winning.

Millions of people kept coming out in Rangoon after the violence had abated. Hundreds of thousands were turning out in Mandalay and other cities as well. By the end of August, it was not just "isolated and sophisticated Rangoon speaking out. What sounded was the voice of an entire nation."[66]

It was into this vortex of violence and upheaval that an unlikely protagonist stepped: Aung San Suu Kyi, the daughter of independence hero Aung San. Aung San Suu Kyi had lived abroad since age 15, mostly in India, then the United Kingdom, where she married Michael Aris, a professor at Oxford University. She happened to be back in Rangoon taking care of her ailing mother when the protests began. Compelled to act by the intensity of the crisis, she ended up addressing a huge crowd at Shwedagon Pagoda on August 26 and convincingly laid forth her credentials as a genuine patriot and democrat, while not shying away from her time abroad.

She famously stated the country was undergoing its "second struggle for national independence." But she also stressed forgiveness and understanding, despite all the violence.[67] She was charming and beautiful and spoke with clarity. The country and then the world quickly fell in love with her.

Meanwhile, there was a lull in conflict but people kept demonstrating into September. With the army pulled back and government no longer functioning there was genuinely a moment of anarchy. Then, on September 18, the military staged a coup (of sorts) and under Saw Maung set up the Bond-villain-named SLORC, or State Law and Order Restoration Council. Troops flooded back into the cities, shooting freely. Again, thousands were killed.[68]

One doctor who was caroming around town in an ambulance trying to save people recalls coming upon the aftermath of a massacre near Sule Pagoda: "It is a scene that I can never forget for the rest of life. There were a lot of bodies and injured people on the street ... a photo of our Bogyoke [Aung San] was on the street, our fighting peacock flag [the symbol of the student movement] was also down, sandals were scattered and pools of blood were everywhere."[69]

Soldiers also shot at unarmed protestors in front of the U.S. Embassy, smashing the perception that this spot was safe: people had felt it had become something of a sanctuary for democracy advocates.[70] The *Tatmadaw* had reasserted its physical and symbolic power. The cost, as well as thousands of innocent lives, was its legitimacy.

The violence and repression also created an exile class. Students and other organizers went in the thousands to join ethnic groups in their struggle against the Burmese military. Others left the country, creating large communities of activist exiles, particularly in Britain and Thailand.

One such exile, Win Naing Oo, currently works for the BBC World Service Burmese section in London. Many of his friends over the summer of '88 had decided they would go engage in armed struggle if there was a coup. When there was, they left for the jungle, taking a train to the town of Ye and then walking nine days and nights to reach a Mon stronghold. *Tatmadaw* defectors taught them the basics of how to fight.

Win Naing Oo left home without telling his recently widowed mother, unable to see in her face the heartbreak of her eldest son leaving. He lived in the jungles and border regions for 15 years until he won a scholarship to study in the United Kingdom in 2003. He finally returned home in 2012. By that point, his mother "didn't want to talk about it." Everyone agreed not to linger on a subject so painful. "But many families suffered through that, suffering the loss of a son or daughter to jail, to the jungle." And, of course, to the army's bullets.

The events of this period also brought international opprobrium down on what had previously been thought of as just a poorly run single-party state. (A later chapter will look at the types of sanctions imposed on Burma/Myanmar for these actions in more detail.) Perhaps one catastrophic, bloody event was not enough to cement a country's position as a pariah. The follow-ups to 1988 would.

1990 Elections and Beyond

SLORC, perhaps surprisingly, noted that it had heard the wishes of the people and pledged to move to a multi-party democratic system and hold elections. This echoed 1958: the coup was meant to be temporary and lead towards a democratic transition. Laws for registration of political parties were quickly drawn up and more than 100 political parties had registered by early November.[71] SLORC facilitated the registration of the pro-military National Union Party and made sure that it could campaign with ease.

3. Becoming Pariah States

By contrast, SLORC was soon limiting campaigning by the National League for Democracy (NLD), a party founded by Aung San Suu Kyi, Tin Oo and Aung Gyi. NLD leaders and members were imprisoned because their huge rallies violated executive order 2/88, forbidding more than four people from gathering outdoors.[72] Arrests of democracy activists were common. Harassment was also common, with Aung San Suu Kyi's motorcade often held up at checkpoints and her meetings disrupted by agitators making noise or otherwise causing commotion. In one incident that fueled her legend, she walked to her appointment through a line of soldiers blocking her way, despite being warned by the officer in charge that she would be shot if she continued. She had a "death-defying obstinacy" and sense of duty.[73]

Aung San Suu Kyi also had incredible instincts for personality politics. She campaigned with a vigor and passion matched only by the respect and adoration she garnered from the citizens of Burma, or as it became officially known in 1989, Myanmar.[74] Direct contact between her and the people was put to an end on July 20 when she was put under house arrest for considering an alternate, non-official event to commemorate her father's death.[75]

In January 1990, the government ruled that she was ineligible to stand for election after a National Unity Party candidate accused her of being connected to rebel student organizations, not being a resident of the country, and, in essence, of being a foreigner.[76] It was too late. On Election Day, May 27, her NLD won 80 percent of parliamentary seats and 60 percent of the total votes.[77] It was a landslide. Embarrassingly, the NLD even won on the Coco Islands, which are almost entirely populated by military personnel and their families.[78]

SLORC, despite its many promises, prevaricated about the results. In a bad omen, official media weren't carrying vote tallies as they came in, nor did they report a statement made to foreign journalists that the army would give up power after a new constitution was adopted.[79] (It had earlier said that process could take two years.[80])

SLORC also tried stalling by suggesting transfer of power should be delayed until economic reform was complete. It also claimed that only eight million out of 20 million eligible voters cast ballots for the NLD, offering a "silent majority" to SLORC. It stated that staying on was a "historical requirement," recalling the state of affairs in 1958.[81] In the end the constitutional imperative provided the government with the best excuse it could find: it began claiming the election was for a constitutional assembly to draft a new constitution: transfer of power, logically, could not happen without a constitution.[82]

In response to this, the NLD began making plans to convene a parliament. The authorities countered by sweeping in and arresting several of its candidates, particularly the younger ones. The youth wing of the party never recovered.[83] Meanwhile, Saw Maung's health began to deteriorate; he also would not recover. He stepped down in 1992, replaced by Than Shwe as the maximal leader.

At the risk of equating the duplicitous actions of the military and the shortcomings of Aung San Suu Kyi, issues were emerging early on with the NLD's icon. Ethnic leaders complained that she was not dealing with them as equals; she failed to encompass other parties into a unified coalition; she failed to incorporate U Nu into her party and in the end several 8888 leaders also rejected her leadership. But her close association with the democracy movement and intense connection to her supporters meant that she personally became conflated with democracy, elevating her opinions to an unchallengeable status.[84]

Longtime Burma-watching journalist Bertil Lintner argues that Aung San Suu Kyi revealed "political weakness" in some of her judgments early on and that she lacked "political acumen and strategy."[85] Yet nobody wanted to see this: "She was already becoming a saint who was above criticism."[86] Almost everyone this author has met who has directly interacted with her describes her as stubborn, self-righteous, and unwilling to listen or delegate to others.

These traits certainly helped her survive years of house arrest: they don't necessarily make for a great politician. Indeed, the tension between being a virtuous icon of democracy and having to move in the muck and compromise of elite politicking would come to define her later years when the military allowed multi-party elections to take place again.

Critics, though not often in public fora, would later complain that her principled stubbornness prevented a compromise democratic system from emerging earlier than it did. Other critics, mostly abroad, once she entered the political fray after 2010, hammered her for compromising on the issue of human rights for the Rohingya, particularly since the forced exodus of hundreds of thousands of them since late 2016. Since her party took power on April 1, 2016, there has also been disappointment that defamation lawsuits have increased or that a visa blacklist still remains for activists and journalists.

Long before that peaceful handover, as early as 1995, when SLORC released Aung San Suu Kyi from house arrest, it seemed clear that their ability to control the domestic environment was linked to how brave they felt about granting leeway to the opposition. Yangon had recently signed 11 ceasefires and had not seen any student protests of any note. At the time, Aung San Suu Kyi asked a *New York Times* reporter after she was released, "Was it just a publicity stunt? Or was it designed to get more investment from abroad? Was it merely a way to lighten international pressure, or was it really for the good of the nation for all of us to work together? I certainly hope it is the latter, but only time will tell."[87]

The opening was brief. A few months later, journalists were again banned from the country and Aung San Suu Kyi faced restrictions.[88] In 1998, tired of their calls for the 1990 election to be respected, the NLD led the formation of the Committee Representing the People's Parliament. This body seemed a little too much like a shadow cabinet to the authorities, who as of 1997 went by the name State Peace and Development Council, or SPDC. The SPDC, consisting of eleven senior military officers, responded by shuttering 43 NLD offices and saying dissolution of the council was a precondition for any talks.[89] They also refused to grant Aung San Suu Kyi's dying husband a visa to see her, saying she was free to leave the country to go to England. She stayed. Michael Aris died of cancer in 1999. Suu Kyi was detained again the next year.

Aung San Suu Kyi was next allowed to leave her dilapidated lakeside villa in 2002. After a quiet feeling-out period, the NLD reaffirmed its commitment to the Committee Representing the People's Parliament and began demanding the 1990 elections be honored and political prisoners be released. The NLD also refused to promote tourism or call for an end to sanctions, perhaps the SPDC's greatest hope. Over the next 11 months, Aung San Suu Kyi toured the country, visiting 95 townships, all the while being harassed by the government-backed party, now called the Union Solidarity and Development Association (USDA).[90]

That harassment sharply escalated on May 30, 2003, at what became known as the Depayin Massacre. Depayin, a small town in Sagaing Region, was where up to 5,000 USDA supporters lay in wait, well armed and prepared to mete out violence against Aung San Suu Kyi and her entourage as they passed through the area. Two withering attacks left perhaps 70 people killed, with unknown numbers injured and others whisked away during the carnage. The government attempted to frame it as an incident in which her vehicles plowed through a crowd, inciting them. They also claimed only four people died, far below what eyewitnesses would testify to during an Ad Hoc Commission organized outside the country.[91]

Paul Harris, a barrister and chairman of Hong Kong Human Rights Monitor, was asked to advise the Asian Human Rights Commission on the preliminary report of the Ad Hoc Commission on the Depayin Massacre. He wrote, "There seems little doubt that the murders committed by those who attacked Aung Sang Suu Kyi's convoy would fall within the definition of the crime against humanity of murder."[92] He urged that more testimony be recorded and a larger collection of evidence be accumulated should someday there be the chance to prosecute the perpetrators. That day has not come and public opinion may not equal justice, but Depayin added to the infamy of as well as domestic and international pressure on the regime.

Key leaders of the NLD were soon locked up again. Aung San Suu Kyi went back into the "gracious protective custody" of the regime.

Saffron Revolution

Four years later, just as it did in 1988, a poorly thought-out economic policy triggered protests. On August 15, 2007, the government removed fuel subsidies overnight and without forewarning. The price of gasoline rose from 1,500 kyat (U.S. $1.17 at the time) to 2,500 kyat (U.S. $1.95) per gallon, while diesel rose from 1,500 kyat to 3,000 kyat per gallon.[93] Suddenly, transportation was in a state of chaos. Prices of other goods rose sharply and confusion and uncertainty reigned.

Citizens began hitting the streets in August to protest and numbers grew in early September, with Buddhist monks getting involved. This was a key difference with 1988: the early involvement of large numbers of the clergy, widely and deeply respected in a very religious country. This, and the early focus on a specific economic hardship, led to some restraint on the part of the authorities, though as a precaution they did begin imprisoning activists from the '88 generation of students in late August and early September.

However, when it started to become clear that the protesting monks were also campaigning about broader issues, perhaps even in favor of the NLD, the regime cracked down, raiding monasteries and rounding up monks in the night, away from cameras.[94] Monks in Pakokku briefly took government officials hostage in response. They gave the government until September 17 to apologize, and when the deadline expired, the monks began to protest in much greater numbers, intensifying the crisis.[95]

Something of a laypeople-monk coalition soon formed. Young people and students would sometimes form a "protective cordon" around long lines of marching monks, who were turning out in cities across the country. Surprisingly, at one point they were even allowed to march past Aung San Suu Kyi's house. She poked her head out of her gate to acknowledge them.

The monks also refused to accept alms from the military and their families. Collecting alms every morning is a regional Buddhist tradition. It is the daily link between the spiritual and the temporal. Laypeople support the monks with food while monks provide people with access to the spiritual realm, to a form of salvation, if you will.

Emphasizing this, the monks began marching with their alms bowls turned upside down. Western literature has often referred (perhaps condescendingly) to these lacquer bowls as "begging bowls." They are much more than that: they are a daily affirmation that a layperson is doing the right thing by supporting the monks and working towards a karmic reward. Being denied that connection to the spiritual is a catastrophe for a pious person. The military had tanks and guns that could shatter one's body, but the monks had the keys to one's spiritual existence and were very symbolically snuffing it out.

The crackdown, hitherto fairly quiet and confined mostly to monasteries, wouldn't stay hidden away for long. Soon the authorities would strike back in the open. A key difference between 2007 and 1988 would be that this time the world was watching in near-real time, hampered only after the regime cut access to the Internet on September 29.[96]

By September 24, crowds had swelled nationwide, with at least 100,000 people on the streets of Yangon. The military began issuing warnings and then unleashed a violent response on September 26. A wave of shootings, beatings, and lootings occurred across the city; monks and monasteries were not spared.[97] In some places thugs were involved, in others the military directly.

It was widely held that the government used agents provocateurs dressed as monks to incite and invite violence. As Kaung Thet, at the time a medical student, recalls, "I saw myself—all the monks were so peaceful. Even if someone was shouting a slogan with some hatred, the monks would stop them. We saw video on DVB, however, of troublemakers throwing bricks and getting others to follow them."[98]

Video and satellite were important because mobile phones, digital cameras and the Internet were used to get images out to news agencies and then back into the country via satellite TV, which had become common in cities despite technically being illegal.

The world and the country watched in revulsion. The beating and shooting of monks was simply unconscionable. Images of bloodied youths and monks shocked people. Melancholy freeze frames captured a street of bloodied flip-flops and Japanese journalist Kenji Nagai, prone and dying from a gunshot wound, amplifying the horror. Altogether, the total number of dead, injured and imprisoned will never be known, but reasonable estimates are of 140 to 200 killed nationwide and over 2,000 locked up.[99]

The last tenuous threads of legitimacy for the military unraveled. Many younger people, with no direct experience of 1988 and who had spent their lives heavily propagandized to, did not—could not—trust their leadership in the same way again. The government, suffering economic and political malaise, could no longer grope towards religion for legitimacy, as Burmese rulers had for centuries and the Generals had attempted to do during the 1990s and early 2000s.[100] And then somehow, things got worse.

Cyclone Nargis

A few short months later, in May, Myanmar was hit with a cyclone of biblical proportions. Most global news consumers recall the 2004 Asian tsunami, with a staggering 250,000 dead, the destruction and chaos stretching across so many countries. Our screens were dominated by its aftermath. Far fewer recall Cyclone Nargis in 2008. Perhaps 140,000 people died in a single country in May of that year, but the lack of access allowed by the government kept it out of the global imagination. The regime's unwillingness to react quickly and accept outside assistance during a truly epic natural disaster added to its notoriety at home and abroad.

A common explanation is that the regime feared a foreign force using the humanitarian crisis as a pretext for a limited invasion. Ever since 1988, when a U.S. aircraft carrier appeared some 90 nautical miles south of Rangoon, the leadership was suspicious that unrest could spark foreign intervention.[101] This also speaks to their core security concern. A toppling of the *Tatmadaw* would probably lead directly to ethnic groups redoubling their armed struggle to secure as much territorial control as possible in the power vacuum.

A leaked military document from 2005 suggests that after Condoleezza Rice's "Outposts of Tyranny" speech, the leadership spent some effort in considering how a U.S. effort to topple the regime might take place, coming up with three scenarios: through agitating its citizens; in an alliance with insurgents and ceasefire groups; through a multinational coalition-led invasion.[102] The document also identified Thailand as its "nearest enemy." While that might sound paranoid, it is worth remembering that Thailand, China and the United States all supported various insurgencies in the post-independence period.

Paranoid or not, the result had calamitous consequences for the country. Some 2.4 million people in the Irrawaddy River Delta were severely affected by the storm and left without food, water and adequate shelter. Over 400,000 hectares of farming land was severely damaged. The storm made landfall on May 2, but the government was extremely reluctant to call for or cooperate with aid-givers. Visas for foreign experts were delayed.[103] Often, foreign journalists or aid workers who did manage to get to Yangon then found that authorities would not grant them permission to leave the capital or pass roadblocks to get to the delta.

The regime started communicating that aid was welcome, but aid workers were not. The first American aid plane was only allowed to land in Yangon on May 12. Meanwhile, eyewitnesses were sending out reports and images of dead bodies lined up in mass graves and bloated corpses floating but trapped amidst the mangrove trees.[104]

Ten days after landfall, the United Nations estimated it had only been allowed to reach 10 percent of the affected population and complained that aid was being held up in Yangon. U.N. Secretary General Ban Ki-Moon lamented the "unacceptably slow response" by Myanmar.[105] He made it to Naypyidaw on May 23 to press for more access. This seemed to work, as leader Than Shwe announced that all aid workers would be allowed in, though only civilian ships would be allowed to dock.[106]

Still, huge amounts of foreign-sent resources and expertise went to waste in the weeks after the disaster. Non-approved NGO workers had to slink around town, hiding their actions and operating semi-covertly just to send supplies to the delta. Other frustrated aid workers found themselves up against a range of bottlenecks that often kept them stuck in Yangon, milling about at restaurants and bars in the city.[107]

Civil society groups from around the country had tried to fill the gap in providing aid. Sometimes successful, sometimes impeded by the military, they all went back to their hometowns with tales of how little the authorities were doing or how obstructionist they were. The county's leaders had missed a huge chance to mend at least part of their tattered image, even as they were simultaneously focused on inching towards democracy.

The plan was their roadmap to democracy (discussed more in Chapter 6) and a referendum was long set for May 10. As David, a Chin employee of the Ethnic Affairs Institute puts it, "After the Saffron revolution and Nargis there was so much anger at the government and many demands from the people for change, both in the main lowland areas and the hill areas, but they had this plan for a long time."[108]

Despite being hit with an unprecedented natural disaster, the referendum went ahead, except for the 47 townships (40 in Yangon Division and seven in Ayeyawady Division) severely affected by the Cyclone. The millions without homes, workplaces or steady food supplies were munificently given a couple extra weeks to ponder the constitution, until May 24. Officially, and implausibly, the battered areas still found a way to turn out to vote: 93.44 percent of eligible voters cast their ballots. Only 6 percent voted against the constitution.[109]

On May 28, the government extended Aung San Suu Kyi's house arrest for another year.[110] Resolution to the country's crisis of legitimacy appeared just as far away as ever. For some years yet, Myanmar would remain Southeast Asia's embarrassment, its pariah state.

4

Ideologies

> "Well, this country has nukes. So after reunification, I think Korea can be very strong, because the South is an economic powerhouse and the North is..."
> "...an ideological powerhouse!"
> —Author, trying to flatter North Koreans, interrupted by a Pyongyang taxi driver in 2013.

> "This is a bullshit China government, only does what China wants!"
> —Yangon taxi driver, when asked if he appreciated that the military-backed government was moving towards democracy in 2014.

As the DPRK and Burma became independent republics in the late 1940s, leaders in both searched to craft national narratives and state ideologies that would bind their citizens together. North Korea was incredibly successful at this, creating a story of resistance to outside influence that continues to resonate, even past the economic collapse of the 1990s. Burma/Myanmar, however, with its ethnic diversity and early economic failures, was never able to create a story that its people could fully embrace. Ultimately, this failure contributed to the leaders' consideration of an alternate social and economic model.

All societies rely on some mix of coercion and consent to function. If they are doing a good job, the groups of people at the top of society convince the vast majority of the rest of us that the political, economic and social order is legitimate. Subordinate—or subaltern—groups generally accept whatever theory justifies society's organization and don't take steps to disrupt that order. The European concept of the *divine right of kings* was an extremely powerful concept, for example, asserting that a monarch sat atop a social order legitimized by God himself. The prospects of a revolt seeking to overturn the social order of pre-enlightenment Europe were virtually nonexistent; there were simply no competing ideas for the disaffected to draw on. People were taught that the hierarchy of monarchy-gentry-peasantry was *natural*.

"Theory is always *for* someone and *for* some purpose," as international relations theorist Robert Cox puts it. Someone always benefits from a theory or ideology at the expense of another group.[1] A theory or ideology that convinces subordinate groups of the naturalness of any particular social arrangement is far better than using brute force. Across most societies, keeping women in the home and economically subordinate to men was not achieved by controlling the locks to the front doors. It was by getting women themselves to believe in and agree with the "natural and obvious superiority" of the male in the social order. This was usually achieved through a complex of religious, familial and state structures.

In modern liberal democracies, things are more complicated than in the days of the divine right of kings, but generally people are kept from restlessness through a mixture of civic duty, political participation, entertainment, the promise of social mobility, and the "naturalness" of inequality, among other factors. The victory of the capitalist societies over the communist countries in the last century was in no small part because the latter had to resort to state repression to maintain rule and order too often. Far more consent is given in liberal democratic countries.

Modern states also rely on a national narrative as part of this mixture. A national narrative is in essence a story or set of stories that help bind a nation together in what Benedict Anderson called an "Imagined Community." A nation is imagined in the sense that most members will never see or interact with the vast majority of other members, yet the people in it have a self-image that they belong to a coherent whole.[2]

National narratives are extremely important in new nations, such as those that emerged after the colonial period. These stories often ride a line between victimhood and triumph. They emphasize both past glories and visions for the future while inviting citizens to imagine themselves as active participants. A national hero who embodies the positive values and achievements of the nation often personifies the narratives. We may not think about how these forces work in Western, developed countries very often, but they are there. Just look to the mural titled *The Apotheosis of Washington* in the U.S. Capitol in Washington, D.C., that depicts George Washington ascending to heaven and becoming a god, so righteous was his struggle to break the yoke of the evil British.

4. Ideologies

Historically, the Burmans lived under a Buddhist form of divine-right-to-rule, wherein the King's right to rule was the direct result of merit he'd accumulated through previously incarnated lives. The faith and the nation were intimately connected through the king, whose role it was to embody and protect both.³ Social order was derived from this, with the *Sangha*—the monastic community—playing both a constantly confirmatory role for the monarch and in some senses mediating between subjects and the government.

It was absolutely crucial for Burman kings, therefore, to be seen as supportive and protective of the Sangha community, continuing to act appropriately in their role as defender of the faith. In terms of the practical management and application of resources and power, this could sometimes be a tricky relationship. For instance, some kings transferred too much wealth to the monasteries, damaging their capacity to rule.⁴ Usually, though the relationship was a symbiotic one.

Choson Dynasty Korea (1392–1887), heavily influenced by Confucian thought, borrowed China's *mandate of heaven* concept for its monarchs and their right to rule over people. This idea not only emphasized the naturally ordained quality of a monarch's rule but also the moral obligations of a king. Indeed, the concept even allowed for the occasional overthrow of a monarch by a righteous revolt, should heaven's mandate be removed due to the monarch's poor behavior.

Morality, rather than genetic inheritance, may have had the bigger role in Choson Korea, but Korea in the 14th century was a pluralistic place. The dynasty founded in 1392 drew not only on Confucian ideas but also on Buddhist, animist-totemist and Taoist justifications for its rule. It also emphasized the unique martial prowess of its founder, Yi Seong Gye.⁵

The feudal states of both Burma/Myanmar and Korea suffered a colonial interregnum and emerged as republics on the other side. At this time, the links between the monarchy, religious/moral guardianship, and subjects was severed. The leaders of both states—as with the dozens of new states (re)emerging after the second world war—found themselves in need of a national narrative, an ideology and a mix of coercion and consent that would stabilize and justify the new social and political order. Before we look at how coercion and consent were applied in both countries, we have to understand the ideologies that existed in both and the stability—or lack thereof—that those doctrines provided.

Kim Il Sung, his cohorts and then his progeny created a national narrative that worked exceptionally well for most of the country's existence and has continued to work fairly well with adjustments since the famine of the mid-1990s. In short, North Korea had the ability to formulate an impactful national narrative and ideological framework to earn the support of most of its populace by appealing to a range of very specific sentiments.

This is something that the leaders of Burma/Myanmar never quite managed to figure out. It was difficult enough, given the multiplicity of cultures within its borders at independence and the quick solidification of ethnic divisions. Its military rulers engendered increasingly little support from 1962 to 1988 by propagating a form of socialism that was largely uncompelling. They then massively undermined what support they had with traumatic violence—against monks and civilians alike—in 1988. The 1990s and 2000s saw an attempt to build a pan-ethnic union-first national ideology. It was, again, largely a failure. But 1988–1990 gave birth to Aung San Su Kyi and her National League for Democracy, an opposition force with astounding emotional appeal both at home and abroad.

North Korea employed an ideology that rode the edge of the political spectrum horseshoe. Socialism, autarky and authoritarianism through a single party state was combined with fierce ethnic nationalism and expressed through the Juche idea, a mishmash of all of the above. Juche was packaged as a successor to—and surpassor of—Marxist-Leninist philosophy.

It was adjusted in the face of famine in 1996–1997 to a form of military-firstism: essentially an abandonment of economic performance as they groped and grasped towards regime survival. This far more compelling ideology and unifying national story, combined with extreme repression—to a degree not found in Burma/Myanmar—has made holding the reigns of power easier for North Korea's elites.

Understanding the ideologies and national narratives in both countries is crucial. The narrative in North Korea was from early days cogent, monolithic and emotionally compelling. It underpins the DPRK's legitimacy and continues to do so even if the social contract that is supposed to consolidate the material and ideational aspects of life has largely broken down. It contributes strongly to regime survival. The leadership of Burma/Myanmar was not so fortunate, if one can use that adjective. They never found a compelling story that would inspire and act upon the majority of its citizens. This failure was compounded by economic mismanagement and repression. In the end, this meant that not only were ethnic minorities skeptical of the national narrative, but eventually many Bamar were, too.

Burma's End of Democracy, Muddled Ideology

Aung San's union began to fall apart almost as soon as it became independent. Before ethnic armies began to fight against the Rangoon-based government, a communist insurgency developed. Prime Minister U Nu and his government's tactical ideological response was to position itself as the defender of religious tradition in general, distributing over a million leaflets to that effect that targeted not only Buddhists but also Christian and Muslim communities. The basic message was as follows: the godless communists could not be trusted.[6]

This campaign abated as the crisis over the communist insurgency wound down, and the 1950s ground on without an ideology that really bound everyone together. This might be due to the sheer turmoil of the day: the government in Rangoon was beating back insurgencies, both ideological and ethnic in character. These wars were prosecuted with some success and the central government went from controlling just 10 percent of Burma's territory in the early 1950s to about 90 percent by 1958.[7] However, there was little time left over to consider a unifying ideology.

After the "constitutional coup" of 1958 and the return to power of U Nu through elections in 1960, an unfortunate attempt at ideology formation based on religion was made. U Nu pushed through a constitutional amendment that made Buddhism the state religion. If the Muslim and Christian minorities had felt ambivalent about the state, this was sure to convince them that Burma was not a country for them and that they were not welcome to participate in the nation-building project.[8]

Among zealous Christians, this was the beginning of the darkness for Burma. As a Christian Karen graduate student put it in 2016:

> U Nu in 1960 said "I'll turn this into a Buddhist country." God was displeased, so he left the country for 40 years. Myanmar was a top country at the time. U Nu was maybe a good leader, but the Christians displeased God a lot, so he left. As Christians, we had to pray, pray, pray, and fight for the country. So it was a kind of spiritual warfare for the last 40 years. It was a very dark place. But God taught us how to conduct spiritual warfare.[9]

This author is not convinced that the spiritual stakes in Burma's conflicts were quite so high, nor that this was the reason for the country's failures, but Burma/Myanmar is a place in which, broadly speaking, religious passions run high. U Nu's promotion of Buddhism was clearly a watershed moment for minorities with high non–Buddhist populations. (U Nu later initiated a constitutional amendment guaranteeing religious freedom, but by then it was too late.)

After U Nu was ousted by the considerably less constitutional coup of 1962, the *Tatmadaw* (Burmese military) formed the Revolutionary Council and groped towards finding a justifying ideology. Ne Win was convinced some form of socialism was the way forward, but the same men he tasked with communicating the new government's goals had been the ones running anti-communist propaganda in the 1950s.[10] They began work on elucidating what would become "The Burmese Way to Socialism."

Ne Win drew up plans to nationalize and collectivize agriculture and industry while allowing the prosperous classes to retain their position in society. He urged his team "to avoid using the word 'imperialism' too frequently," as his goal "was to strike a balance between capitalism and Eastern European style socialism."[11]

If this sounds somewhat half-baked, conceptually speaking, it was. Ne Win's men created an ideological justification for military rule in a matter of days, one that attempted to balance between the two global camps as had been Burma's strategy since independence.

The key problem for the Burmese Way to Socialism was that it incorporated many of communism's weakest points, such as gross inefficiencies in state-owned enterprises, and a single, exclusive cadre party (the Burma Socialism Programme Party), without any of the aspects that were inspiring populations across the world in the mid-twentieth century, namely a redistribution of wealth, intense political participation of the working or peasant classes, and a promise of secular justice against oppressors, wrapped up in the noble goals of equality and fraternity.

The foundational document for the Burmese Way to Socialism included aspects such as:

3. In its activities the Revolutionary Council will strive for self-improvement by way of self-criticism. Having learnt from contemporary history the evils of deviation towards right or left the Council will with vigilance avoid any such deviation.
6. The fundamental concept of socialist economy is the participation of all for the general well-being in works of common ownership, and planning towards sufficiency and contentment of all, sharing the benefits derived therefrom. Socialist economy aims at the establishment of a new society for all, economically secure and morally better, to live in peace and prosperity.

8. Socialist economy does not serve the narrow self-interest of a group, an organization, a class, or a party, but plans its economy with the sole aim of giving maximum satisfaction to material, spiritual and cultural needs of the whole nation.
17. Attempts must be made by various correct methods to do away with bogus acts of charity and social work for vainglorious show, bogus piety and hypocritical religiosity, etc., as well as to foster and applaud bona fide belief and practice of personal morals as taught by eithics [sic] and traditions of every religion and culture. We will resort to education, literature, fine arts, theatre and cinema, etc., to bring into vogue the concept that to serve others' interests is to serve one's own.
21. On the full realization of socialist economy the socialist government, far from neglecting the owners of national private enterprises which have been steadfastly contributing to the general well-being of the people, will even enable them to occupy a worthy place in the new society in the course of further national development.[12]

Highly vague, the coup leaders ambitiously looked to not deviate too far left or right, provide prosperity for all, provide spiritual as well as material satisfaction, tidy the nation's morality and increase common ownership without damaging the capitalist classes. This poorly thought-out program was coupled with an economic management system that was manifestly deleterious for large swaths of the population.

Any rapidly implemented politically ideology needs early success stories and in stark contrast to the economic growth that accompanied North Korea's ideologically formative period, the main product of the early (and later) years of the Burmese Way to Socialism was poverty.

U Mohammed, a fourth generation Indian-Burmese living in Yangon, recalls having to send one family member to spend two hours in a queue to get bread, while another family member would be dispatched to stand in a lengthy queue for cloth, or some other necessity, "all just trying to find a way to survive, selling or earning money any way we could."[13] This sort of privation meant the Burmese Way to Socialism didn't have a chance at becoming an ideology that would bind the multi-ethnic country together.

Small business owners such as U Mohammed's family and larger enterprises found themselves nationalized and housed under 23 state corporations. Military men and bureaucrats ran these companies poorly and production and export rates quickly plummeted.¹⁴ The state set prices for many goods that were too low for the producers to survive, so they turned to the black market to find customers willing to pay better prices. Hiding production from the state became the norm and corruption helped keep the black market vibrant and viable.¹⁵

Many of the most capable bureaucrats were also purged in 1962, exacerbating the mismanagement of what were anyway inefficient policies.¹⁶ Bureaucrats who remained had to try to survive on wages similar to what they were in prewar days while the cost of living was at least four times as high. Support from any social class with savings was destroyed with a decree in 1964 that made larger bank notes invalid, wiping out funds stored in cash.¹⁷

The military also drove away future intellectual leaders rather than co-opting them and perhaps even turning some of them into good propagandists. University students had emerged as a political unit and force for intellectual confrontation during the colonial period. That tradition had continued after independence and student groups maintained an active dialogue with U Nu and the governments of the 1950s. The military viewed this activism as a threat rather than an opportunity and after the coup in 1962 moved to reorganize the administration of the universities and impose a number of restrictions on the students. The students protested, the military cracked down hard, hundreds died.

In 1962 the *Tatmadaw* blew up the student union building where most meetings at Rangoon University were held.¹⁸ The harshness of the crackdown severely damaged the military's stature in the eyes of the public. (In 1974, a massive student-led protest of the regime's handling of the burial of U Thant, former UN Secretary General and longtime object of Ne Win's opprobrium, confirmed how shaky Ne Win's legitimacy remained in the face of student organization.¹⁹)

The *Tatmadaw*, meanwhile, was becoming a social class of its own, but it was failing to convince the rest of the population to join it in building Burma. "From the late 1950s on," writes Mary Callahan, "the military has continuously preached discipline and responsibility to a citizenry that—in military eyes—has responded with little better than indifference."²⁰ With little passion for socialist-organized society, the military or the union among the populace, the potential for system-change would always remain latent, lying in wait for an opening.

The economic failures of the state also impacted ethnic politics, especially as extractive industries were the only major exporters and hard currency earners. As one speaker at a Diversity Conference in 2015 stated:

"At least when the British colonized us they built us roads and schools. Now we are being colonized by the Burmese. But they don't build us anything. They just take our resources."[21] Or as notorious Shan State drug kingpin Khun Sa once said in an interview: "Burma and Shan are not the same. Our houses were taken by the British; we threw them out. After the British went, the Burmese started acting the same way."[22]

Finally, and perhaps most damagingly, the junta also failed to manage the government's relationship with Buddhist institutions, particularly the Sangha, Buddhism' highest organizational authority. As one well-known monk complained in 1989, "from 1962 until 1988, the military regime tried unsuccessfully to crush the Sangha, and on three different occasions, in 1962, 1964, and 1967 there were attempts to undermine the Sangha in the name of purification, with monks accused of immorality, stockpiling of weapons or of being communists. The object of this exercise was to undermine the standing of the Sangha with the people."[23] It didn't work. And for the Buddhist majority, the righteousness of the faith stood in relief from the uselessness of the Burmese Way to Socialism. The more the military antagonized the ecclesiastic community, the more illegitimate they became in the eyes of the majority.

In the 1970s, following the opening up of the Burma Socialism Programme Party into a mass organization, the regime attempted to be more inclusive of Buddhism, but by then it may have been too late. Compounded by continued economic mismanagement, Ne Win's regime had failed to inspire its populace with an inclusive ideology or national story. This finally came to a head in 1988, when the violence in Rangoon turned the country sharply towards pariah status.

The Juche Idea

Another night in Pyongyang ends up at Karaoke. The cheap yet tasty local beer, Taedonggang, is the choice for some of us. Others prefer the hard stuff, the soju. More shots get pounded by candlelight as a power cut forces a pause in the singing action. The lights come back on, the machine reboots, and someone chooses Frank Sinatra's "My Way." Typical. It seems every soju-filled night with North Koreans includes "My Way." Anyone who's ever studied English (and many who haven't) know and love the Sinatra classic, which trumpets the auteur's independence, creativity and uniqueness in the face of opposition.

"My Way" is probably the most North Korean Western song because it so neatly encapsulates the *Juche* idea, the DPRK's state ideology. Juche has three pillars: independence, self-reliance and self-defense. The importance of these elements is trumpeted through slogans around the DPRK and espoused by all loyal adherents. Some other key aspects include Korean-ness-first, loyalty to a monolithic leader and party system, and socialism. Well crafted for and compelling to its domestic audience, it has formed an enduring bedrock that legitimizes the North Korean state to its people long after the death of Communism elsewhere.

Malleable. Vague. Amorphous. Yet exercised and considered nearly every day of every North Korean life. What is this paradoxically empty yet potent idea? It is a set of fairly simple tenets expanded—or more accurately, bloated—into a difficult-to-read and unnecessarily complicated political theory. (This isn't unique to North Korea, of course: one might feel that way about at least half the social science texts one reads in Western graduate schools.)

The idea was first mentioned in an explicitly DPRK context in 1955, during a speech Kim Il Sung gave to his propagandists, titled "On eliminating dogmatism and formalism and establishing Juche in ideological work."[24] In it, he asks: "why do our propagandists and agitators fail to go deeply into matters, only embellishing the façade, and why do they merely copy and memorize foreign things, instead of working creatively?" It was the beginning of Kim's articulation of a vision in which North Korea's socialism was an independent project not beholden to the USSR or anyone else for its ideology. There had been some tension with the Russians during the Korean War and in the mid–1950s, and the Koreans felt they had too much influence. It was also a period in which the Soviets were becoming more accepting of "national roads to socialism" and consciously acceding to greater freedom of action among communist states.[25]

The speech in 1955 was the first "authentic statement to enunciate explicitly the Juche principle," but it wasn't until the 1960s that the term was redefined to be the central organizing concept for the DPRK.[26] It was 1965 when the term Juche was referred to as an ideology for the first time.[27] Its conceptual breadth—some might even say its lack of concreteness— allows it to explain or justify a wide variety of choices made not only by the state but also by other organizations and individuals as well. The commitment to self-reliance and the specifically Korean revolutionary masses had extraordinary resonance with the people of North Korea. Moreover, during the decade and half after the Korean War, reconstruction proceeded apace and the economy grew rapidly, reinforcing the perception of the correctness of Juche. The country exceeded its projections for its three-year development plan (1954–1956) and completed its subsequent five-year plan (1957–1961) 18 months ahead of schedule. The Korean people couldn't know, of course, just how much of this economic miracle was dependent on Soviet grants and loans. Eighty percent of imports from 1954 to 1956 were aid, for example.[28]

So what are some of the claims that Juche makes? Well, initially it seems fairly Marxist-Leninist and it's worth looking at one of Kim Jong Il's definitive texts on the matter:

> Kim Il Sung discovered the philosophical principle that man is the master of everything and decides everything. He explained a new law which governs social movement, the movement of the motive force, and he thus put socialism on a new, scientific basis. The socialist and communist cause as clarified by the Juche idea is the cause of the popular masses for their complete independence. Socialism as scientifically systematized by the great leader Comrade Kim Il Sung is man-centered socialism and socialism centered on the masses. Ours is a socialism where the popular masses are the masters of everything, where everything serves them, and which is developing through their united efforts. The Juche-oriented theory of socialism scientifically clarified the essence of socialism and the law governing its development, by placing man at the centre. On this basis, the theory explained that if the building of socialism is to succeed, a vigorous struggle must be waged to occupy the two fortresses of socialism and communism, the ideological and material fortresses, and that here, absolute precedence must be given to the struggle to take the ideological fortress.[29]

So, the popular masses come first, and communism follows so-called scientific principles. The break with mainstream Marxism of the time, however, is the emphasis on ideology. Ideas take primacy over the material, which more traditional Marxist-Leninists focused on.

Then, this, a greater elucidation on what Juche was, from Kim Jong Il's *On the Juche Idea*:

> An age had passed and the revolutionary movement had gone a long way since the birth of the revolutionary theory of the working class. Revolutionary practice in the new era demanded that the revolutionary theory be developed in a way which was suitable to new historic conditions. The Juche idea propounded the basic principle of revolution that the masses of the people are masters and the motive force of the revolution and construction and, on this basis, rendered it possible to evolve new revolutionary theories required by our time.
> The Juche idea, the revolutionary world outlook representing a new era in history, the Juche age, is rightly leading the onward movement of mankind aspiring to independence and sovereignty, socialism and communism, while sweeping away all the reactionary and counterrevolutionary currents of thoughts.[30]

A grand set of assertions, but here Kim Jong Il, in what North Koreans regard as perhaps the seminal text on Juche, captures much of what the idea was designed to do. It was supposed to improve on traditional Marxism by being more applicable to Korea's situation.

Its "originality" was also to elevate Kim Il Sung to the forefront of both domestic society and the international community, first to socialist societies. "Kim Il Sung thinks more deeply than others about the position of the socialist camp and the international communist movement," one hagiographer bluntly puts it.[31] He was also cast as a thought-leader for any number of small states seeking to maintain independence. The word independence appears 144 times in what is barely an 80-page text.

It was also designed to fill the Koreans with pride at how fortunate they were to have such a genius as their leader. After all, "The revolutionary ideas of the working class are originated by distinguished leaders."[32] This is a key part of Juche; there is a strong concern for independence of man, but this independence can only be expressed socially, or collectively, and the collective is expressed through unity behind a singular leader. In North Korea, there is no room for debate on this principle.

Juche is so commonly referenced in North Korean life that it has become an institution, which, like all institutionalized ideas, "fundamentally shapes the boundary within which actors define their interests while at the same time constraining the range of strategies available to them; and the interests pursued and the strategies chosen by the actors, in turn, reproduce and reinforce the institution."[33]

We might say at the national-strategic level, North Korea's central goal is to avoid Juche's partial antonym, *Sadae*, which roughly means sycophancy or dependence on the powerful. Sadae was embodied by Choson Dynasty Korea's reliance on China, which proved disastrous when China was unable to protect it from Japanese imperialism, leaving Korea prostrate. This situation is North Korea's "never again"; their entire society is set up to resist foreign influence and domination.

The reluctance to rely on others, even close allies, is perhaps best expressed through Pyongyang's nuclear program. Loathe to depend on China or Russia for its defense against a more powerful enemy, nuclear weapons are seen as the ultimate guarantee of freedom and independence for the DPRK. It also helps explain just how fractious Chinese-North Korean relations can be. One might think that North Korea, so dependent on China economically, would take care to ensure that Beijing is never angry with its small ally. Instead, we see North Korea often frustrate the

4. Ideologies

Chinese, as if to purposefully demonstrate that Beijing's leverage has no real value.[34]

When it comes to social organization, Juche justifies the DPRK's relatively closed nature (which we will explore more in the next chapter). As a self-proclaimed foreign spokesman for North Korea, Alejandro Cao De Benos, stated in a documentary: "You say … 'it's a mysterious country. You know, it's a secret country.' OK, that's fine, it's true. It's a secret country—you can see that. It's a fortress. We are very much protecting our system."[35] In other words, the only way to create an independent society is to firewall it from the rest of the world.

The need for North Korean society to have monolithic system with a maximal leader is also deeply felt and reflexively expressed. As one North Korean earnestly told the author in 2012, "Foreigners just don't understand the relationship we have with our leaders. They really do everything for us and we do everything for them."[36]

Juche also exercises an influence on how individuals think about their daily lives. For example, during a consultation in summer 2011, a motorbike factory manager was not deterred by a visitor's comment that it would be hard to achieve growth without capital investment to buy parts from China. The factory manager, who lacked such capital, enthusiastically exclaimed, "It doesn't matter if we can afford the Chinese parts! We'll find a way to make them ourselves! We've been taught that when we can't get help from somewhere else, we have to rely on our own creativity and ingenuity. That's the Juche idea!" There was almost certainly an element of performance in his monologue, putting on a brave face for the foreigners. But even so it was clear the prospect of solving problems in his own way invigorated him. We weren't able to follow up to see how his business developed, though one suspects he was unable to make the parts himself.

The idea that "we do it ourselves, in our style" is a prevalent one in terms of industry and culture too. Cultural products, influenced by this idea, reflect it and create a powerful feedback loop. The North Korean film *Centre Forward* might be a good example of this, wherein the protagonist—a football player—learns how hard he has to work on his own, but also with his team, in order to win respect.

Any success at industry can be framed in these terms also. This includes Juche Steel, for example, which apparently uses a different type of oxidation process in order to utilize domestic brown coal in its production.[37] It may also be at the Taedonggang Beer brewery, where if you point out to the

North Korean guide that the entire facility was imported from Burton-on-Trent in the UK she will quickly retort, "Yes, but we made our own changes to its assembly line and to the recipes we use, which suit local tastes."

Finally, Juche can be felt in Pyongyang's Karaoke rooms through a legendary Italian-American crooner.

... But Do They Believe It?

This is the million *won* question and one, frankly, without a satisfactory answer. The question is somewhat like asking, "Do Americans believe in the American dream?" Such a yes/no question would be difficult to answer adequately in any survey and becomes even less simple once a conversation about it develops. The relationship of most individuals to the societies in which they live is a complicated one. How much an individual buys into the metanarrative she is presented with depends on her station in life, her personality and her intellect.

However, it is fair to say in North Korea that there was virtually universal acceptance of the national narrative through the mid–1990s. From independence until this time, the state ideology developed in parallel to a robust social contract, in stark contrast to what occurred in Burma. Even when the economy began to slow down in the 1970s and 1980s there was essentially 100 percent employment; healthcare and education were taken care of as were clothing, housing and basic rations. The persuasiveness of the ideology was of course supported by intense levels of indoctrination and a coterminous censorship of alternative viewpoints. Kim Il Sung sought to create what the North Koreans were calling a "monolithic system" and Juche became a synonym for that.[38] It was shorthand for that social contract and from the 1970s to the 1990s mentions and references to Marxism-Leninism were gradually phased out. Marx's portrait was finally removed from Kim Il Sung Square in 2012.

With the 1995–1996 famine, however, the social contract broke down. People turned to market activities to survive. Defection and border crossing (with China) increased. Consumption of illegally imported foreign media became common. Suddenly, what was probably the least corrupt society in Asia became one of the most, in terms of bribery. The monolithic system could no longer hope to claim people's material lives were superior to their neighbors' as they knew it wasn't true. But much of the narrative remained intact, leaning on how the American imperialists were attempting to destroy the country, subjugate its people, and destroy its culture and society the way the Japanese had.

Finding the answer to "do the Koreans still believe it?" is a tricky one: surveys in-country are impossible and frank conversations between North Koreans and outsiders are rare and isolated. (With the largely unfettered access and freedoms of speech and association in Myanmar today, researchers can get access, though in the past it was also difficult to ascertain.) It is a contentious issue among North Korea watchers.

In today's DPRK, things are further complicated by the nature of the two kinds of North Koreans that the rest of the world interacts with directly (again, due to the DPRK's relatively closed nature). The first group is that of defectors. One doesn't wish to overgeneralize, but by and large this group is made up of DPRK citizens who are the most cynical, the most desperate, or both. They are the ones who have risked their well being, if not their lives and perhaps their families' livelihoods, to escape their country. They find themselves abroad, facing a political situation limiting their prospects of returning home, perhaps ever.

The second group is made up of citizens who have permission to deal with foreigners, usually in Pyongyang or abroad. They tend to be the most fortunate and privileged class of people in the country and have received significant training in how to convey the party line to foreign guests, even if they don't always stick to it.

Media and commentators critical of engagement tend to call these people "elites," given that they have government permission to live in the capital city or abroad. This term conflates a wide range of classes, however, from core elites with access to yachts and overseas healthcare to those who live essentially upper-middle class lifestyles with German cars and imported food to those with office jobs but limited spending power to low-skill workers who have very few material comforts.

In general, as a foreigner, you get little more than the party line from a North Korean you meet for the first time, given the perspective that North Koreans are obligated to convey to a visitor. As friendships or working relationships develop, one does find that people usually have complex, nuanced views of their state and its ideology.

The more one gets to know North Koreans, the more one hears expressions of both doubt and belief, often housed in the same person. For example, this author has had the same person say, "Beijing is such a cosmopolitan city now ... no one could have imagined it would be this way 30 years ago. Someday Pyongyang will become a cosmopolitan city."

But also, "We have to run our society like this or the Americans will wipe us off the map. It's America's fault." The former statement is exemplary of the subtlety with which North Koreans express reservations about their system and hopes for a different society.

Another example might be a young lady who once stated, "Results are more important than method." This is a fairly frank admission by a North Korean regarding her commitment—or lack thereof—to ideology. Following traditional North Korean thinking, results are only valid if they adhere to Juche principles. (North Korea has yet to have its pithy Deng Xiaoping revision, wherein the color of the cat doesn't matter and only the result—catching mice—is of interest or importance.)

However, other Koreans in this Pyongyang group are far more committed to the ideology in which they've been raised. Such people, upon complaints of the rules and limitations foreign visitors face, make sincere appeals to understand their "organized society." Genuine tears are shed upon recalling the sacrifices of the leaders for the people. Impassioned arguments for their right and need to possess nuclear weapons are made.[39]

Overall, among the groups of Pyongyang-based individuals who work with or around foreigners, it is fairest to guess that most subscribe roughly to parts of a national narrative that suggests that they could be like China except for the unique military pressures they face. They could also be developing rapidly, but half of their territory is occupied by a hostile power. They have had to spend so much to keep the country safe, had to sacrifice so much, that they haven't been able to develop like China has. Indeed, the *Songun* (military first) era, which began in the mid-nineties, saw deep economic turmoil for most of the population while precious resources were diverted to keep the military strong. But now things have changed—North Korea is a nuclear power, the fatherland has the ultimate deterrent. Everybody's sacrifice has been worth it, according to this story.

Since 2010, the economy has been improving and expectations have changed. Higher hopes may ignore the realities of centrally planned economies and how radical the reforms in China have been, but it's not just a propaganda line. It's a shared story that most people accept, to varying degrees. Those "varying degrees" depend very much on the individual.

In 2014 an extremely rare type of survey was conducted by a South Korean newspaper of 100 North Koreans legally residing or visiting China.[40] These people will be from a range of classes but likely quite privileged; they would probably not be waitresses in North Korean restaurants or textile workers residing abroad as those groups would find it extremely

4. Ideologies 103

hard to find a few moments of privacy in which they could speak to an interviewer.

Again, this is a small sample size. But among this group 69 percent of respondents said they support capitalism over socialism, only 19 percent preferred socialism outright, while 11 percent said they support both equally. However, 65 percent of respondents stated that they were either "exceedingly proud" or "moderately proud" of the Juche idea. This indicates what many visitors to Pyongyang can testify to anecdotally; while there are reservations about how North Korea is run, there is still a high degree of pride in what is, after all, *their* country.

One keen observer concludes that the survey adds evidence to the claim that North Koreans "do not want their state to disappear; their interest is predominantly in seeing it develop. Respect for the *Juche* idea, synonymous as it is with (arguably false) impressions of autonomous development in the era of Kim Il Sung, arguably implies that collective memory of what North Korea once was is sufficient to maintain its popular legitimacy today."[41]

Among defectors, impressions of their home country are also complicated, though, as you might expect, they are far from a random sample. First, they are essentially a self-selecting group: people who ideologically or materially were so displeased with their country that they took enormous risks to leave it. Second, there is a degree of pressure that defectors face from human rights groups and government agencies to emphasize or even exaggerate portions of their life story. There is, essentially, a market for stories that highlight the grimmest, most horrible aspects of North Korean life.

This statement is not meant to diminish in any way the experiences that defectors have gone through or their opinion of the country from which they came. Critics of defector testimonies often display a remarkable lack of empathy or understanding and are quick to focus on inaccuracies while ignoring the ample, verifiable or coherent evidence this group provides. We do, however, have to be aware that there are no neutral actors in trying to understand the complex narratives of North Korea.

Defectors, almost to a one, don't believe in the core principles of the ideology with which they were raised. Even so, there is often deep ambivalence about their homeland. Those who've escaped North Korea, particularly older ones who experienced the good years of the 1970s and 1980s, often become genuinely emotional when recalling Kim Il Sung's death. Kim Il Sung's charisma was formidable and the sense that he was really a man of the people remains, even among many defectors.[42] Or as one director of a regional NGO that helps resettle defectors and provide jobs training said, "When I ask defectors who they would fight for if war broke out between North and South, they cry. They can't answer."[43]

Many defectors struggle to believe that it was the DPRK that kicked off the Korean War in June 1950, for example. That the U.S. imperialists started the war and that peace-loving North Koreans defended themselves is a foundational tenet of the DPRK. One defector, in a column for NKNews, notes that, "Even if you try to tell the truth about the war to North Korean people, no one would be likely to believe it. It was unbelievable even for someone like me, who voluntarily left North Korea."[44] Another, in a panel during a Heritage Foundation conference, cited it as "the most surprising thing she learned after moving to the South."[45]

The question of who started the Korean War is central to the DPRK's existence as a righteous state in the minds of its citizens. Still, one wants to understand how North Koreans feel about their country today, and defector opinions can be useful in that regard, also. The most current edition of an annual survey of new defectors by Seoul National University, published in 2015, suggests that that public support for the third generation of leadership under Kim Jong Un may be fairly solid. Among the respondents, 33 percent guessed that over 70 percent of North Koreans support the leadership, 47.4 percent thought it was between 30 percent and 69 percent, while only 19.6 percent said support was below 30 percent of the population.[46]

A survey of 11 defectors by NKNews in 2014 suggested something similar, with that sample guessing that somewhere in the range of 20 percent to 50 percent of people in North Korea still believe official government propaganda. Again, this is hardly scientific but suggests that even long after the traditional DPRK model of zero outside information and total state planning has broken down, aspects of its ideology continue to inspire and arouse support.

We can conclude from what we glean from defectors and Pyongyangers today that even after the crumbling of the social contract, the *Juche* ideological foundation still has motivational power in North Korea. This is a major part of the reason that the DPRK has managed to survive, against the expectations of most outside pundits and observers. While the material deprivation of the last twenty years, increased corruption and wider access to outside information has eroded the monolithic system, its core tenets are still convincing enough that the North Korean system retains some legitimacy, even today, among no insignificant portion of the populace. This has made it remarkably resilient in the face of tremendous outside pressure, uniquely so among so-called pariah states.

Burma to Myanmar

Around the time of the retreat of global Communism, when North Korea's hard times began in earnest, the military leaders of Burma made several decisions that shredded any legitimacy that they may have earned despite their fragile ideological foundations.

The first was economic. Saddled with debt and laden with underperforming state-owned enterprises, in September 1987 the government declared many of its banknotes invalid. (They left only 45 and 90 kyat notes; if that looks weird, it was the result of a superstition-driven currency revaluation two years prior based in part on the fact that Ne Win considered nine his lucky number.) This damaged everyone with cash savings, including university students.

Tensions brewed for months, with farmers also remonstrating against a squeeze on agricultural prices. Student-police clashes had seen some violence, but when student and civic groups launched a full nationwide strike for August 8 things came to a head.

The second major decision was when Ne Win unleashed the military on the mostly unarmed protestors in August 1988. Estimates vary, but hundreds, if not thousands, of people were killed in a five-day crackdown.[47] News of the violence spread quickly around the country and the bloodshed "had a profound psychological influence on its participants," as one author puts it. "Before 1988, the police and intelligence agents had been widely disliked, but after the troops killing of students and monks, the military itself became hated."[48]

Aung San Su Kyi, who was in Rangoon in order to nurse her ailing mother, emerged as an opposition figure and democracy activist in the following months. The regime offered a major concession—multiparty elections—that her party, the National League for Democracy, went on to sweep in 1990. The results were not honored and she spent most of the next two decades under house arrest, refusing to leave the country. In the process she became something of a secular saint, a democracy icon.

This created important changes in Burma/Myanmar. The regime's actions horrified the world and it took its place as a pariah in the international community. But it also set the stage for the country's eventual emergence from that status. An opposition party had taken and kept the moral high ground and the concept of democracy as a fundamental goal for society took hold.

Civil society was allowed to flourish and provide services to the public as long is it remained apolitical. The socialist experiment was terminated. The military began trying to build a national consciousness and end many ethnic conflicts. And the generals began considering what would come next.

Unfettered democracy was not on the table; it was considered too great a threat to the primary concern of preserving the union. The ruling elites' ever-eroding legitimacy, however, was also unsatisfactory. They seem to have realized that some sort of change would be necessary to secure the loyalty of a greater percentage of Myanmar's people. The military had to begin thinking about a "roadmap to democracy" that would offer some concessions but still preserve the *Tatmadaw*'s primacy. Had they been able to craft a national narrative and ideology as the North Koreans had, they may not have found themselves in such a position.

Of course, some system of propagation of these ideologies was necessary, and both countries sought to limit competing ideas through censorship. For those who remained unconvinced by the party lines and sought to express that discontent, a system of punishment was developed. Again, when we look at the coercive side of the coin, we will see that the DPRK created a system of control over propaganda and resistance that was incomparable to anywhere else in the world, even Myanmar.

North Korea was, and remains, relatively insulated from pressures to change because it has a potent national narrative and the means to compel adherence to it.

5

Propagation and Control

"Welcome to Orwell's country," was how a journalist greeted me when I arrived in Yangon in 2015. Perhaps this was out of a long, bitter habit: it wasn't all that Orwellian where we met for coffee. People spoke freely over espresso and tourists meandered among hawkers on the street while raucous cars and construction kicked up dust in the background.

George Orwell is intimately connected to Myanmar and North Korea. His experiences as a police officer in Burma in the 1920s are what gave him his keen sense of exploitation and injustice. His experiences as a cog in the colonial machine led him to write Burmese Days, a novel whose main character is both embedded in and deeply distressed by colonialism and oppression. Orwell loathed repression and his prescient suspicions of both National Socialism and Communism inspired him to write his more famous novels, Animal Farm and 1984. The latter, perhaps the classic dystopian novel, describes a state that has near total control over its people and requires constant crisis to survive.

From it we have drawn the very vocabulary we use to describe an oppressive state: Big Brother; Thought Police; Newspeak. "Orwellian" itself is an abbreviation for state oppression.

Many have seen elements of his vision in both Burma and North Korea. It is particularly apparent in the DPRK, given how deeply the state was able to penetrate into the lives of its citizens, guiding their thoughts with a nearly perfect totalitarianism. Christopher Hitchens used to grimly joke that Kim Il Sung must have gotten his hands on an advance copy of 1984 and thought: "Hmmm ... good book. Let's see if we can make it work."[1]

"What's the lie that angers you the most?"
—Off-camera filmmaker

> "It's that our Korean people, my comrades, they are forced to believe in our system. Like there is someone ... a soldier with one machine gun pointing at each one of our citizens to force them to follow our system."[2]
> —Alejandro Cao De Benos

Despite such sentiments by pro–DPRK foreigners such as Alejandro, the corpulent boss of the Korea Friendship Society, North Koreans are oppressed, even if they don't (usually) have a gun to their head. North Koreans cannot freely leave the country, nor can they easily or legally access information from outside official channels. Both Burma/Myanmar and North Korea created systems to prevent the flow of information in and out of the country while using the judicial system to punish potential political opponents. Information restrictions helped the regimes to project their visions of the world with minimal competition. At the same time, punishment for political crimes would prevent potential competitors and create a climate of fear among the population.

The DPRK and Burma/Myanmar went about this in different ways, however, with North Korea's information blockade and punishment system becoming far more extensive that Burma's. Post-famine, the Korean information cordon and restrictions on movement have broken down somewhat, but it has remained potent and effective in key areas. As with its ideology, Burma/Myanmar's efforts were both less comprehensive and less successful. The rules have changed in Myanmar during the transition period, of course, and now freedom of speech, association and travel are enjoyed, though with some problematic limitations, such as harsh defamation laws.

This chapter examines some of the tools used in the DPRK and dictatorship-era Burma/Myanmar for propagandizing to and controlling their citizens. These include limitations to freedom of movement, control over media and telecommunications, and access to the country by foreigners. It also discusses the organizations responsible for surveillance and punishment of dissent as well as the nature of the education systems meant to help prevent dissent from developing.

It is also important to note that propaganda, rules and enforcement change over time. As such, the list of coercive tools below cannot claim to be comprehensive. Instead, it tries to offer an accurate glimpse into the types of controls imposed on the citizens of the two countries.

Freedom of Movement

In Burma's early years of independence, international travel was not restricted. That was to change. "Following the coup of 1962, contacts were not encouraged. Within about a year, the government began to restrict the entry of foreigners and the exit of Burmese, except those specially approved. Internal travel was greatly reduced." Meanwhile, the minorities on the fringes of the country increased contact with foreigners in this period.[3] The Burmese state did (and does) not control many border regions, forcing minority groups and ethnic armies in those regions to pursue international trade for survival. Over time, international NGOs became involved with groups along the borders of Burma, given that they were largely restricted from working in the country.

The BSPP forbade most travel abroad. After 1988, it became more feasible, but was still arduous. First, in order to get a passport, you had to have a letter of invitation from a company or organization abroad, giving you a concrete reason to leave. This ended up creating a whole industry, with Burmese abroad running "invitation factories" and selling invitations for $50 to $100. Next, you'd have to fill out paperwork and verify that you were up to date on your taxes, weren't a political troublemaker and that neither you nor your immediate family had a criminal record. Finally, your district police officer would have to endorse you as a suitable person. Sometimes, your passport would be stamped, indicating where you planned to go. If you returned with stamps from other countries in your passport, you'd have to explain yourself. It was sensitive to visit certain countries like the UK or U.S. Getting a passport could take months and then was often only valid for 3 years, to maximize control.

Foreigners were also restricted from travel to many areas. Essentially, any region in which the military thought a foreigner might be consulting or aiding a group opposed to the regime was off-limits. Kayah state only opened to foreign visitors in 2015, for example.

In North Korea, travel abroad is severely restricted. Certainly, international travel for leisure is a non-starter, except for perhaps a few hundred people from extremely important families. Among the rest of the populace, anyone wishing to go abroad must have an official or semi-official reason. This means a letter of endorsement from their company or organization, which is then taken to the Ministry of Foreign Affairs and to State Security for processing. Family background, professional qualifications, previous jobs held and previous travels abroad will all be considered in the decision. Even if one has a passport, one has to get an exit visa or a visa that allows one to live abroad. Upon returning, a North Korean must turn over their passport to the Ministry of Foreign Affairs.

Recently, under Kim Jong Un, it appears that the number of people allowed to travel and live abroad for work has increased. Business trips have become more common. More people are staying in China or elsewhere for long-term stints to run businesses. Contrary to many claims about "families being held hostage back in Pyongyang," businesspeople can increasingly live abroad with their families. Finally, more laborers are being sent abroad to work in construction or textile manufacturing, particularly in the Middle East for the former and China for the latter.

That last development is often decried as slave labor, which is both untrue and shortsighted. People compete for these positions: there is considerable anecdotal evidence showing that laborers even pay bribes to get chosen.[4] They also earn a wage, meager though it may be and with their state claiming a huge percentage for itself. Even though these laborers live under controlled conditions, they still get exposure to the outside world in ways that would not be possible at home.

It is worth noting that both the DPRK and Myanmar have restrictions on domestic travel as well, though for different reasons. In Myanmar, it is due to a lack of control. People cannot always move back and forth freely between areas held by ethnic armies and the *Tatmadaw*. Myanmar has a huge problem with internally displaced people, who have fled their homes amid fighting or troop movements. Often, in fluid conflict areas, whole communities have their freedom to move restricted as one side or another controls access to roads and communications. At the end of 2017, some 120,000 Rohingya were living in Internally Displaced Persons (IDP) camps, with thousands of others outside camps but under restricted movement rules. Nearly 100,000 more people were in IDP camps in Kachin and Shan states.[5]

Sometimes a much more stable condition develops in an ethnic-controlled area. For example, the Wa Autonomous Region, bordering China, is a de facto independent state. The *Tatmadaw* has been unable to defeat the region's main military force, the United Wa State Army (UWSA), or its predecessor, Burma's Communist army. The UWSA defends its territory with some 25,000 soldiers and even advanced radar and missile technology.[6] Profits from the opium trade fuel its de-facto independence, and the UWSA also built casinos catering to Chinese gamblers and SEZs for more legitimate international trade to sustain its autonomy.[7] Some Myanmar government presence exists, such as a hospital and school, but locals speak almost no

Burmese and use Chinese RMB exclusively. There are checkpoints and restrictions moving between Myanmar and the Wa region.

The DPRK always maintained a much firmer grip on internal travel, which not only controls its people but provides an asymmetric advantage against its enemies, the United States and South Korea. This is one more restriction that makes infiltration or intelligence gathering on important areas unusually difficult. Before the great famine, ordinary citizens could not travel beyond their neighboring county without securing a travel permit. Now, defector testimony suggests that with the rise of corruption and the market economy, it is much easier to travel around the country, though Pyongyang and the border regions remain sensitive and more difficult to access.[8] Having said that, in 2016 NGOs based in-country have reported bottlenecks due to rural partners being unable to travel just to the nearest major city to pick up parts and supplies.[9]

Control Over Print Media

In both countries, importation of foreign media was extremely limited and tightly controlled. Control over domestic media was tight also.

In North Korea, all publications and broadcasters are state-owned. In effect, it is the Korean Worker's Party that controls media outlets, primarily through the Propaganda and Agitation Department (PAD). The department ensures that all content that appears in the media is ideologically sound and adheres to the goals of the KWP.

First, the department coordinates with other agencies to make sure personnel are ideologically acceptable and can be trusted to execute the appropriate role of the media, which is to support and promote the goals of the party. News and entertainment, therefore, all have extremely tight messaging in support of regime goals.

Second, both the PAD and sub-agencies (the General Bureau of Publications Guidance for print and the Radio and TV Broadcasting Committee for broadcast media, for example) take content well in advance of it being made public and subject it to multiple, rigorous checks. For print, censorship staff embedded at the publication will vet material first before sending it to General Bureau of Publications Guidance staff for inspection. It is then sent back to the publication for a final review and proofing before it can go out to the public.[10] This constant feedback and coordination between the PAD, its sub-organizations and media outlets ensures that there is no room for alternative messaging or individual viewpoints to enter news or entertainment products.

The DPRK's relatively small size and limited number of newspapers and magazines increases the state's ability to control print media. While Pyongyang has several different newspapers, most provinces or major cities will have a only a single local publication. It is also important to note that the importation, registration and sale of printers or print materials is strictly controlled. It is impossible to imagine an underground newspaper, 'zine, or other variation of *samizdat,* being distributed.

Myanmar/Burma, by contrast, has a lively and diverse publishing scene, most of it privately owned since the 1990s. As one might expect, the freedom of speech guaranteed by the first constitution after independence was undone following the 1962 coup, eventually replaced by freedom of speech "to the extent that the enjoyment of such freedom is not contrary to the interests of the working people and of socialism."[11] In practice, this grim turn of phrase meant anything the military did not like was prohibited.

Nonetheless, control was still less ideological and more permeable than in North Korea. Prior to 1962, there were over 30 daily newspapers and multiple magazines and other periodicals; afterwards the private press was eventually nationalized and brought under the Ministry of Information.[12] But by then, a degree of combativeness between the press and regime had been inculcated. After 1962 the media still covered political maneuvers with a degree of accuracy although the 1962 Printers and Publishers Registration Act was being used to pressure them. That act set up the system for pre-publication censorship and punishments for violators. Still, in 1969 you could read U Nu's critical comments about the dictatorship in the press, for example.

After the 1990 elections, when private ownership was encouraged again, the diversity of publications increased, though the practice of censorship persisted. Uniquely, most publications had to be submitted to censors *after* printing, creating a laborious process in which editors would have to go back and *physically* remove objectionable material on all copies.[13] Burmese journalists who in 2009 met with staff from the Committee to Protect Journalists (CPJ), an international advocacy group, estimated that 50 news publications and 130 other papers or magazines were being published at that time.[14] These would have had varying reach but speak to the diversity of ideas and actors involved in media production.

The rather frankly named Press Scrutiny and Registration Division (PSRD) carried out censorship, though it is assumed Military Intelligence stood closely behind it. One Myanmar literary critic, while in Europe in 2002, described the process of censorship for a monthly magazine thus:

> You must go three times a month to the PSB (Press Scrutiny Board) office: once for proof censoring, second for printing, and the third for delivering. If you are absent or delayed, your magazine will definitely be banned for months, years, or for life.[15]

But "never mind, we are used to the threats," said a retired newspaper editor to a CPJ researcher in 2002. "If you haven't been in jail you haven't been a reporter here."[16] The very fact that CPJ researchers were in country, communicating with media professionals, also speaks to the defiant nature of media in Burma/Myanmar. Cautiously antagonistic Myanmar reporters and editors maintained links with the outside world in a way that the far more hermetic DPRK would never tolerate. Particularly in the 2000s, the media environment in Myanmar was a pluralistic one, with different organizations seeking to be more or less cooperative with censorship, even if ultimately the censors had the last word.

One means of subverting the censored discourse was through newspaper comics and illustrations. Many of these, given the limitations, were banal and safe. Some, however, truly pushed boundaries and signaled messages of discontent, at least to some readers. "Cartoons require leaps of understanding. As with all forms of subtle, implicit expression, they imply and create a community of people with shared knowledge and sensibility: a community of people who 'get it.' Cartoonists draw for this community, confident that their humour will be understood."[17]

Later, a term was even developed for the art of sneaking information past the censors: Sandwich reporting, wherein "just like a sandwich, which puts a filling between two slices of bread, we insert into our stories messages that are missed by the censors," according to an anonymous journalist.[18] Anagrams and acrostics were used to sneak messages into stories. This, in terms of information dissemination, was pointless. In terms of demonstrating resistance and non-compliance, however, it had great value.

Advance censorship ended in 2012, with the dissolution of the PRSD, though post-publication monitoring by the state still takes place.[19] Disappointingly, a clause in the 2013 Telecommunications Act is now being used to hinder criticism and debate, by allowing up to three years in prison for "extorting, coercing, restraining wrongfully, defaming, disturbing, causing undue influence or threatening any person using a telecommunications network." Since it was passed, and with much of Myanmar now hooked on Facebook, it has been used to prosecute over 70 individuals for defamation for articles or Facebook posts.[20] The vast majority, distressingly, have come while the NLD has been in power.

Radio and Television

Both regimes understood well that outside information represented a threat and both sought to control it. That began with radio. For poor countries, radio is perhaps the key source of news and entertainment. Both countries would frequently jam foreign radio broadcasts. However, since signal jamming is an imprecise and uneven technological solution, other measures had to be taken as well.

Prior to 2001, people in Burma/Myanmar could legally only listen to a single state-owned radio station. In 2001, Yangon City FM broke this monotony/monopoly, though it was still state-owned.[21] (In the transition period, radio stations have proliferated.) Nationwide, people in the DPRK still have a choice of just a single radio station.

Moreover, in North Korea, all radios sold legally are physically fixed to receive authorized broadcasts only—probably the most extreme measure taken anywhere to prevent access to foreign broadcasts. Tampering with the mechanism that does this is a punishable offence, as is listening to foreign radio broadcasts on a smuggled radio.

A foreign tourist to the DPRK in 2010 recalled that his guide, Ms. Kim, was fascinated with a Korean-English electronic dictionary he'd purchased in South Korea. By the end of the week she'd worked up the courage to ask if she could buy it. The tourist, aware of her relatively meager salary, offered to give it to her, eliciting a huge grin. Having read enough about the country, however, he thought it best to warn her that the dictionary had a radio function. Her face dropped as she awkwardly decided she didn't need the dictionary after all.[22]

A 2004 survey of defectors found that 19 percent had used foreign broadcasts as their main source of news, while 21 percent claimed to know someone who had tampered with their fixed radios to listen to other broadcasts.[23] Other surveys around that time found over 50 percent of defectors had listened to foreign radio broadcasts.[24] Some activists suggest that 30 percent to 40 percent of people are listening to unrestricted radios.[25] These sources are self-selecting, but it is fair to assume that a significant minority of North Koreans now listens to foreign—primarily South Korean—radio broadcasts.

Television in the DPRK is also heavily controlled and, subjectively speaking, quite boring indeed. It is largely focused on Korean Central Television, the main channel, where news, music, dramas and movies generally play. Korean Central Television broadcasts usually from 3 or 4 p.m. until sign-off at 11 p.m. It or its predecessor has been broadcasting since 1963 and is the only nationwide TV channel.[26] As of 2016 there are three other channels, generally available only on weekends. This includes an educational channel and, as of 2015, a sports channel that broadcasts for six hours on weekends.

The most popular station is Mansudae, which since 1983 has broadcast a mix of light entertainment, documentaries and movies, often foreign. There is quite a bit of global content on Mansudae. For example, several months after Felix Baumgartner's amazing 39-kilometer free fall in 2013, a documentary about it was shown. Unfortunately, this channel is quite hard to get outside of the Pyongyang area.

In Burma/Myanmar, sales of radios weren't restricted in any way. However, citizens were not supposed to listen to foreign radio broadcasts and getting caught doing so could be grounds for punishment.

Some Myanmar citizens, such as political activist Thet Swe Win, who grew up in the 1990s, recall the role of radio thus: "Listening to foreign radio was a crime, but my father listened to it in the house at night time with very low volume and with all the family around."[27] News about Burma would then be discussed cautiously for fear of intelligence personnel overhearing. Emerald Hsu, a high school teacher from Ayerwaddy, recalls listening to foreign broadcasts such as Voice of America, Radio Free Asia, and the BBC at home. "We wouldn't talk about it with friends ... but we would discuss with the family."[28]

Supplying foreign radio stations with information was a much more serious crime. In one case in 2002, a sting operation was set up in Kawthaung to catch individuals suspected of crossing into Thailand to share information with broadcasters abroad.[29]

It was common for state-owned broadcasters to actively attack foreign broadcasts, with scrolling banners on TV or brief bulletins on the radio. During intense periods of propagandization, such as the 2007 protests, it could even become part of the official news stories. For example:

> The government has also been fighting back at foreign broadcasters beaming news into the country using shortwave radio. The state-run New Light of Myanmar newspaper reported on 9 October that speakers at pro-government rallies had said that "internal and external destructive elements have aired fabricated news in collusion

with BBC, VOA [Voice of America], RFA [Radio Free Asia] and DVB [Norway-based Democratic Voice of Burma] and have provoked the people." New Light of Myanmar newspaper reported on 9 October ...

All the people have seen the cunning habits of BBC, VOA, RFA and DVB. Therefore, all participants in the rallies unanimously denounced acts of BBC, VOA, RFA and DVB which air skyful of lies and those countries that have manipulated them," the paper said.

Burmese state radio and TV were running the same captions that have been on for some time—"BBC lying, VOA deceiving.... The public be warned of killers in the airwaves"—while including reports on the pro-government rallies.[30]

This tactic seems to have had little effect, given the lack of trust most people had in state media. It may have even backfired: political and social activist Zwe Nay Naung, recalls that "on the radio, they always used to say 'VOA is a liar and BBC is a traitor!' They used to mention it every few hours on the radio. For that reason, we all listened to them!"[31]

Through anecdotal evidence and limited survey data it appears as if listenership was quite high throughout the decades of dictatorship. In 2003 it was reported that an Intermedia survey on behalf of the BBC and VOA found that 39 percent of the country's 52 million people listen to the BBC and 30 percent to VOA.[32] In 2010, the BBC was boasting 8 million listeners per week.[33]

Television in Myanmar was just a single government-controlled channel, MRTV, before the introduction of a second station in 1995. Throughout this time, TV was heavy on news and propaganda extoling the virtues of the leadership for building pagodas or infrastructure. Locally produced movies and dramas tended to be quite martial in nature, usually featuring righteous Bamar warriors fighting ethnic villains. Imported children's shows such as *Tom and Jerry* were quite popular among kids, though foreign content was generally quite minimal. Again, under the transition, the number of TV channels is growing.

Internet

Poverty is the biggest reason why much of the world does not use the Internet and Myanmar and North Korea are both certainly poor countries but were (and are) also extremely suspicious of outside information. This led them to take steps to control the influence of the Internet. North Korea took a far more comprehensive approach than Myanmar.

5. Propagation and Control

In societies where people can afford smartphones, computers and data services, the Internet has become a far more important source of information than radio or TV broadcasts. Indeed, not only news information but also the information needed to run a business, to conduct research or conduct daily errands is increasingly web-based.

This may seem like a trite axiom in 2017, but it is a fact of which most North Koreans are unaware. With the exception of North Koreans abroad or a select group (who number probably no more than a few thousand), people in the DPRK simply do not have any access to the Internet. If they are aware it exists, they tend to have no concept the degree to which it has penetrated and enveloped modern society. Post-transition Myanmar, by contrast, is becoming perhaps the most rapidly connecting society in history.

Prior to the opening up of the telecommunications sector in Myanmar, connectivity was a different story, of course. Dial-up Internet service was only introduced in 1999, but high costs made it prohibitive but for a few denizens of urban areas. In the early 2000s the government granted a private company, Bagan Cyber Tech, a license to provide Internet services alongside Myanmar Post and Telecommunications (MPT), the state-owned telecommunications enterprise. Some blocking of political and pornographic websites would take place, though ironically it was the private company that was more aggressive in censoring content. Internet users from that era attest that the system for blocking websites was relatively unsophisticated and not too challenging to circumvent. Users worried that their activities online were being monitored and it appeared as if 65 percent of Internet users were using techniques or programs to make IP addresses "untraceable."[34]

Zwe Nay Naung recalled in an interview that in the early 2000s, "people were afraid to have an email and people didn't care or understand about having an email. You had to go to an Internet café or Public Access Center, so they could screen everything you do." His colleague Thet remembers his family getting online in 2000, though at first it was only an intranet. About a year later they had full Internet access and he'd spend much of his time at the computer, waiting 5 or 10 minutes for pages to load up so he could read about politics.

Why did the government allow this? "Maybe they were not aware of the power of the Internet," suggests Thet, "but also they wanted to show the world they were opening or changing."

The North Korean leadership, by contrast, seems very much aware of the power of the Internet. The first hint of awareness, at least, might have been when Kim Jong Il asked U.S. Secretary of State Madeline Albright for her email address in 2000. It was shortly thereafter, in 2001, that a China-based Korean company, Silibank, began providing email service for organizations in North Korea. This store-and-forward email service initially transferred email to Pyongyang only once every hour and charged $1.50 per basic email. Over time, however, delivery became more frequent and prices more reasonable.[35] North Korean organizations still have to pay a fee for each email they receive from abroad, however.

The DPRK Ministry of Posts and Telecommunications in 2009 formed the Star Joint Venture Company being with Thailand's Loxley Pacific and now administers North Korean websites and in-country Internet access.

Regarding Internet access, there is a balancing act for the leadership. Kim Jong Un is more concerned with economic growth, but still has to worry about ideological purity and especially the strategic asymmetric advantages they hold over their enemies by having very little online and vulnerable to cyber-attack.

The social control that the limited Internet access provides is potent. As one particularly cynical manager at a trading company noted in 2014, "if they opened the Internet, this government wouldn't exist in six months." Whether that's true or not, the leadership has consistently leaned towards security.

Estimates are that only a few thousand people have unfettered Internet access, either for their work in security and monitoring or because of their extremely privileged social position. If an organization or company has a "legitimate reason" to contact foreigners, it might be granted a company-wide email address. Employees at such companies then share a single email address, which ends with ".star.kp." Employees don't have access to individual emails or the web other than in exceptional circumstances.

North Koreans do have easier access to *Kwangmyong*, a domestic intranet service. However, this author has asked dozens of North Koreans whether they have used the portal and only a couple replied in the affirmative. A few years ago, one tended to hear statements such as the following, "You have the international Internet while we have our domestic Internet." While this illustrates a deep lack of understanding of how the Internet functions in other societies, it also shows the power of the state. The concept of the Internet has been hollowed out in North Korea and filled with an ideologically safe alternative: for all most people understand, their intranet is the same as the Internet.

There is the growing realization in the business community in Pyongyang, at least, that the Internet is crucial for business, research and efficiency in a range of fields. But even if more cosmopolitan North Koreans are starting to hope for greater access, they tend not to understand just how deeply Internet connectivity has penetrated the lives of people elsewhere. One North Korean, who had not been abroad since the early 2000s, had never heard of Facebook or Google but said to this author in 2015, "I know my country won't really develop until everyone has the Internet."[36]

As of 2017, limited access to the internal DPRK network could take place on smartphones: users could download the daily newspaper, get the weather forecast or order food and other products from their phones. As of 2017, it appears as if some companies are being allowed to use a native chat app, *Saebyol*, to contact business partners in China.

Mobile Phones

As in other countries, mobile technologies are opportunities for control as much as for freedom. They are also increasingly how people interact online, so require special attention from states that wish to control their citizens.

Mobile phone use in Myanmar has exploded in recent years and is perhaps the most visible impact of the country's transition. Before 2010, state-owned MPT held a monopoly and sold SIM cards for roughly $1,200 dollars. Given the limited availability of these cards, resellers on the black market would charge even more: up to $5,000. Data and voice services were expensive and far out of reach for the vast majority of people. According to UNICEF, in 2008 the lowest ranked country in the Asia Pacific for mobile phone penetration was Myanmar at just 0.74 percent.[37] One has to suspect that the government was creatively using its state-owned enterprise to limit information access through these high prices.

This has since changed since the political transition, along with the plummeting costs of handsets. In 2014, the government tendered two contracts to foreign companies, Qatar's Ooreedoo and Norway's Telenor, allowing them to compete with MPT. Costs for SIM cards soon dropped to less than $1.50 in a little over one year and mobile penetration skyrocketed.

There were 28.1 million SIMs as of March 31, 2015, representing a penetration rate of 54.6 percent. This was up from 32.9 percent just a year earlier.[38] Six percent of new mobile users worldwide in 2014 were in Myanmar.[39] To get a SIM card, one did not even need an ID until March 2017. Interestingly, with these millions of people getting connected, Myanmar currently has the freest Internet in Asia: no websites are blocked at all.

North Korea has seen modest but significant mobile growth since 2008, when Orascom, an Egyptian company, formed a joint venture, Koryolink, in order to set up and run a mobile network in the DPRK. Previously, Loxley Pacific had done the same, but that network was largely shut down in 2006. Orascom has run into problems remitting its profits, though by 2015 subscribers had topped 3 million people.[40]

North Korea monitors communications of individuals of whom it is suspicious, even if it cannot monitor everyone. There are also some restrictions that are unique to North Korea. For example, each SIM is registered to a single phone. If it is inserted into another phone, however briefly, it is flagged to authorities, who can either immediately call to demand an explanation or who can quietly put the person on a list to monitor more closely.

Foreigners, who have been able to purchase SIM cards easily since 2013, have mostly unfettered Internet access via the 3G network. However, they can only call other foreigners in-country or abroad. It is impossible to call a Korean mobile phone or land-line. Foreign businesspeople are sometimes faced with the absurdities of having a Korean partner make a domestic phone call and then yelling into the Korean partner's phone, just to speak to someone a mile or two away. Another solution is phoning their office abroad from Pyongyang to have them call a Pyongyang company's international landline.

The DPRK is the only country in the world with these sorts of limitations. Mobile phones have certainly made market activities more efficient and increased the speed at which news and rumors can move around the country. However, the key restrictions that exist have thus far ensured that the proliferation of mobile phones hasn't increased the possibility of unrest or anti-government sentiment.

The restrictions on communication can be a frustration, of course, such as this scenario, described to this author by a businessperson:

> We work with an organization that has a few hundred employees. You call the central Pyongyang switchboard, which transfers you to the "international communications

room" of your partners, which is just a room with a fax and phone line. Maybe, of course, no one picks up. If they do, though, you ask for your person, then they say hold on. You hear footsteps. You wait, sometimes a couple minutes. Then you get the person you're trying to reach, or you get the first person back, who says call back later. This can take four or five minutes and therefore cost seven or eight dollars.[41]

The inability to contact North Koreans can be far more melancholy, of course. Most people in the DPRK will never be able to make or take an international phone call. International letter writing is also extremely limited. Take, for example, Korean-Japanese Myongfa Kim, who studied at the pro–DPRK university in Tokyo, Chosun University. She stayed in Pyongyang for five months as an exchange student in 1993. She recalls, in a March 2016 interview with the author:

> My cousin, who was in the army, would come visit me at my hotel every day. He would always bring me kimchi, rice cake or a boiled egg, something a bit special in the early 1990s. I kept trying to buy him a nice dinner at the hotel restaurant—something quite special for him—but he always said, no, I've eaten already, let's just sit and talk. We would talk about family and what our relatives were doing. When I said goodbye before going back to Tokyo I was filled with sadness. I knew I would probably never get to see him again.

She never did. This personal tragedy is not rare. Korean diaspora relatives of North Koreans cannot call their families nor expect contact by mail. Visits of Koreans abroad to see family usually take months of coordination and take place under controlled conditions.

Foreign Journalists

The access to the country of foreign journalists is also far more limited in the DPRK that it was in Burma/Myanmar. In North Korea, journalists are officially invited on special occasions to cover major events or celebrations, such as the 60th anniversary of what Pyongyang calls "Victory in the Glorious Fatherland Liberation War." On occasions such as these, swarms of Western journalists arrive and cover events as scripted, with occasional side visits allowed by the two minders who accompany every journalist team at all times. Perhaps the widest latitude given might be being "allowed to roam ... with a government minder" when in a department store.[42] Sneaking around certainly isn't possible.

Western journalists do on occasion perforate the DPRK in a tourist group, either by deceiving foreign tourist agencies or by promising to write carefully so as not to expose anyone to undue risks. Either way, tours are so tightly scripted, with freedom to move around or even to converse with locals so limited, so useful reportage rarely emerges.

In Myanmar, official journalist visas were also almost impossible to obtain. However, the *relatively* open nature of Myanmar meant that for journalists, sneaking into the country was far more plausible and potentially fruitful than in North Korea. For example, Emma Larkin (a pseudonym) has written several engaging books by visiting on tourist visas and traveling cautiously around Myanmar. Entering thusly usually required the falsification of one's resumé and a plausible non-journalistic backstory.

Even during the devastation of Cyclone Nargis in 2008, when the authorities were in some real sense paranoid about foreign involvement, journalists were still sneaking in to the country on tourist visas. Many found themselves unable to find ways down to the Irrawaddy Delta, where most of the devastation had taken place, and thus milled about in Yangon; others were found to be journalists and deported.[43]

In the aftermath of Nargis, few journalists from Western news agencies got further than Yangon, but some did. For example, Choe Sang-hun of the *International Herald Tribune*, a South Korean citizen, made it down to the flood-hit areas. He was helped by a Korean friend of his who had run textile factories in Myanmar: in 2007 the friend gave Choe's information to a former employee, who nervously helped him cover the Saffron Revolution in 2007.

He called on her again during Nargis and she came up with the idea of enlisting her former Yangon University classmates and friends to rent a van to drive to the delta. They dressed Choe in traditional Burmese clothes, told him to keep his mouth shut and pretend to be asleep at military checkpoints, and proceeded to drive him to areas where he gained exclusive access on the cyclone's devastation and the regime's anemic response.[44]

Such defiance of the state to help a foreign journalist would be unimaginable in Pyongyang. An unauthorized North Korean making contact with a tourist at a hotel would be instantly noted and reported. Similarly, a tourist wandering away from his hotel or being picked up by a random car would be noticed. Then, the rigidity of checkpoints is such that any sleeping "citizen" would be woken to show her identification. The punishment for her interlocutors getting caught would be severe. Also, given the restrictions on telecommunications, a former factory owner would not be able to call or email potential helpers to ask for such a favor in the first place. If they remained at their workplace, they might have a shared company email address, but it wouldn't be a private one.

State Security Institutions

There were (and remain) several services with intelligence roles in Myanmar. This most powerful is Military Affairs Security. It has a broad mandate to investigate nearly anything, including and especially political issues. Anything related to the NLD has been a primary focus since 1988. MI also keeps close tabs on political parties and groups or civil society organizations that have the potential to mobilize people. Student groups have always been of particular concern and university campuses around the country are saddled with informant networks and sometimes (still) even a uniformed military presence. MI also actively infiltrates and gathers information on ethnic organizations as well as maintaining spy networks in neighboring countries.

MI has been through a few iterations in name. It was redubbed "Military Affairs Security" after a 2004 purge, though most Myanmar citizens just refer to it as Military Intelligence or "MI." In fact, purges of MI were not so uncommon—the head of such powerful networks had access to such breadth of information, the maximal leaders—Ne Win, then Than Shwe—had to worry about the possibility of coups emanating from their intelligence services, a potential "state within a state."[45]

Indeed, in a point of convergence with Korean history, the intelligence service was at a relatively weak point in 1983: Ne Win had purged the head of MI in May, which "effectively decapitated the country's intelligence apparatus and undermined its operational capabilities."[46] It was October of that year when North Korean agents planted three bombs in an attempt to assassinate South Korea's president, Chun Doo-hwan, who was on a state visit to Rangoon. The blast killed 17 South Koreans; Chun only escaped death because his vehicle had been delayed. Newspapers and media coverage of the event were "amazingly frank and surprisingly prompt"[47] in accusing Pyongyang of the assassination attempt. (One can neither imagine such an event being pulled off by foreign agents in the DPRK nor frank media coverage of it if it were to somehow occur.) This was the event that led to Burma severing diplomatic ties to North Korea until 2008.

There are other intelligence agencies in Myanmar as well. The Bureau of Special Investigation exists for investigating financial crimes, government officials, and corruption issues. It was founded by the British and is under the Ministry of Home Affairs. Importantly, the 2008 constitution stipulates that this ministry is controlled by the military along with the Defense and Border Affairs ministries. Myanmar's Police Force controls the Special Intelligence Department, or "Special Branch," another British legacy. Special Branch handle mostly criminal cases, but they can also be assigned to political crimes.

Usually, the more important a case, the more likely it is that it will be passed up to or taken over by MI. MI was widely feared by the citizenry and commanded extreme respect, given their ability to investigate, detain or harass nearly anyone they encountered.

In one example of its reach, Ko San Lwin, a driver for tourists, once hosted a Mexican visitor for a few days in 2004, taking him around town. Ko San Lwin could speak some Spanish and during the course of his general banter described both the military and the government as "mucho loco." According to San Lwin, the Mexican happened to be a journalist, who wrote up the experience in an article, describing his interlocutor as a "Spanish-speaking driver outside the Kandawgyi Lake Hotel."

"It was too easy for them to find me!" San Lwin exclaimed mirthfully in 2017. "They put me in prison for six months."[48]

The North Korean State Security system is even more pervasive than in Myanmar. It is also multilayered, with overlaps and silos—intentional isolation of information between agencies—to ensure that only the maximal leader has a full picture of domestic intelligence.

Perhaps the most important institution is the State Security Department (SSD), also known as the Ministry of State Security. This focuses most of its energies on activities that might harm the state or system and deploys perhaps 50,000 staff across the country to this end.[49] It monitors a variety of institutions and collects information abroad as well as keeping a close eye on people who have returned from foreign countries.[50] The State Security Department also runs the *kwanliso* prisons, of which there appear to be six as of 2017, although two are relatively small (Tongrim-ri in Kaechon and Camp 25 in Chongjin).[51] Some closures, amalgamations and movement of the camps have taken place in recent years. The SSD handles "serious" political crimes that can be rehabilitated but also have separate sections in their prison camps for political crimes from which there is no return. Prisoners in these sections of the sprawling camps are expected to work in servitude until they die.

Another institution that deals with law and order is the Ministry of People's Security. This is more like a normal police force tasked with everyday law and order issues. However, the Ministry of People's Security also covers surveillance over things that could cause disturbances, such as market activities and transportation, that sometimes border on what the North Korean state considers political crimes. People who commit such offenses are held in facilities more like penitentiaries.[52]

There is the Military Security Command. This organization is embedded within the North Korean military and is responsible for internal security within the Korean People's Army, ensuring that individuals who might be disloyal or present some other threat are quickly found out and punished.[53]

Finally, the extremely powerful Organization and Guidance Department (OGD) should be mentioned. The OGD can investigate elite Workers' Party Members and party institutions in a way none of the other organizations can.[54] It also vets candidates for any position of significance, including in the military, acting as sort of a human resources department for the country. One prominent defector even claims the OGD is the ultimate power in North Korea and goes so far as to say Kim Jong Un is subordinate to the OGD.[55] (This is probably not so.)

Physical Surveillance

A North Korean proverb, "The bird listens during the day and the mouse does at night," illustrates the degree to which words are dangerous: you never know who is listening on behalf of someone else.[56] Criticism and frank speech are something that are at best confined to ones immediate family or closest friends. Trust is extremely difficult to build in North Korea, so even if you have doubts about something sensitive, say, something on the news about a successful infrastructure campaign, one usually keeps quiet on the matter.

It is generally assumed that "North Korea has a policy of inspection known as the 'one in five household' system."[57] As the name suggests, perhaps 20 percent of people or households are regularly called on to inform state security personnel about the actions of neighbors or co-workers. Tips can lead to "random" inspections for contraband. Since the marketization of North Korea began in the late 1990s, bribes can often get one out of trouble during an inspection. This is not always the case during periodic crackdowns, when inspection units are cobbled together from different institutions to prevent graft or leniency.[58]

The most sensitive contraband shared between North Koreans is South Korean or religious material. Sharing unauthorized media via USB or DVD is common but is usually limited to just one or two people. Families have to be more careful than in Myanmar, where listening to illicit radio broadcasts was common, for example. In North Korea, the family unit's function is to reproduce the state/party system. Even inside the family it is often unsafe to explore ideas that are ideologically heterodox.

There are also semi-professional informants. Historian Andrei Lankov believes, based on defector interviews, that perhaps some 250,000 to 300,000 citizens are at any given time paid informers.[59]

In Myanmar, British laws from 1907, the Village Act and the Towns Act, handily provided authorities with near unlimited power to search a residence at any time. This lasted throughout military rule and still persists. Any homeowner or renter also has to notify the state to host overnight guests. Generally, one week was the most frequent duration granted for guests, though it could be longer.[60] This system made it much easier for authorities to track the movement of individuals around the country and those who did not register could be presumed to be up to something. Foreign guests were not allowed at all, the same as in North Korea.

Authorities could (and still can) not only deny guest registration for individuals of whom they disapprove but also use the rule as a pretext to inspect homes at any time, searching for contraband, people, or merely to harass perceived political or economic opponents. This intrusive practice is often referred to as "midnight inspections."[61] Neighborhood or village "chiefs" were expected to know the comings and goings of all people in their area and make regular reports to the authorities.

It has proven difficult for the government to abandon some of this control, even in the post–2010 liberalization and post–2016 civilian government. The law was renewed in 2012 and updated as the Ward or Village Tract Administration Law. In May 2016, parliamentary debate on the matter left things unresolved though anecdotally the number of inspections and punishments has declined a great deal. Relationships matter when it comes to enforcement, also. One interviewee told me that his mother, "who was kind of important on our street since our family had lived there for over 100 years," would always get a warning from the neighborhood chiefs before the authorities would stop by to look for guests or contraband.[62]

By way of personal experience with the laxness in enforcement, during a 2014 visit to Myanmar, we'd put the address of a friend with whom we were staying on our visa applications. As we turned them in at the dingy window of a cramped Myanmar consular section in Bangkok, built for a time when few foreigners were bothering to visit, the lady pinched her brow and said, "Actually, tourists are not allowed to stay at private residences."

I stuttered, slightly flustered: "Ah, I, um..."

"...but here's the name of a hotel!" she cheerfully interjected. "Just cross out your friend's address and write this." As of 2017, the rules for hosting foreigners are being tightened again, in part to protect politically connected hoteliers from small businesses and services such as Airbnb.

Civil Society and Protests

Published in 2014, a UN Commission of Inquiry (COI) report interviewed more than 240 people privately and had more than 80 people testify publically on the human rights situation in North Korea in an effort to be a defining marker on human rights in the DPRK.[63] The report catalogues a huge list of abuses, stating, "There is almost complete denial of the right to freedom of thought, conscience, and religion as well as of the rights to freedom of opinion, expression, information, and association."[64]

In particular, the report found that suppression of freedom of religion was uniquely important to the state, concluding that:

> The State considers the spread of Christianity a particularly serious threat, since it challenges ideologically the official personality cult and provides a platform for social and political organization and interaction outside the realm of the State. Apart from the few organized State-controlled churches, Christians are prohibited from practising their religion and are persecuted. People caught practising Christianity are subject to severe punishments in violation of the right to freedom of religion and the prohibition of religious discrimination.[65]

People who illegally cross the DPRK-China border to trade, if caught, face far more serious punishment if they admit to any involvement with either South Koreans or Christians. Two show-churches exist in Pyongyang, but they appear mostly as an exercise in foreign-facing propaganda. (A third, Russian Orthodox Church, exists and is actually used by a handful of Russians living in Pyongyang.)

It's not just religion that is oppressed: any capacity to organize activities outside state control is not allowed. While markets, semi-private enterprises and grey-area private ownership of assets has grown since the famine and been tolerated and even encouraged under Kim Jong Un, there remains essentially no such thing as civil society in North Korea. There are no organizations that exist outside the state and thus no means to develop or transmit complicated political ideas contrary to those propagated by the authorities. It is true that physical markets allow for gossip and rumors to flow far more freely than before, but this in no way approaches anything like a capacity to organize resistance or defiance towards the system.

The UN report found some evidence of small-scale protests taking place around the country, but these were not in any direct sense political—"these random protests are mostly about economic conditions rather than direct criticisms against the state."[66] A public display of disaffection with the state, the party or the leadership remains nearly unthinkable in the DPRK on an individual level. Some of these small protests in response to relatively minor grievances against minor officials may flirt with criticisms of broader policies, but there isn't really evidence to suggest that flirtation crosses over into broad and explicit criticism.

Regardless, not only are there no extant institutions to act as a platform for a protest movement, creating a new institution or organization is impossible. This is compounded by the limits on communications and communications technologies that prevent the potential for a protest movement to develop.

The landscape for both civil society and protest are vastly different in Burma/Myanmar. Independent Burma was born out of a student protest movement. Aung San, U Nu and other national leaders of the generation that won independence began their political lives as student leaders. Interestingly, Ne Win did not have a politicized university career though he did publish some articles, the contents of which are now unknown.[67]

Both before and during Ne Win's military-socialist regime, the concept that university students bore a moral obligation to be political and work for justice remained strong. In perhaps the most dramatic example, the government's refusal to give U Thant, the former Secretary-General of the United Nations, a state funeral, led to student protests in 1974. Students essentially stole the coffin and marched it to the Rangoon Arts and Sciences University.[68] The government declared martial law and violently crushed the protests, echoing the crackdown that took place in 1962.

It was then, immediately after Ne Win's coup, that students conducted a series of protests against the new military regime. This ended with hundreds of deaths, thousands of incarcerations and the explosive demolition of the symbolic and historic Rangoon University Student Union (RUSU) building, the wellspring of the independence movement under the British.

Even though MI and police had forced serious activism into dormancy, students again led the massive 1988 protests. The potential for political opposition emerging from student groups was such that the government largely forced Rangoon/Yangon University to close between 1988 and 2013, when undergraduate classes resumed with an intake of 300 students.[69]

Regardless, as Ne Win's government retreated from its socialist program after 1988, it consciously allowed civil society to blossom. Since the government was unable to create or allocate revenue for public services, it allowed civil society groups to fill in these spaces. This was acceptable so long as these groups did not approach the persistently forbidden area around politics. Activities conducted by civil society ballooned, filling in gaps in healthcare, public works, agricultural development, education, social activities, and on and on.

Groups accepted "political domination in exchange for space to pursue coping agendas. Their lack of political expression comprises a spectrum: all the way from being democrats-in-hiding, unwilling to act without the proper conditions; to groups generally indifferent to 'big-P' politics; to groups actively opposed to participating in political processes."[70]

In turn, the authorities' acquiescence ranged from specific ministries turning a blind eye to civil society groups to active collaboration between the government and such groups, depending on the sector in which they operated. This had several important effects on the populace, beyond the provision of useful services. It reinforced the unreliability of their state, for example, while instilling a spirit of social enterprise or social entrepreneurship. It also created networks of individuals mobilized around particular issues of concern.

At the same time, after the 1990 landslide victory by the NLD, political organization became taboo. Actual politicking or any organizing that could lead to political activity was crushed and NLD activities became crippled. The NLD itself was forced into "a painful choice: NLD leader Suu Kyi saw value in remaining a continual symbolic reminder that there was something else in Burma besides the military's version of history and the future."[71] She and her colleagues chose to act as a symbolic locus of resistance while they were either cowed into quiet submission, imprisoned or in self-imposed exile. (Of course, Aung San Suu Kyi spent most of the 1990s and 2000s under house arrest.)

This was of huge significance because even though it could not be articulated in the public sphere, her determination to represent an alternative to life under the military and their cronies provided a sense of hope to a disaffected citizenry. This quietly undermined the legitimacy of the regime. It was a form of latent political power, one that only people of extreme stubbornness and commitment could endure. Suu Kyi also became the fulcrum around which external actors could campaign and build alternative visions of political legitimacy in Myanmar.

Thus, an opposition political force endured, even if it was severely restrained. At moments of great tribulation, such as after Than Shwe's disastrous removal of fuel subsidies led to widespread protests in 2007, this idea that alternatives were possible were part of the zeitgeist. The *possibility* of another, more legitimate system inspired people. The bloodshed during the 2007 Saffron Revolution only served to reinforce the illegitimacy of the regime.

An opposition political consciousness wasn't always expressed so dramatically or traumatically. For example, the 88 Generation—student activists who organized the 1988 protests and were then involved in the electioneering of 1990—remained organized if harassed. Early in 2007 they ran the so-called "Open Heart Letter Campaign," which over two months encouraged ordinary Burmese citizens to write letters to senior general Than Shwe and other members of the State Peace and Development Council politely expressing their grievances and struggles to the leadership.[72]

Throughout the 1990s and 2000s there remained both apolitical civil society organizations, opposition networks, both overt and underground, and activists abroad. These were crucial for creating an environment conducive to the eventual transition.

Imprisonment and Forced Labor

The operation of prison systems for those deemed political opponents of the state were also vastly different; and again, North Korea's system exceeds Myanmar's by a great deal.

DPRK officials refuse to acknowledge the existence of the country's prison camps. Thus, knowledge of the DPRK prison system comes largely from defectors. (Only two foreigners are known to have experienced the ordinary prison system, in the late 1960s. The Westerners detained in North Korea more recently are held elsewhere.)

There is a small cottage industry of human rights groups that has tended to publish and make definitive statements on very limited evidence about the prison system. Perhaps 15 years ago, there may have been sufficient grounds to doubt many of the claims of abuse and widespread human rights violations that such groups make. Now, however, the body of testimonial evidence is so great that the issue is undeniable, even if the details can be difficult to parse and the field of human rights remains deeply politicized.

One widely testified fact is that of the "three generations" principle of punishment for severe political crimes. Both biblical and Confucian in its discrimination, not only can offenders get incarcerated for their crimes, but family members can too. Such is the desire to ideologically protect the state that this formalized system came into being in the 1950s and appears to have been prevalent through the 1980s. Various testimonies suggest this principle is no longer as common, including those collected in the 2014 United Nations COI report.

That COI report found the use of torture was widespread on political prisoners, both before and after conviction. The report confirmed what was already widely known: that as well as smaller, "normal" prisons, there are two types of detention centers for what we would term political prisoners. The first are called *Kyohwaso*, or re-education camps. In these facilities, prisoners can be rehabilitated and mix with non-political criminals. They either work in prison factories or farms. They are also forced to endure meager rationing, intense labor, and often arbitrary punishments.

Kwaliso are usually larger internment camps for the more serious types of political prisoners. Most of these include life-imprisonment zones, with no chance of rehabilitation. Life in these camps is incredibly hard, with deprivation and cruelty rampant.

Estimating numbers of political prisoners is very difficult and requires the triangulation of defector testimony, satellite imagery and guesswork. They vary from "zero" among pro–DPRK groups to 200,000. The latter number probably includes some 70,000 people arrested for "normal" crimes, leaving 80,000 to 120,000 political prisoners as a now-common estimate.[73] Regardless of the exact number, it is a huge percentage of the population.

By contrast, a widespread gulag system never developed in Burma, in part due to the relatively weak ideological commitment to the revolution. Instead, the country relied on a system targeting political prisoners to instill fear of challenging the status quo in specific ways. The targeted system meant that at any time "only" a few thousand people were usually behind bars for political crimes.

If, however, intelligence services decided you were a political threat, one could expect a short trial. Activist Bo Kyi, in a 2012 interview, described his 1990 trial thus: "The Military officer asked one question: 'did I commit a crime?' I replied, 'absolutely no.' Then he replied, 'three years imprisonment with hard labor.' That's all. Finish the trial."[74] Frankly, he got off lighter than some. Many of his cohorts in 1988 and 1990 received much longer sentences.

Compared to the DPRK, where idle chatter among friends can bring serious consequences; someone in Burma/Myanmar would have to be transgressing political boundaries in a more serious manner to face incarceration. Political activism or organization was a clear way to get on MI's radar, as would be publishing or producing critical writing or art. Relatively minor crimes, such as owning a satellite TV dish in the 1990s or discussing politics with friends would go ignored, provided there was no connection by the transgressor to any more serious crimes. If a person were suspected of more serious activity, the litany of minor offenses would be dragged out into the light, however. Political conversations in teashops, always conducted with caution, would cease altogether during periods of fear, such as after the 2007 Saffron Revolution.[75]

If the number and range of political crimes as well as detention was small relative to North Korea, this was likely not much comfort to inmates, who endured awful conditions. Many prisoners ended up suffering back problems from sleeping on stone floors, recalls artist Htein Lin, who was incarcerated from 1998 until 2004. Disease and healthcare were also problems, and he suffered a debilitating stomach problem while in prison. Still, what was the worst aspect in his personal experience? The toilet situation. "Just a bowl in the corner that multiple people had to use. And when it got hot …" [implying the stench].[76]

Htein Lin was nonetheless able to smuggle materials in to create art. Some four hundred of his works of art were also smuggled out. In Myanmar, even political prisoners usually had family visitation rights, sometimes fortnightly, if separated by a wire grate. Sometimes, family members could reach through and touch fingertips.[77] Prisoners could have personal items, such as the knitting needles and crochet equipment kept by Ma Thanegi, once personal assistant to Aung San Suu Kyi, which helped them make it through difficult times.[78]

Regarding forced labor, the most common instances in Myanmar take place when either the *Tatmadaw* or rebel armies compel locals who have the misfortune of being near the frontlines of battles into taking part in building projects or working as porters to transport war materiel. In a very real sense villagers in war zones ever since independence have suffered forced conscription or "porter" work, as it is known colloquially. This remains an ongoing problem.

There are officially 48 labor camps holding roughly 20,000 prisoners who work on farm plantations or in quarries. Bribery is rife in these institutions and an informal system exists in which a prisoner can pay to receive less abuse. There is also some evidence that prisoners at some facilities are forced to do unpaid labor for private companies, for which the prison guards get a share of the profits.[79] The ILO also received reports of forced labor in the construction of Naypyidaw.[80]

Education

Schooling in North Korea is an exercise in indoctrination. All state education systems are such, of course, with particular views of history and civic responsibility never far from core curricula. However, the DPRK's education is particularly intense. The fatherland or the leaders feature in almost all aspects of education. The schools invariably have large entrance signs that read "Thank you Kim Jong Un" (since 2012) and/or "Let's Learn for Korea!" Kid's songs include titles such as "I want to see Comrade Kim Jong Un" but there may also be songs about butterflies or potatoes. (Of course, the potato song includes a line about the starch being "given from the bosom of the General's love.")

Science and mathematics classes are basically pretty standard, though even math story questions can include ideological training. For example, "During the Fatherland Liberation War [North Korea's official name for the Korean War] the brave uncles of the Korean People's Army killed 265 American imperialist bastards in the first battle. In the second battle they killed 70 more bastards than they had in the first battle. How many bastards did they kill in the second battle?"[81]

Geography and history classes also are fairly normal and have a global sweep. Though, as you might expect, history in particular focuses on a leftist view of the world, with the most attention being paid to "Revolutionary History." Revolutionary History is, essentially, a personal hagiography of Kim Il Sung.

In the DPRK, in classical 20th Century Socialist fashion, all children are automatically enrolled and involved in state youth groups. From age nine, one joins the Young Pioneer Corps, a process in part depicted by the documentary *Under the Sun*.[82] Central to the film is the swearing-in ceremony for the Youth Pioneers, wherein the youths are called on to "be reliable reservists of the Juche movement" which is passed on "from generation to generation," an injunction emphasized by the tying of the iconic red scarf around the kids' necks by elderly war veterans. In a very real sense it is their introduction to an intense, state-organized life: until death or infirmity they will be enrolled in state/party-run organizations, either through their school, neighborhood association or workplace. These organizations will mobilize and indoctrinate them.

In Myanmar, schooling was less comprehensive in its indoctrination. The righteousness of Aung San's struggle against the British and the Japanese was a focus in service of building a national identity, until 1988. After the emergence of Aung San SuuCed and the renaming of the country, Myanmar history touched on Aung San in elementary school and then generally ignored him, leaning instead on a much longer historical timeline wherein an essentially unified Myanmar (under Bamar leadership) struggled against foreigners, primarily the Siamese. Ethnic groups featured mostly as rebels and problems that Burmese kings either had to conquer or civilize.

Regardless, it is unlikely that ethnic minorities were absorbing and accepting this unifying version of history. Many could not speak Burmese very well, yet all schooling was conducted in this, for them, foreign language. Many Kachin students in Myitkyina in the 1990s, for example, could speak better English than Burmese.[83] (The issue of language of instruction remains a hot topic today.)

Schooling also became very easy in the 1990s, with teachers told to pass virtually all students. The narrative on the recent violence was that the military had to put down student agitators to keep the country together. This could be persuasive for students who did not receive a counter-narrative from family or outside media. One student from Yangon recalls fighting with her school friends about the nature of the military, having "been told another version by her aunts and uncles."[84]

There were youth organizations with government backing, but these were voluntary. In the BSPP period, the biggest was Lanzin Lu Nge, a group that around 50 percent of all students joined. It focused on community services such as taking care of the elderly or rubbish collection. Participants were generally seen as being "the good kids."

There was also an elite youth group–*Kin Htauk Tat Pwut*–which was very exclusive and seen as grooming future leaders. Just a handful of students were selected from each school district for this group. They had to have good grades but also family with money to support nationwide travels and activities when the government subsidy was insufficient.

As noted, Yangon University was closed in 1990 along with other tertiary education institutions following the 1988 student-led protests. It was reopened leading up to the 75th anniversary of the institution in 1995 and then closed down again following student riots in 1996. Other universities were gradually allowed to reopen, but Yangon University and the Rangoon/Yangon Institute of Technology remained shuttered until 2013 and 2012, respectively, taking in graduate students for much of the interim but no undergraduates.

Universities can function as hubs for intelligent, motivated young people to gather and exchange new ideas. They can also foment critical thought. The junta did a splendid job of denying a nerve center for this to take place, but it also crippled the country by ensuring a generation of top technocrats, business leaders and scientists could not easily develop. It helped ensure that institutions outside of military influence were not a pathway to social advancement, either.

By contrast, in the DPRK an extensive system of universities and colleges has functioned essentially very well, even during the difficult period of economic collapse, privation and social change of the late 1990s. As in Burma, you need recommendations to attend university; in North Korea also "you must have a reference letter and be endorsed by the National League of Students and your high school." Then, the "university makes an admissions decision based on your family background, extracurricular activities and your grades."[85] Contrary to common Western media portrayals, and as powerful as the propaganda apparatus is, education in North Korea is not all propaganda, especially at the higher echelons. Science, mathematics, geography, languages and the like have sound curricula and qualified teachers, for the most part. As noted earlier, other topics—history, economics and social sciences are perhaps more propagandistic in nature, true from primary school up through university. In poorer areas of the country where teachers are forced to engage in market activities or charge for classes to survive, it is much harder for students to advance and have a chance at getting in to university.

Prospects for Change Under These Systems

The intensity of education and organizational life in North Korea, combined with severe limitations on foreign information and harsh punishments for even the faintest hints of opposition to the state, makes for an extremely robust system. As one prominent defector puts it: "Why North Koreans are so ignorant? Are they have any questions about the regime ... why they live as modern slaves today?" She answers her rhetorical question thus: "When growing up in that environment, no matter how smart, how genius ... you become ignorant ... because from the moment you are born, all you see is that environment."[86] The sealed-off, indoctrinated population didn't even really challenge the state as it oversaw the devastating famine of the 1990s.

This simply wasn't the case in Myanmar. With porous borders, armed resistance groups, a flourishing civil society (from the 1990s) and more open information technology, there was simply no realistic way to prevent people gaining alternative interpretations of their state, especially as it led the country into economic ruin. The intelligence system targeted a handful of activists and created a climate of fear, but ultimately the pressures and desires for social and political change could not be destroyed.

Even when North Koreans do develop doubts about their system, there are no platforms for them to express or explore political thought. The people with whom a North Korean would articulate doubt are *extremely* few in number. Even sharing alternative views with family or close friends presents risks. Any kind of publishing or distribution of non-sanctioned ideas remains heavily punished. Even consuming media about those ideas is dangerous: the sheer extent of the prison system attests to that fact.

Much hope rests on how the marketization of North Korea has created a paradigm shift for DPRK citizens, who seek opportunities to earn rather than commit their lives to party or military careers. There is strong evidence to suggest that many Koreans are more exposed to media from abroad, smuggled in via DVDs, USB drives and radio. This has created arguably the least ideologically committed generation since the founding of the republic.

However, the vast majority of information and news North Koreans get is still from official sources. Most have no legal, cheap or easy means of communicating with outsiders or getting outside information. Those who do have limits to what they can share and with whom they can share it.

In Myanmar, alternate viewpoints and discontent among the population were constantly being beaten back by the ruling elites. These issues exploded into violence during student demonstrations and other protests in every decade since the Ne Win coup of 1962. The existence of a legitimate (if cowed) opposition since 1988 meant that general discontent had an avatar, a focal point, in the personage of Aung San Suu Kyi. This was constantly a threat to the state as conceived by the *Tatmadaw*.

By contrast, North Korean elites are almost completely insulated from public opinion, except in very exceptional circumstances.[87] With a much-diminished need to react to popular attitudes on important social issues, Pyongyang's ruling class has greater freedom of action. The threat of an alternative narrative, much less an uprising, is kept extremely low by the controls on information and the deep penetration of the state into any form of organized life.

The leaders in Pyongyang have developed a superior system for not only ensuring that a unified view of the world is disseminated among the citizenry, but also that that view goes unchallenged. When conflicting information does enter, it is mitigated, first by the comprehensive national narrative and then by an incredible apparatus of repression.

Myanmar's leaders didn't have these tools and so faced much greater pressure from within for system reform. North Korea's leaders don't face that problem to nearly the same degree, so concomitantly don't need to seek a reform-and-opening solution.

6

Sanctions

If storm clouds are overhead, rain may fall without anyone's help. If moisture-laden clouds are in the sky, chemical seeding may bring forth rain. But if the skies are clear and dry, no amount of human assistance will produce rain. Similarly, sanctions may be redundant, productive, or useless in pursing foreign policy goals, depending on the economic health and political stability of the target country.[1]

The Use and Utility of Sanctions

Sanctions are an expression of coercive power, employed when one state (or states) wishes to influence the behavior of a state or punish it for behaviors deemed unacceptable. The state(s) imposing sanctions are generally called "senders" and those being reprimanded called "targets." Both Burma/Myanmar and North Korea have become sanctions targets in the late 20th and early 21st centuries, for the reasons we've looked at. Being the target of sustained sanctions binds these two states together in a unit as much as anything: they were the only long-term pariahs and certainly the only near-universally condemned states in the post–Cold War political-economy of the East Asia region.

But what effect did these sanctions regimes have? In order to answer that we'll have to briefly look at what sanctions are *supposed* to do. We'll then look at the debate over their effectiveness generally in order to contextualize how they actually impacted the two Asian pariahs.

Ultimately, sanctions have thus far failed in North Korea because as much as the state and the people endure hardship due to sanctions, the leadership has made nearly no gains to speak of in terms of solving their fundamental security dilemma. For the leadership, the reasons they are sanctioned—their nuclear and missile programs—are seen as central to their existence as a state: the programs are the only way to ensure survival in the DPRK's struggle against the United States. In Myanmar, with the sanctions connected entirely to human rights, democracy and the fate of Aung San Suu Kyi, the regime was able to tackle their core security issues—the threat of the country's dissolution or fracture—before turning to the issues of social and political change that concerned the sanctions senders. The two issues could be divorced and sequenced.

By contrast, the social and political change many hope to see in North Korea is retarded by the sanctions regimes. North Korean people, first cut off from the outside world by their government's policies, now find themselves with less access to the outside world due to sanctions. Their nuclear program continues to develop and their state survives, in many ways unchanged. On those terms, the sanctions have to be judged a failure. The international relations of North Korea are dynamic, sanctions have gotten significantly stronger since late 2016 and Kim Jong Un may yet have a breaking point, though this has yet to be seen.

This chapter discusses heavily the United States. This is because since World War II, the United States has been the country that has been most keen to use sanctions to try to coerce behavior. Often strategically compelled, since the 1970s the United States has seen human rights become a priority goal of sanctions policies. In this era, the United States has levied sanctions against six Western hemisphere dictatorships, yet failed to dislodge or change the behaviors of those regimes, with the possible exception of Nicaragua.[2] In the 1990s, sanctions focused on human rights issues in Africa became more common, often in coordination with the European Union. (These met mostly with failure, also.)

The European Union, United Kingdom and other Western countries are often aligned in sanctions policies. But with the United States as the most important international actor, "U.S. presidents seemingly feel compelled to dramatize their opposition to foreign misdeeds, even when the likelihood of changing the target country's behavior is remote. In these cases, sanctions often are imposed because the cost of inaction—in terms of lost confidence both at home and abroad in the ability or willingness of the United States to act—is seen as greater than the cost of the sanctions."[3]

Leaders in the global system feel obligated to take action against states whose norms are judged to be too far outside acceptable bounds or whose actions challenge the order or security of that global system. Sometimes this is primarily based on values, such as when human rights violations drive sanctions forward. Along with South Africa, Burma/Myanmar is probably the best example of this vector. Its pariah status was almost entirely due to human rights violations, even if for the United States isolating Myanmar was strategically difficult to justify (as we will see).

Sanctions also often flow from strategic rather than moral concerns. The case of Russia in 2014 is a good example of this. The United States and European Union wanted to punish Moscow for Russia's annexation of Crimea so imposed restrictions on major Russian state banks and companies. Blacklisting dozens of senior officials and firms was designed to impose a strategic cost on Russia, though they could or would not challenge Russia and her proxies in Ukraine through war.

Often, but not always, it is both strategic and moral, and the lines can be blurred. Strategic concerns can help create the conditions in which sanctions over human rights can be implemented. Conversely, human rights violations can justify sanctions that also provide a strategic advantage to the sending country. After all, it is much easier to focus on the human rights violations of a country when doing so aligns with strategic goals. North Korea falls into this category: its nuclear program is the primary justification for sanctions, but its treatment of its own people allows a "second front" to be opened as the United States and other actors take action against the country.

By contrast, pressure over human rights is less likely when a potential target's strategic value is thought to be too important to try to coerce. Saudi Arabia, by any measure a gross violator of human rights, is perhaps the best example. Despite it being a country that exercises capital punishment for witches, warlocks and atheists, discussion on the issue of Saudi human rights is generally muted and there has never been a serious attempt to sanction the oil-producing Kingdom.

Either way, sanctions are levied when the opprobrium over the target's actions does not align with a strategic position that would justify kinetic action. Or to put it more simply, sanctions are used when a state wishes to coerce another state for strategic or moral reasons but is unwilling to go to war to defend those reasons. In this sense, national strategies play the primary role in determining whether sanctions will be implemented.

Finally, it should be noted that domestic political imperatives also play a role, of course, as leaders throughout the 20th century "often launched sanctions to answer domestic outrage and to prepare the public for sterner measures."[4] For both audiences, domestic and foreign, applying sanctions can "provide a satisfying theatrical display yet avoid the high costs of war." Sanctions allow politicians to look active without bearing much risk.

Do Sanctions Work, Generally Speaking?

The most comprehensive study on 20th century sanctions concluded that sanctions were "at least partially successful" in 34 percent of the cases recorded. The researchers broke that figure down into several categories, which had varying results. When the goals are modest policy changes, the number is higher, with a 51 percent success rate. When democratization or regime change is the goal, the rate drops to 31 percent. Disruption of "military adventures" is the least successfully prosecuted goal, with only 21 percent success. Sanctions seeking military impairment or "other major policy changes" are effective 31 percent and 30 percent of the time, respectively. This is a mixed bag to say the least, and perhaps unsurprisingly, sanctions are most likely to coax minor policy changes out of target states.

Failure to achieve goals *seems* to come when there is a lack of global buy-in. It is commonly thought that when sanctions are unilateral or applied by small coalitions, target countries can find other trade and investment partners that help keep the economy afloat and the leadership ensconced.[5] Essentially, that there are escape routes when the sanctions aren't multilateral.

Not everyone agrees with this assessment. Even multilateral sanctions episodes are primarily driven by a single state and they require coalitions to implement. These states have different interests and goals, however, which can lead to a coalition that is weak or cannot stand the test of time. "This fragility gives the target state the incentive to wait out multilateral sanctions to see if the sender coalition collapses," argues one influential scholar of sanctions, Daniel W. Drezner.[6] He argues that multilateral coalitions tend to break down as various senders' interests often do not align for long. As cracks appear, even the main sender is pressured to give up rather than pursue an isolated and probably futile sanctions policy.

He concludes that several tests have shown "no link or a negative correlation between cooperation and sanctions success," while "no statistical test has shown a significant positive correlation between policy success and international cooperation among the sanctioning states."[7] However, unilateral sanctions are not as effective as multilateral sanctions, *if the multilateral sanctions have the backing of an international organization.* This is because an international organization "can convert a fragile cooperation equilibrium into a more robust one. International organizations prevent backsliding by giving wavering states the means to resist domestic pressures and by reassuring states that a cooperative equilibrium will be maintained."[8] International organizations can provide moral and legal authority for the main senders to pressure less committed states into staying the course.

The issue of multilateral vs. unilateral sanctions aside, it is generally assumed that the pressure on a target state's leadership should be enough so that the costs of persisting under sanctions exceed the cost of changing the policy that the sender wishes altered. As one scholar puts it:

> One state (the sender) seeks to obtain concessions from another (the target) by holding hostage some benefit the target values. Conceding on the policy of interest to the sender is costly to the leadership of the target. The leadership would only concede if the cost of noncompliance exceeds the cost of granting the sender's demands. For coercion to work, the political stability of the target should suffer more from coming under pressure than from conceding.[9]

This may seem obvious, but leaders of target countries have proven surprisingly resilient and willing to endure a great deal of pain when conceding would *seemingly* benefit them and their social or political allies a great deal. This raises several questions that are extremely difficult to answer: when do domestic conditions create pressure on leaders? What happens when the pain of sanctions is externalized through costs imposed throughout society? How do leaders of targeted countries evaluate their options? Furthermore, if the target "stoutly resists" modifying the policy or behavior the sender wishes changed, "sanctions are of limited utility."[10] How does one deal with such intractability?

Some scholars explain this capacity to suffer through the expectations that develop between adversarial countries.[11] Adversaries see no prospect for improved relations and perceive their conflict as zero-sum. As such, decisions flow from the expectations of both the sanctioning and sanctioned states that they are in an escalating conflict. Compromise then becomes less likely from the state under sanction, which tends to see acquiescence as hurting its reputation and weakening its position in future—unavoidable—conflicts.[12]

Domestically, it allows leaders to create a "rally round the flag" kind of atmosphere, where all manner of policy failures can be blamed on the outside world. Whether or not this is successful depends very much on the social and political fabric of the target country.

The privation caused by sanctions tends to benefit political allies of the regime. Under the blanket sanctions endured by Iraq, Saddam Hussein and his family still enjoyed large collections of sports cars, gold AK-47s, and women as their playthings. Ordinary people struggled to survive. Even the now en vogue "targeted sanctions," which go after specific individuals or corporate fiefdoms close to leaderships, tend to have this effect: "the targeted regime shelters its cronies, while the rest of the population suffers."[13] Following the Ukraine Crisis in 2014, for example, Putin's allies who found themselves in the sanctions crosshairs were simply given new concessions to compensate; concessions that inevitably were taken from somebody else with fewer connections to the regime.

Given that the impact of sanctions appears to be borne largely by the citizenry, the uneven distribution of the suffering caused by sanctions raises ethical dilemmas. For example, sanctions tend to exacerbate income inequality in target states.[14] This leads some to argue on utilitarian grounds that sanctions are never valid because the number of losers exceeds the winners, while acknowledging that utilitarian ethics is not a precise tool.[15] It is very hard to even agree on what constitutes gains and losses, much less measure them.

Both North Korea and Myanmar descended into their respective pariah statuses in the late 1980s and early 1990s and were sanctioned by the international community as a result, both unilaterally and multilaterally. Broadly speaking, both Myanmar and North Korea turned to the same escape valve during their sanctions experience: China, a country less concerned with human rights than other international actors and with a different strategic outlook. This led to an over-reliance on China for both pariahs, making the leaders in both countries extremely uncomfortable with their international strategic positions. Both countries felt trapped by China's embrace.

Myanmar's internal strategic gains against insurgent foes in the 1990s and 2000s, however, meant that the leaders in Yangon/Naypyidaw could in the end begin taking steps to undo the sanctions regime and find other international partners. North Korea's ongoing standoff with the United States, still without resolution, means it cannot follow Myanmar's example. It remains trapped.

Myanmar Sanctions

With regards to Myanmar, this section will look primarily at U.S. sanctions given that the U.S. relationship has been so crucial to Myanmar. The European Union and other Western states tended to follow suit but with weaker sanctions than the United States.

After the transition to civilian rule had begun, the major sanctions senders reviewed their positions. In 2012, the European Union lifted almost all sanctions, though preserved a ban on arms sales. The United States has been slower to lift sanctions, recognizing that to give up all sanctions meant abandoning its leverage. In 2011, Secretary of State Hillary Clinton visited Myanmar, beginning a series of signals that continued progress on democratization would bring sanctions relief. In 2012, the United States issued a general license, allowing investment and trade in Myanmar. In 2013, Washington suspended a 1996 visa ban and clarified some of the new permissions in publications by the U.S. Treasury in 2014. By 2015, only nine people had been removed from the Specially Designated Nationals (SDN) list, essentially a blacklist of people or entities that Americans are not allowed to deal with. Two of those were taken off because they had died. As of late 2016, some restrictions apply, primarily focused on remaining SDNs connected to narcotics.

Myanmar's position as a sanctions target was almost entirely due to its violent suppression of protests in 1988 as well as its invalidation of the 1990 elections and subsequent repression of political activism related to the opposition, centered on Aung San Su Kyi. In 1988 it was actually more in the U.S. interest to engage Burma and help guide it out of isolation and pseudo-socialism to an orientation towards the market economies and U.S. allies in South East Asia. David Steinberg sums it up thus:

> Had not the military coup been so brutal in 1988 in repressing the popular riots throughout the country, the United States and the industrialized world would have welcomed the most important economic policy change by the military since 1962: the abandonment of socialism and the opening of the economy to both the foreign and domestic private sectors.[16]

Strategically, even if Burma maintained an official policy of neutrality, Rangoon's willingness to open its economy after three decades of socialist isolation would certainly have given the United States and the West a chance to enmesh the country into financial flows, trade relationships and cultural partnerships that would have increased the relative value of America and its allies to Burma.

Instead, on August 8, 1988, the military massacred protestors during the 8888 uprising. With remarkable rapidity—just three days later—the U.S. Senate passed a resolution calling on President Reagan to take action.[17] Less than a month later, the U.S. House of Representatives passed a resolution calling on the executive branch to review assistance programs in Burma. The Reagan Administration quickly concluded that all U.S. aid to Burma should cease. The following year, just two months into office, President George Bush removed the country from the U.S. Generalized System of Preferences (GSP) program.[18]

After the 1990 election, the United States also refused to nominate an ambassador to be stationed at the U.S. embassy in Burma. This remained the case until July 2012 when Derek Mitchell became the first U.S ambassador to Myanmar in 22 years.

As the mid 1990s approached and Aung San Su Kyi languished under house arrests, with many other "88 generation" activists in prison or exile, the United States began withholding funds from international organizations working in Burma/Myanmar. Five years after the election, the intensity of activity in both the target and the primary sender increased dramatically.

In late July 1995, the Free Burma Act was introduced in the Senate, which would have placed a broad range of sanctions on Burma, including a ban on U.S. investment and assistance, the suspension of GSP privileges and normal trade relations, the prohibition of all imports of Burmese goods, travel restrictions to and from Burma, and U.S. opposition to all multilateral assistance. The United States was the fourth-largest investor in Myanmar, after France, Singapore and Thailand, at the time.[19]

According to some, the severity of the sanctions proposed in this bill was sufficient to persuade SLORC to release Aung San Suu Kyi from house arrest on July 10, 1995, though her freedom of movement was restricted. Ultimately, the bill didn't pass. Another sanctions bill, the Burma Freedom and Democracy Act of 1995, also failed to pass in December.

In 1996, the Burmese military cracked down on the NLD again, as the party began planning a May conference with a few hundred delegates. They arrested perhaps 2,000 political activists in order "to prevent unrest." Had the military been able to avoid this somewhat nervous reaction and taken a more sanguine approach to the meeting, the next round of U.S. sanctions might have been avoided.

As it was, the following year, a major sanctions bill did become law. The Foreign Operations, Export Financing, and Related Programs Appropriations

Act of 1997 imposed a number of specific sanctions on Burma and gave the president discretionary power to decide if and when human rights and democracy standards had been met. This act authorized and required the President to prohibit new investments in Burma, which Bill Clinton duly did by executive order, though after some prevarication. (Speculation had it that he was worried about being vulnerable to criticism over a double standard regarding China, where he had specifically divorced economic relations from human rights considerations.[20])

Regardless, from 1997 all new U.S. investment into Burma was banned, explicitly linked to the large-scale repression of or violence towards the Democratic opposition. Aung San Suu Kyi's well-being is specifically mentioned in the act. There was no expiration on the bill, but it did require the president to report to the chairmen of the Committee on Foreign Relations on the situation in Burma regarding democratization and quality of life, implying that changes on those fronts could lead to a relaxation of the sanctions. ASEAN (Association of Southeast Asian Nations), which admitted Myanmar into the regional association in 1997, opposed these sanctions, as did Japan.

Meanwhile, the European Union introduced sanctions after 1990 and strengthened them in 1996, creating a blacklist on investment with designated entities and a travel ban for named individuals. A suspension of high-level visits to the country was also introduced. In 2000, the EU expanded the visa ban to include members of a lower military rank and a policy of opposing loans to Myanmar from international financial institutions. They also made it difficult to invest in many Myanmar state-owned enterprises.

The United States slapped another more severe round of sanctions on Myanmar in 2003, after the Depayin Massacre. Aung San Suu Kyi had been unconditionally released from house arrest in May 2002 and began travelling, visiting local NLD branches and inspiring impassioned supporters across the country. Just over a year after her release, during a tour in the middle of the country, her supporters and entourage were set upon by a group of several thousand attackers at Depayin. She escaped largely unharmed; others were not so lucky. Many estimates suggest 70 people died that day and rumors still persist that it was ordered from "very high up."

The Burmese Freedom and Democracy Act of 2003 was a direct response to this brutal affair and prohibited the import of any Myanmar-made product into the United States. President George W. Bush implemented the act on July 28, 2003, which froze the assets of certain Burmese officials and banned the provision of financial services to Burma.

Also in 2003, Myanmar was designated a "primary money laundering concern" under section 311 of the U.S. Patriot Act. This effectively cut off Myanmar from the U.S. dollar system by denying "Burmese financial institutions access to the U.S. financial system through correspondent accounts." Correspondent accounts are how global financial institutions move U.S. dollars through New York. The ruling not only stopped U.S. banks from conducting transactions, but it also extended "to any correspondent account maintained by a U.S. financial institution or any foreign bank if the account is used by the foreign bank to provide a Burmese financial institution indirect access to the U.S. financial system."[21] Two banks, Myanmar Mayflower Bank and Asia Wealth Bank, were the first specific foreign financial institutions ever designated under section 311. They wouldn't be the last.

This meant that from then on, Myanmar transactions would either have to avoid U.S. dollars or make sure they were laundered through multiple layers, imposing costs on the transaction. Part of this could be done by only using RMB: the Chinese, after all, were the biggest investors in the 2000s *and* the biggest consumers, though at points Thailand officially imported more than China.

The number one import by China has been jade, of which they are by far the biggest purchaser. Chinese data suggested that by 2014 the country was importing $12 billion a year worth of jade; a Global Witness report estimates the figure to be closer to $31 billion in part due to rampant smuggling.[22] That report also elucidates how Chinese partners are willing to help make the jade business opaque, including through financing.[23]

Singapore was also an important outlet for Myanmar elites, with a banking system that was far more welcoming that the Americans would have liked. Suspicions long lingered that Myanmar's leaders were stashing billions of dollars in Singaporean banks, forcing Singapore's prime minister to publically address the issue in 2007.[24] A 2009 report by Earth Witness estimated that $4.8 billion dollars was earned by the *Yadana* natural gas field in the 2000s that didn't appear in the national budget. The report alleges that the funds are kept in two Singaporean banks, the Overseas Chinese Banking Corporation and the DBS Group.[25] The banks and the Monetary Authority of Singapore denied this particular accusation. Singapore became Myanmar's third largest trading partner in 2009–10, with bilateral trade reaching $1.86 billion.[26] Singapore consistently argued against sanctions on Myanmar.

The final significant sanctions applied to Myanmar came after the Saffron Revolution. Building on previous sanctions, in September 2007 President George W. Bush announced the United States would be going after more individuals and promptly designated and froze the assets of 14 Burmese officials. The following year, The Tom Lantos Block Burmese JADE Act was passed. It not only focused on Myanmar's valuable jade industry but also found a way to turn "jade" into an *exceedingly* clever acronym: Junta's Anti-Democratic Efforts. Specifically, this act forbade Myanmar gemstones from being imported to the United States, including via third countries. It also expanded the list of officials under a travel ban to the United States.

The effects of The Burmese Freedom and Democracy Act of 2003 illustrate some of the ambivalence and irresolution that accompanies sanctions regimes. The most affected sector was the textile industry, which employed some 400,000 people at the time and sent 80 percent of its products to the United States, worth about $400 million annually.[27] Most of the employees worked in terrible conditions but would have no alternatives once factories began shutting down.

A 2008 study of the garment industry in Myanmar sought to look at the impact of these sanctions on "virtually the only industry that practices modern mass production-based manufacturing as part of the global supply chain," even if the sector overall remains underdeveloped.[28] The study found that as the market for garments shrank, competition became more severe. This hit smaller companies hardest, as bigger companies with better connections or stronger ties to foreign companies were better able to adjust and squeeze out competitors.

Companies exporting $10,000 or less dropped from 41 firms in 2000 to just nine in 2004. The top five firms' market share grew from 15 percent to 20 percent in the same period.[29] Layoffs were also higher at smaller companies. Ultimately, the paper concludes that sanctions did not have as much of an impact on military-related enterprises as they did on domestic private firms," with the former "more entrenched in their position in the industry than they were before the sanctions."[30]

As in several other cases of sanctions, the elite could consolidate their positions through connections to the regime, as they were handed bigger slices of a shrinking pie. Moreover, some argue that because the nascent and growing civil-society did not have access to significant flows of foreign capital, they couldn't make gains vis-à-vis the military in several fields, including infrastructure and civic institutions.

Instead of promoting positive political change, the U.S. unilateral sanctions have made the military government stronger relative to the civilian population, further entrenching its role as a state-building institution. Rather than impacting the sectors of the Burmese economy under total state control, the U.S. unilateral sanctions exact their toll on parts that are controlled by the private sector before sanctions.[31]

Furthermore, critics charge there has been a lack of clarity in U.S. sanctions:

> The goals sought by the U.S. comprehensive sanctions against Myanmar could be a combination of any of the following: to change the military regime's policies on human rights and democracy, to inflict economic hardship on Myanmar, to punish the leaders of the military regime, to induce a regime change, to legitimize Daw Aung San Suu Kyi and the NLD, to rally support for democratic forces in Myanmar, or to make human rights activists in the United States feel good.[32]

Certainly, the goals were vague and broad on the one hand and narrowly connected to the fate of Aung San Suu Kyi on the other. The preamble of the Burmese Freedom and Democracy Act of 2003 lists a number of overarching goals: "[t]o sanction the ruling Burmese military junta [the SPDC], to strengthen Myanmar's democratic forces and support and recognize the National League [for] Democracy [NLD] as the legitimate representative of the Myanmar people." The goals expressed in the preamble are supplemented by additional conditions that must be met before the sanctions are disengaged: that the SPDC make "substantial and measurable progress to end violations of internationally recognized human rights."

The U.S. sanctions on Myanmar had taken on a very emotional quality in which the personal fate of Aung San Su Kyi was an avatar for human suffering: and no one could be seen voting for human suffering. Her fate and her opinions drove U.S. policy. Sanctions were seen as giving her leverage: she supported them, judging that they gave her bargaining power. Her moral authority meant that as long she kept a pro-sanctions position, no U.S. politician could really be seen as arguing against it.

To quote Steinberg again, "For about two decades there was almost no public policy dialogue on alternative policies on Myanmar in Washington, in contrast to all other foreign policy issues in troubled areas. Policy was traumatized and focused on democracy, human rights, and the role of Aung San Suu Kyi."[33] As long as Suu Kyi and the military seemed to be immovable objects (even though the military was altering on-the-ground realities, as we've seen), it was very difficult to think about sanctions being unwound.

Meanwhile, the lack of trade and investment options with the West meant that Myanmar became over-reliant on China. In 2009, trade between the two countries reached $2.9 billion, an increase of 10 percent from 2008, but heavily unbalanced: Chinese exports were valued at $2.3 billion while exports from Myanmar were just $646 million.[34] This was an upward trend and only Thailand was a similarly important trade partner for Myanmar, though it didn't have the surpluses that China did. Thailand was the biggest importer of Myanmar goods before the 2010 elections.[35] This hampered the effect of sanctions in terms of regime collapse—China was the outlet with ever-growing trade and investment filling the vacuum left by the United States and Europe.

In turn, this apparent stalemate allowed the *Tatmadaw* to maintain its position as the only organization capable of achieving anything on any large scale: The *Tatmadaw* remained the center of not only political life but commercial life as well.[36] Certainly, only an institution connected to the military could develop exporting jade mines, for example, or gas fields and pipelines to produce Myanmar's biggest export from that period, natural gas.

Critics argue that the usefulness of sanctions was weak precisely because the environment of greater privation was spread among the citizenry, while the benefits and monopolies only went to extremely well-connected people. For ordinary people, access to markets was tougher and prices were higher. Myanmar's economy was largely isolated under the socialist period, but under sanctions ordinary people were unable to engage in trade or entrepreneurship. They then found themselves cut off from the outside where they were once cut off from the inside.

In terms of daily life, as one Yangon University professor put it: "Sanctions meant the cost of every thing was higher, which was difficult because we were low income. So we could only get products from China. Everything was from China and low quality. But we had to pay high prices for that low quality. Under sanctions, I had to spend 1600 Kyat for a big bottle of Coca-Cola. Now it's 800!"[37]

Even the relatively privileged faced those higher prices. As a journalist recalls: "Everything was difficult. Buying a car ... my mom bought a car for me. It was $50,000 USD for a car in 2007 that was a 1990 model. My telephone number and phone were like $5,000."[38]

Such prices didn't seriously harm the people at the very top, of course. But as insulated and well-off as dictator Than Shwe, the generals and their cronies were in the 1990s and 2000s, sanctions did play a role in their strategic thinking as they considered their options, in two key ways.

The first was that over-reliance on China. Middle states often seek to balance between more powerful allies—North Korea was a master of this during the Cold War Sino-Soviet split—and to be too dependent on a single patron risks limiting policy options, both politically and economically. This is not a complicated concept: the more a single country is responsible for your economy, the more leverage it has in your bilateral relations. The European Union, United States, United Kingdom and Australia were largely absent from the market. Other actors, such as Japan and South Korea, did not impose economic sanctions on Myanmar but were restrained in their economic interactions by the United States and their own concerns over human rights violations.[39]

This relatively isolated position worried the leadership in Yangon and was part of the impetus for change. Over the 2000s this situation began to impel the regime towards finding a way out of the over-reliance on China. As one observer puts it: "A long tradition of nationalism, self-reliance and even xenophobia suggests Rangoon had no intention of becoming a Chinese pawn, and that as soon as conditions permitted, it would move to reduce its dependence on Beijing."[40]

If trade and investment with Thailand and Singapore were still significant, the trend towards Chinese dominance was clear and troubling. According to Chinese statistics, in 1989 bilateral trade was just $313.72 million, by 1995 it was $767.40 million, and by 2008 it was $2,625.43 million. China has always run surpluses with Myanmar, though some speculate that this is balanced by illegal drug trading or other hidden, off-book investments.[41]

Anecdotal evidence suggests that Chinese firms could command below-market prices for their imports from Myanmar as they had monopsony power, though comprehensive studies on this subject are lacking.

China became Myanmar's major source for military hardware, also. A report in 2007 suggested that since 1988 Myanmar imported $1.69 billion in military goods from China. Yangon/Naypyidaw have diversified their weapons purchases somewhat: since there were no UN prohibitions, other countries such as India, South Korea, Israel and Russia have made sales, also.[42] The Chinese sold the widest variety of weapons, however, including radar systems, fighter jets, missile systems and tanks, and in quantities that far exceeded those of other suppliers.[43]

With the Asian Development Bank, World Bank, European Union

and United States absent, China stepped into the void to provide infrastructural development assistance as well. It was Chinese expertise and financial backing that underpinned Myanmar's ambitious infrastructure program of the 1990s.

> China was involved in establishing state-owned enterprises such as sugar plant, textile factory, plywood plant, rice mill, coal-fired power plant, pulp and paper mill, mobile liquefied petroleum gas plants, agriculture equipment plant, and other light industrial factories. China also provided coastal liners, irrigation pumps, construction materials, an auto telephone exchange, and a satellite ground station. Construction of the Yangon-Thanlyin Bridge, Mandalay International Airport, a gymnasium, a theatre, and upgrading of roads.[44]

The full extent of Chinese investments is very difficult to assess since much cross-border trade is arranged and executed locally, without the knowledge or oversight of the Myanmar Investment Commission.[45] Even though the central government ended up controlling more of its northern territory, a great deal of China-Myanmar trade operated through local ethnic strongmen and businesses based in Yunnan province: trade and investment relations between Beijing-Yangon was one axis, but the Kunming-Northern borderlands axis also became a economic lifeline for Myanmar.[46]

Even though Myanmar's political transition was many years in the making, Myanmar's improvement in relations with the United States was sudden enough that it dramatically shook up the strategic relations in the region. Myanmar began to achieve the breakout it wanted from China's overwhelming influence.[47] (Beijing is on the one hand concerned about losing influence vis-à-vis other competitors, but it is also likely pleased that the transition could create stability in the long term.)

The second effect of sanctions was that they became the object around which relations between Aung San Suu Kyi, the United States and the junta orbited. Because Aung San Suu Kyi supported sanctions, this helped give them some acceptability domestically. This was despite the sense among many people that they were suffering because of sanctions. The generals tried to paint sanctions as Aung San Suu Kyi's fault, but the stratospheric legitimacy and adoration she carried among the people of Myanmar meant that argument carried little resonance, along with their various other attempts to besmirch her reputation.

David Steinberg once claimed that, "she essentially determined U.S. policy toward Myanmar until the Obama administration."[48] This may be a slight overstatement but not by much: it was certainly the case that with her continued endorsement, maintaining sanctions was the only politically viable option for both presidents and Congress. Sanctions were seen as pro–Aung San Suu Kyi, and who could risk to be seen as against her, Asia's icon of democracy? Various people who interacted with her during the transition period have claimed she had to be talked into their relaxation when the United States was finally ready to begin unwinding them as the transition to civilian rule began in 2010. Certainly, the status of U.S. sanctions has been the subject of much cooperation and consultation between Washington and Aung San Suu Kyi over the last several years. Even as late as 2016, the sanctions were still seen as carrots—leverage to ensure the transition to civilian rule stayed on track.

In May 2016, as the United States decided to maintain a portion of its sanctions, she still said: "We are not afraid of sanctions, and we are not afraid of scrutiny. We believe we are on the right path. We believe all sanctions will be eased if the time arrives. We have no difficulty with those issues. I assume the U.S. is our ally. *I believe the sanctions imposed on us are providing help for us.*"[49] (Italics mine.) She was standing next to U.S. Secretary of State John Kerry at a joint press conference at the time.

Prior to the 2010 elections, sanctions did play the crucial role of forcing the regime to deal with Aung San Suu Kyi. The dynamic of her endorsement of sanctions and U.S. endorsement of her role in government meant that she could not be ignored if and when the leadership decided to rejoin the international economic mainstream. Her position on sanctions softened gradually following 2010 as ongoing talks between her, the military and international actors took place. The United States removed some sanctions in 2012, eased others in 2015 and then eliminated all remaining non-arms related sanctions late in 2016, after the NLD had taken office. The European Union was quicker to cede leverage and welcome Myanmar back, having removed its sanctions in 2012. (Both the United States and European Union still have arms embargos on Myanmar.)

What eventually emerged was a compromise: the military would not turn over all the power of the government to her, nor allow her to assume the presidency, but they have ceded a significant role to her, which she accepted. She also accepted their compromise 2008 constitution that allows the military 25 percent of parliamentary seats and control of key ministries.

This lengthy and difficult road might have been avoided, along with all sanctions regimes, had it not been for the brutality of 1988 and the poorly thought-out plan to hold elections two years later. Myanmar's leaders might have emulated the South Korean or Chinese-style development-dictatorship model. Sanctions denied that path. The triangle of the United States, Aung San Suu Kyi and the military meant that Than Shwe had to find a path to some degree of democratic reform before genuine economic development could take place.

Did sanctions work? Other factors were more important to Myanmar's transition—the strategic gains against insurgents being the key. It is undeniable, however, that sanctions in a very real way forced a degree of democratization upon Myanmar, eventually. One might say that Myanmar's leaders took their time to find the minimum amount of democracy necessary to have sanctions removed. This can still be viewed as an accomplishment.

Perhaps without sanctions and a developing market economy, a middle class might have emerged in the intervening two decades and that class may have demanded more political transparency and accountability, as happened in South Korea. Perhaps after the gains against insurgent forces and strengthening of the state, the leadership would have tried an experiment in democracy again, given that it is the international norm in the 21st century. Or perhaps not. Other paths were not taken and we cannot know.

What we do know is that once sanctions were applied, the generals gradually came to understand that some form of compromise on their political model would be necessary to gain the benefits of participating in a globally integrated economy and escaping over-reliance on China. In that sense, sanctions did impact their cost/benefit analyses. Importantly, the sanctions and constituents behind them were not related to insurgencies or the threat of national disintegration, their key strategic concern. This allowed them to address those concerns separately, before tackling the issues that generated the sanctions imposed against them.

North Korea

Again, when looking at North Korea, it makes sense to focus primarily on the United States as the sender of unilateral sanctions, though the European Union, United Kingdom, Australia, Japan and South Korea have imposed unilateral sanctions as well. This is because the United States is North Korea's primary antagonist as well as the guardian of the global financial system, which relies heavily on the dollar as the medium of trade and finance.

Through the 1990s, the United States imposed minor sanctions on North Korea for missile technology-related transfers and proliferation, as well as for cooperation between Pakistan and the DPRK. These steps were largely symbolic.[50]

Unlike Myanmar, however, North Korea has not only faced unilateral sanctions measures but also UN sanctions as well. Stronger UN and U.S. sanctions have their roots in the first North Korean nuclear crisis, in 1993–1994, and have progressed alongside the DPRK's nuclear and missile programs. The United Nations was close to implementing sanctions in the spring of 1994 as the United States prevaricated between airstrikes or economic measures in those months.

In 1993, the UN Security Council had passed a resolution stating that the DPRK was in violation of its safeguards obligations and urging the country to return to the Treaty on the Non-Proliferation of Nuclear Weapons (NPT). As the crisis deepened in 1994, Pyongyang made it clear that sanctions would be viewed as an act of war and would provoke a kinetic response. This was most chillingly illustrated when a negotiator from the North said, "Seoul is not far from here ... if war breaks out, it will become a sea of fire."[51] (This threat has been repeated many times since, diminishing its value, but at the time, it had the effect of terrifying the population and leadership of South Korea.)

Viewing the situation with alarm, Jimmy Carter went to Pyongyang, brokered the outline of an agreement and made a surprise announcement that led to a deal. An early provision of the deal was that Pyongyang allowed back IAEA inspectors, who had been kicked out in 1993. Major sanctions, and probably war, had been averted.

With the recession of the 1994 crisis and a period of awkward cooperation beginning, the impetus for sanctions was largely removed. On October 21, 1994, the two old enemies signed the U.S.-DPRK Agreed Framework, which made provisions for several things: the United States would lead a consortium (KEDO—the Korean Peninsula Energy Development Organization) to build light water reactors for energy use and supply fuel for energy during the construction period; the DPRK would shut down any reactors capable of making weapons-grade fuel; the DPRK would rejoin the NPT and allow inspections; and a step-by-step normalization of relations would occur.

It was "awkward" because on November 8, the Democrats lost control of Congress; key Republicans were opposed to the agreement. The Agreed Framework had become, as the first director of KEDO later commented, "a political orphan within two weeks after its signature."[52] Shipments of fuel were late, delays beset financing and starting the light water reactors, and the type of fuel the Americans sent was not what the North Koreans were hoping for. Frustrations with these problems, in part, led to Pyongyang deciding to test a ballistic missile in 1998, which they shot over the Japanese mainland.

For their part, the Koreans were breaking trust by secretly running a uranium enrichment program. The agreement and the KEDO eventually died after the Bush administration revealed in 2002 that the North Koreans had that secret program.

This also led to the DPRK pulling out of the NPT in January 2003. Later in the year, they joined the Six-Party Talks but these ground on with few results. With diplomacy failing, the U.S. unilateral sanctions regime kicked off in earnest in 2005, followed by North Korea's first nuclear test in 2006 and then the beginning of multilateral sanctions on the nuclear issue.

While Six-Party Talks were ongoing under the purview of the U.S. State Department, the U.S. Treasury moved to pressure North Korea. On September 15, 2005, the Treasury labeled Banco Delta Asia, the fourth smallest bank in Macau, as a primary money laundering concern: this was explicitly because of its relationship with North Korean companies.[53] The Macau authorities quickly moved to freeze some $25 million in North Korean funds, which took 18 months to release, much to the consternation of Pyongyang.[54] Banco Delta Asia lost its access to the U.S.-dollar trading system.

This unilateral action has been the most painful for the North Korean state. Almost immediately, the financial world took notice. The risks of dealing with North Korea were suddenly magnified by a huge degree. Any bank dealing with North Korean companies, banks or individuals was suddenly terrified they could lose access to the U.S. dollar system if they were caught out. Given the DPRK's opacity, it is extremely hard for a bank to conduct due-diligence investigations: it is easier just to steer clear of anything with a whiff of North Korea associated with it.

In subsequent discussions, a North Korean negotiator is reported to have said to a senior White House official, "You finally found a way to hurt us."[55] Banks have considered North Korea toxic ever since.

The DPRK responded by conducting missile tests in July 2006, inspiring

United Nations Security Council Resolution (UNSCR) 1695, which imposed targeted sanctions on missile proliferators and associated materials. Pyongyang's first nuclear test came in October of that year and UN sanctions in response in the form of UNSCR 1718. This was a fairly tepid attempt. It expressed "the gravest concern" over the test, though China's role on the Security Council guaranteed it wasn't too punitive.

Generally speaking, the dynamic at the UN Security Council when it comes to North Korea, is that the United States pushes for very strong measures while China resists. A compromise is then negotiated. China's strategic goals diverge steeply with those of the United States. China is unhappy with a nuclear North Korea, but it doesn't want to see its neighbor and ally disappear completely. The strength of the measures and the speed with which a resolution is passed following a provocation by Pyongyang indicate how frustrated China is, among other things.

By 2017, China has become much more willing to punish North Korea, but in 2006 this wasn't the case. Resolution 1718's provisions included:

- A ban on any "further nuclear test or launch of a ballistic missile" and suspension of both programs.
- A call for the DPRK to "return immediately to the Six-Party Talks without precondition."
- The right for shipments of cargo going to and from North Korea to be stopped by U.N. member states and inspected for weapons of mass destruction or other items.
- A ban on imports and exports of "battle tanks, armored combat vehicles, large caliber artillery systems, combat aircraft, attack helicopters, warships, missiles or missile systems" and other military materiel.
- A call for UN member states to freeze the overseas assets of individuals and companies involved with the DPRK's weapons programs and a ban on those individuals from travel.
- A ban on exporting luxury goods to North Korea.

Importantly, there were no measures for enforcement of any of these provisions. Member states were not *compelled* to search and seize DPRK cargo, only *allowed* to. Luxury goods were not defined.[56] A 2009 study concluded it was "virtually impossible to uncover any statistical evidence that the nuclear test and subsequent sanctions had any impact on North Korean trade."[57]

After the DPRK's 2009 nuclear test, the UN Security Council passed Resolution 1874.[58] This set up a panel of experts to assess how enforcement was taking place. It called on member states to prevent the provision of financial services that might contribute to the DPRK's weapons development. It also asked member states not to facilitate loans or grants except for developmental or aid purposes. It was a marginal expansion on the first resolution.

Less than four years later, a similar song and dance took place: in response to Pyongyang's February 2013 nuclear test, the UN Security Council passed Resolution 2094. This, again, "strongly condemns North Korea's ongoing nuclear activities," but only marginally improved on the strength of previous resolutions. The update required members to block financial transactions and bulk cash transfers in support of illicit activity, though burden of proof remained unclear. More strongly, it gave Member States the power to inspect suspicious cargo and required states to deny port access to any North Korean vessel that refused to be inspected. A similar aircraft provision was included, also.[59] The measures empowered states that so wished to identify and impound cargo they deemed suspicious.

During these UN actions, Washington was still active in applying unilateral sanctions. It put 86 people on the Specially Designated Nationals list from 2006 to 2015.[60] Executive Order (EO) 13687, issued on January 2, 2015, allows people to be designated for status, rather than proven conduct, widening the scope of sanctions targeting. Another EO was issued on March 18, 2016, further restricting what U.S. citizens can do with regard to North Korea and leading to the designation of 11 more nationals in May, one of whom was Kim Jong Un.[61]

It was after the fourth and fifth nuclear tests in 2016, that the United Nations passed resolutions with considerably sharper teeth. UNSCR 2270, passed in March 2016, banned coal and iron ore exports, though it had a vaguely worded exception for "livelihood purposes." The measure specifically targeted extractives, North Korea's main exports. North Korea leans heavily on its rich coal, iron ore, magnesite, gold ore, zinc ore, copper ore and other mineral resources, even if their production rates are hampered by lack of investment and poor infrastructure.[62]

As with previous rounds of sanctions, the key question was: "How strictly will China enforce the measures?" A secondary question is: "How does a Chinese economic slowdown affect North Korea?" The DPRK had a good year of coal exports in 2015, thanks in part to a gap in exports to China left by Vietnam. Still, weakened demand and the reduced prices for commodities meant that trade volume with China was shrinking, according to some evaluations.[63] One think tank calculated that bilateral trade was down 14.7 percent from 2014 to 2015 between the two countries, reaching only $5.4 billion.[64] Coal exports to China were worth about $1 billion of that, down from the previous year.[65]

In the months following UNSCR 2270 Chinese imports of sanctioned items fell. Official Chinese customs data shows that imports of coal fell to 28.3 percent year-on-year in May 2016.[66] In April it had dropped by 20 percent year-on-year.[67] By June, however, numbers had recovered and it appeared a system for reporting (or just making up) that coal was "for livelihood purposes" was in place.[68] By August North Korea was exporting record amounts of coal to China.[69] The will to enforce sanctions appeared weak.

Pyongyang then tested a fifth nuclear device on September 9, 2016. Following several weeks of negotiations, UNSCR 2321 passed on November 20. This put a cap on coal exports, imposing a $400 million (or 7.5 million ton) ceiling on the "livelihood purposes" exemption with respect to the exportation of coal, demonstrating a growing ire in Beijing. With coal worth nearly $1 billion and the DPRK's total exports worth $2.7 billion, this represented more than 22 percent of the value of merchandise goods exports. New limits on exports of copper, nickel, silver and zinc worth approximately $100 million a year were also imposed.[70]

The 2016 sanctions on gold exports from the DPRK will also add to Pyongyang's costs. Previously, gold from North Korea was certified on the London Metals Exchange to be traded directly on commodities markets. Now, North Korea will have to find middlemen to falsify the origin of the gold. A diplomat was caught smuggling $1.4 million of gold into Bangladesh in March 2016, perhaps taking part in this process.[71] Pyongyang was also looking forward to the continuing high value of rare-earth minerals, crucial to the manufacture of electronics—this will now be much harder for them.

Following several missile tests in July 2017, the Security Council passed Resolution 2371, which then fully banned its largest export, coal, as well as iron and iron ore, lead and seafood. Altogether, these sectors represent probably over $1 billion, perhaps 25 to 30 percent of the DPRK's export income. Pyongyang responded with a nuclear test a few weeks later, its biggest yet, on September 2.

The UN Security Council in extremely rapid fashion then passed

Resolution 2375 on September 11, 2017. This banned all North Korean textile exports, which according to the United States Mission to the United Nations were "North Korea's largest economic sector that the Security Council had not previously restricted" and "earned North Korea an average of $760 million in the past three years."[72]

Not only did the UN Security Council now ban "over 90 percent of North Korea's publicly reported 2016 exports of $2.7 billion," the UNSCR moved to have North Korean workers, of which there may be over 100,000, sent back home. Member states are supposed to send workers back after their contracts run out and not renew or hire replacements from North Korea. The United States characterizes these people as "slave laborers," though they actually compete for the chance to earn money abroad and also get exposed to things they would otherwise not.

The September Resolution also banned all corporate joint ventures with North Korea, whether in the DPRK or abroad. Resolution 2270 in 2016 had also added a number of new financial pain points. Bankers face new restrictions: the resolution forbids the DPRK from opening new bank branches in member states and it bars foreign banks or companies from taking ownership stakes or maintaining correspondent banking relationships with North Korean banks. Member states also must shut down DPRK banks within their borders. Foreign banks can still maintain offices and accounts in North Korea that already exist, unless evidence emerges that they are supporting sanctioned activity. What that evidence might be is unclear. Most of these remaining legitimate financial channels are Chinese.

Washington, for its part, acted on several legislative options to restrict North Korea's international financial activities. The North Korea Sanctions and Policy Enhancement Act, which President Obama signed into law on February 18, 2016, takes aim at several channels for conducting business with the country.[73] The key action was designating North Korea, as Myanmar had been 13 years before, as a "jurisdiction of primary money laundering concern," essentially extending the same sanction faced by Banco Delta Asia to the whole country.[74]

The United States can now clamp down harder on U.S. dollar transactions through New York branches of any banks dealing with North Korean businesses and to more aggressively target companies and other entities that trade with the DPRK by threatening to cut them off from dollar trading.[75] So while the UN sanctions in 2016 restricted what DPRK bankers can do abroad, the United States can now independently go after foreign bankers and companies who work with North Korea to decrease the options for North Korean businesses.

Banks of any reasonable size will have to worry more than ever that their access to dollars could be cut if they don't comply. The threat of secondary sanctions will be worrisome for banks who deal with North Koreans or their proxies: it is an understatement to say that for any major bank or bank with global aspirations, access to the dollar system is crucial. These U.S. actions will further increase the already high risks for foreigners interested in doing business in North Korea.

Still, North Koreans have learned to navigate through the considerable restrictions imposed since 2005, when the U.S. Treasury Department adopted its landmark sanctions on Banco Delta Asia. The evasive tactics that the DPRK has developed over the last decade speak to a key shortcoming of Washington's increasingly aggressive approach: it can only succeed to the extent that North Korea's neighbors—as well as traders, bankers and regimes around in the world—are willing to cooperate.

As it is, North Koreans regularly skirt financial restrictions by using informal money transfers to banks in third countries. To send money from North Korea elsewhere, an entrepreneur need only contact either a bank in Pyongyang with agents abroad or a foreign financier with unofficial representatives in Pyongyang. The businessperson hands cash to a broker, that middleman takes a commission, and the money then shows up in a foreign bank account with no formal record of origin. This system is largely used in China. If these middlemen perceive greater risk and/or require another intermediary layer to help obscure the transaction, their fees will go up—North Korea's profit margins will correspondingly go down.[76]

South Korea's response to the fourth nuclear test and subsequent missile test was to close the Kaesong Industrial Park, the last vestige of inter-Korean cooperation from the Sunshine Policy era. This was an industrial park located on the North side of the DMZ, where South Korean firms employed North Korean laborers. The Kaesong Industrial Park was launched in 2004 and by 2015 employed over 54,000 people. It paid $120 million in wages to 2015, though wages are distributed to the state before workers were given their portion and it is unclear what percentage they ultimately received.[77]

Following the 2010 shelling of South Korean islands by the North and the sinking of a South Korean naval vessel, Seoul imposed sanctions and cut off all inter-Korean trade except for Kaesong. Still, Kaesong alone by 2015 was worth $2.71 billion in trade: South Korea's exports northward totaled $1.26 billion while its imports from the North totaled $1.45 billion.[78]

If the 2010 sanctions had reduced North-South trade, ceding greater economic influence to the Chinese, the 2016 shuttering of Kaesong has excused South Korea from the game entirely. In the month following the closure, inter-Korean trade dropped 99 percent.[79] This means that China has more control than ever over the DPRK's prospects for economic growth.

Enforcement is a key issue with any sanctions regime. With North Korea, despite the institutional framework of the United Nations, the differing strategic goals of the main actors—the United States and China—affects how sanctions have been implemented. In Washington, it is widely perceived that the lack of enforcement by Beijing is why North Korea has been able to enjoy economic growth over most of the last decade. It is generally true that China is far keener on pulling the DPRK economically into its orbit and trying to induce economic reform, while the United States wishes to isolate the regime more.

If at the United Nations since 2006 the *modus operandi* has been the United States pushing for strong measures with China watering them down, something does appear different in 2017. U.S. President Donald Trump has appeared much more willing to threaten Chinese companies with the prospect of secondary, unilateral sanctions for working with or in North Korea. Beijing, for its part, is more fed up than ever with its neighbor and ostensible ally.

On June 29, 2017, the U.S. Treasury sent something of a "shot across the bow" of the Chinese banking system by sanctioning the Bank of Dandong. This bank only has five branches and no real international footprint, but Dandong is the Chinese city that is the hub for overland China-DPRK trade. The message was clear and since then it appears as if Chinese banks have been aggressively shutting down the bank accounts of DPRK nationals and companies.

But what will these measures accomplish? The noose has certainly been tightened in 2017 but the DPRK's opacity means that data is even more limited than in Myanmar—the study that looked at the garment industry would not be possible in North Korea: this is partly to do with the sanctions regime but also because foreign companies operating in North Korea generally shy away from publicity.

To compensate for this, one innovative study took to nighttime satellite imagery to try to see how wealth was distributed during and after sanctions episodes. It found distribution of light, and therefore electricity, increases towards Pyongyang. Meanwhile, a sanctions event decreases luminosity by about 0.5 percent on average in rural North Korea.[80] A sanctions event increases the luminosity gap by 3.3 percent in Pyongyang compared to 1.1 percent in the province capitals.[81] The capital, where the urban elite and those closest to the regime reside, becomes brighter relative to province capitals, which also increase relative to the hinterland. However, North Korea's urban military bases do not change relative to the hinterlands.[82]

The author surmises that an additional sanction event decreases rural GDP but increases urban GDP, with Pyongyang's relative economic activity increasing the most. The sanctions create hardships in the domestic economy, but the regime compensates by diverting resources—in this measurable case, electricity—to the capital, where loyalists are centered, at the expense of the countryside. The evidence isn't perfect, but as in Myanmar, it does appear as if those closest to the regime are relatively shielded from the effects of sanctions, while those furthest away suffer disproportionately.

This complements anecdotal evidence: public works and development projects are taking place in provincial cities, but by far the greatest amount of investment has taken place in Pyongyang. New buildings and districts have been showcased, new retail and banking options have emerged and considerably more vehicles can be seen on the streets in recent years, even as sanctions have increased.

Another study found that Chinese middlemen have reduced the efficacy of sanctions to prevent procurement of military or dual-use material or components. The ongoing development of the DPRK's missile and nuclear programs certainly suggests that they have little trouble getting what they need. It does penalize procurement by adding to costs, however.

Essentially, a North Korean company will choose a Chinese middleman, either one with operations in the DPRK or through contacts in China. For a fee that is usually around 15 percent, the middleman purchases the desired equipment from a foreign manufacturer and handles all documentation and logistics. Delivery is usually sub-contracted to another private Chinese company to handle all the necessary logistics.[83] This may or may not include "fees for expedited immigration" across the China–North Korea border. Regardless, the subcontracting makes it difficult for the foreign firm to recognize that the end customer is in North

Korea. The author goes on to suggest that this may have actually *strengthened* North Korea's dual-use procurement program, adding a layer of untraceability through the world's second biggest economy.[84] Specifically banned items find their way in, for a premium.

One can already see that "middleman's premium" at work in mundane matters; the price of a coffee in Pyongyang, for example, where a cappuccino can be $6 or $7. The managers of one Pyongyang café near the river lament that instead of buying coffee beans from a wholesaler, they must pay a broker in the Chinese border town of Dandong from an RMB account in China. The broker buys the beans from a wholesaler elsewhere in China and adds a significant markup for the last stage of the process: sending the beans from Dandong to Pyongyang. This gets passed on to the end consumer. And, after all that, their $7 cappuccino isn't even that great.[85] (Not the greatest problem in North Korea, of course, but illustrative.)

The breadth of the sanctions levied on Pyongyang in 2017 mean that it is quite likely North Korean businesspeople will be forced to rely even more on shady Chinese organizations and criminals. The banning of joint ventures and nearly all of North Korea's key exports will force many of these companies underground, contributing to the "gangsterization" of North Korea's corporate world. The economy will contract, probably massively, but North Korean businesspeople have been now told to use any means necessary to continue to do business. The lessons learned from trading in illicit items will be applied to other, formerly legitimate sectors as well.

Sanctions have also made DPRK over-reliant on China, as other countries have banned or discouraged trade with North Korea. China-North Korea trade has increased more than ten-fold since the early 2000s. China accounted for 91.3 percent of total North Korean trade in 2015, according to South Korean estimates.[86] Those estimates excluded inter-Korean trade, but since the 2016 shuttering of the joint manufacturing complex in Kaesong and inter-Korean trade falling to zero, these percentages can be assumed to be accurate.

Clearly, sanctions have not prevented North Korea from becoming a nuclear state, even if they've harmed the development of coffee culture. They have failed not because of lack of will or enforcement but rather "because the sanctions are not appropriate to the size of the policy objective they are supposed to achieve."[87] That said, under Donald Trump there has been an attempt to make them significant enough to have an impact on Pyongyang's decision-making.

"The basic strategic assumption behind the sanctions was that a marginal negative shift in the balance of costs of the North Korean nuclear program compared with what Pyongyang could gain from negotiating it away would be sufficient to compel a change in North Korean nuclear policy."[88] Sanctions thus far have never come close to affecting that balance to such a degree that the leadership in Pyongyang would give up their weapons. Sanctions pressure has shifted from "marginal" to "massive" in 2017, but it is still unclear if sanctions-relief could ever provide as much on the benefit-side of their calculations as does maintaining a cache of nuclear weapons.

The North Korean leadership views the nuclear program as absolutely central to its survival as a class and to the survival of the Democratic People's Republic of Korea as a state. This group can still pass on the costs of sanctions to the broader population.

And of course, imposing costs is one of the functions of a sanctions regime. Sanctions remain punitive and with an attendant "role in delegitimizing the North Korean nuclear and missile programs and in denying them outside assistance."[89] Now all major exports will require middlemen or import partners to obscure their origin. Financial transfers will increasingly require intermediaries to hide transactions' origins or end points. Sanctions will eat into DPRK profit margins when North Koreans can find ways to keep exporting.

Could they someday help achieve denuclearization? It is extremely difficult to see how they would. There is reasonable evidence that throughout the 1990s and early 2000s, Pyongyang was willing to use its nuclear weapons or parts of its program as a bargaining chip. At least, nuclear weapons gave Kim Jong Il a package of options, including bargaining, deterrence, prestige and asymmetry with South Korea.[90]

As mentioned previously, the fact that North Korea's facilities were visible suggests they *wanted* the world to know about them early in their development and discuss them. If they wanted to secretly develop a deterrent, they would have done it underground: the Israeli nuclear program is a blueprint for this sort of WMD program and the North Koreans have become master tunnel makers and underground builders.

Now, however, the period where the weapons were on the table appears ever receding in history's rearview mirror. Pyongyang seems to have moved towards an assured retaliation doctrine for its nukes and missiles rather than other postures that have diplomatic, rather than strategic-military goals.[91] There has been an evolution of thought in Pyongyang, wherein now the possession of nuclear and missile programs are seen as central to state survival. For Pyongyang's policymakers, the harshness of sanctions in 2016 and 2017 may only testify to the awful nature of their republic's enemies.

Certainly under Kim Jong Un, Pyongyang has unambiguously communicated that it views its nuclear status as irrevocable and permanent. It has frequently stated that its nuclear cache is central to survival in a hostile world, even that it is "the nation's life."[92] In 2012, the DPRK enshrined its nuclear status in a new constitution.[93] The country consecrated itself "a state with nuclear power."

When sanctions are explicitly tied to an issue that Pyongyang now seems to consider non-negotiable and central to state survival, what room is there for bargaining? A scholar and former George W. Bush administration official, Victor Cha, puts it thus when discussing the incentives that both the Clinton and Bush administrations tried:

> This bargain has been—give up your nuclear weapons and you potentially will get a peace treaty formally ending the Korean War, normalization of relations with the United States and Japan, energy assistance, economic assistance, and a place at the table as a normal member of the international community.[94]

For Pyongyang, "potentially" getting a peace treaty with an enemy they fundamentally do not trust is simply not as attractive as maintaining a nuclear and missile program for guaranteeing the survival of Kim rule and the system built around it. Essentially, Pyongyang prefers to live under sanctions but with a nuclear arsenal to no sanctions and no nukes.

It also, however, is possible to imagine a near-future scenario wherein the overlapping sanctions regimes diminish economic growth to such an extent that Pyongyang feels compelled to return to the table to discuss its nuclear weapons programs. This could be for a few reasons, however, all unlikely to lead to full denuclearization. Talks could be, firstly, a tactic to buy time, until the military believes it can strike the United States with a nuclear tipped warhead and can credibly signal that capacity. It is also likely that once Pyongyang reaches that point, they may opt for a quiet period without nuclear or missile tests and let the world forget about sanctions enforcement and to become accustomed to the idea of a nuclear DPRK.

It could also be that Pyongyang's baseline will change and that it is willing to negotiate a freeze and monitoring regime but not the erasure of its previously developed nuclear weapons. Or perhaps to give away some of their fissile material but not all of it. But what kind of sanctions relief could they expect for that? It is unclear if the Trump Administration has given any thought to sequencing an unraveling of sanctions during negotiations.

Publically living with a nuclear North Korea, even if only "temporary," would represent a huge compromise on the part of the United States. Would the North Koreans be able to reciprocally compromise on American troops remaining in South Korea? Would some kind of lengthy timeline for a freeze that allows for trust building be politically possible, in Seoul, Washington or Pyongyang? Would one side or another mess up that trust building?

Prior attempts have failed due to mendaciousness, incompetence and plain bad luck. Pyongyang's elites have internalized these experiences and viewed from afar what happens when dictators give up their WMD in a deal with the West, as Muammar Ghaddafi did, or never acquire them, like Saddam Hussein. The latter was hanged and the former ended up sodomized with a bayonet.

The DPRK has learned that its repressive apparatus and the absolute lack of domestic political opposition in any form has given it considerable leeway in its policy options. Their systemic and political rigidity is clearly a strength. Sanctions and privation can be blamed on the "US Imperialists" and there are no other voices to say otherwise.

It has also learned that thus far, China can be counted on to provide an economic lifeline—a huge fissure in the sanctions coalition—even when Beijing-Pyongyang relations are strained. Beijing has agreed to an unprecedented amount of pressure since late 2016, but one suspects that the Chinese would intervene if a financial crisis or famine was about to take hold. All these factors make it difficult to see how Pyongyang's nuclear and missile arsenal will be undone by either UN or U.S. sanctions. North Korea is perhaps the only country in the world that could see its economy contract by 50 percent and *not* have people hit the streets in protest.

In both Asia's pariahs, years of sanctions created an over-reliance on China. Both Yangon/Naypyidaw and Pyongyang were extremely uncomfortable with this situation, but only one chose to make policy changes that provided sanctions relief. Sanctions are complex and defy easy pronouncements about success or failure. Sanctions against Myanmar did impact the military junta, adding to the pressures to consider some type of democratization. Sanctions thus far have failed to move North Korea to the international community's ultimate goal of denuclearization and, as of 2017, have also failed to encourage the shorter-term goal of forcing Pyongyang to the negotiating table.

7

Why Myanmar and Not North Korea?

Why did Myanmar move towards a more democratic, open system, while North Korea could not? North Korea, as we've seen in previous chapters, has never found a way to mitigate its core security threat of a more powerful South Korea, backed by the United States. This has led it towards militarization and ultimately nuclearization. In turn, this has meant that that it has been unable to escape its pariah status.

Myanmar, by contrast, in the 1990s and 2000s, made significant gains in addressing its core security threat: multiple insurgencies that sought to either weaken or fracture the state. Shoring up the state's position vis-à-vis these threats allowed the leadership to then to focus on democratization and thus its pariah status. A more secure state developed through a series of military victories, won over decades of slowly choking off insurgent groups, as well as several peace treaties and the relocation of the country's capital city.

There may also have been other factors at play, of course, and rumors about the military's opaque decision making are still rife. For example, many people in Yangon speculate that as Than Shwe aged, he could not find a successor that he trusted. Nor did he have a personality cult to bolster his unique position. This opened the very real possibility that without some diffusion of power, the single-leader system he used to rule would be usurped by whoever the strongest and most ruthless general was as Than Shwe grew old and declined. He understood the risk for not only himself but also the interests of his family and network. The fate of outgoing dictators tends to be at the whim of their successor, after all.

Generational values may also have played a role. The adult children of the military leadership did not appear generally to be interested in pursuing military careers. They were more interested in running businesses and living well. In this view, the transition may also be a matter of scale. Than Shwe and his generals recognized that with an open economy that was able to attract investment and find markets all over the world, they could be passing down to their families not just multimillion-dollar business empires but billion-dollar ones.

Some speculate that fear among the top leaders was a motivator. After the Saffron Revolution and Cyclone Nargis, perhaps they were genuinely scared there could be a revolution—one they couldn't keep a lid on. The communications technology and civil society networks that had emerged in the 1990s were too threatening when combined with the broad social discontent that existed.

That seems unlikely or at least only partially true. The regime was invested in some kind of transition from at least the early 2000s, recognizing that the future would need to hold some form of democratization. At the Central Institute of Civil Service, future bureaucrats were studying the workings of democracy and federalism since at least 2002. Kyaw Myat Khaing, a 2005 student, recalls that by the time he matriculated, "on the institute grounds there was free discussion, debate and brainstorming" about such political systems. But, "as soon as the students left campus and went to the tea shop, no talking."[1] Discussion of democratization and governance was not yet allowed in the public domain, but it was happening behind closed doors.

Ultimately, the key reason was that the state was becoming more secure as a territorial entity. The gradual grinding down of insurgent forces through the four cuts policy had contained most of their activities. This was coupled with a series of important peace deals in the 1990s, which in turn put state military forces in a stronger position.

So while we can guess that Than Shwe wanted his legacy to be the opening and enriching of Myanmar, it is clearer that the military position of the union was made much more sound through the end of the 1990s. He could thus turn his attention towards economic and political reform, under which his children and cronies could thrive, safer from the potential retributions of a successor—always a risk in a dictatorship. And in the long run, a more democratic system could return the military to a position of respect that had long been eroded. How did they accomplish this more secure position for the state? Several steps taken since 1989 solidified the state's position: the pinning down of armed resistance groups as well as outright military victories; peace treaties and concessions with key enemies; the construction of a new capital in the heart of the country.

The Four Cuts

In the late 1960s the *Tatmadaw* developed a counterinsurgency strategy called *Pya Ley Pya* or the four cuts. This was officially adopted in 1968 and is still in effect. The four cuts was a doctrine designed to sever insurgents from their key inputs: funding, food, intelligence and recruits. In practice, this meant terrible things for people on the ground in conflict areas.

The four cuts bore striking similarities to counter-insurgency strategies elsewhere in the region in this period, developed most concretely by the British during the Malayan Emergency, when the British essentially remained in their colony an extra decade to fight off a Communist insurgency. There, one tactic used was the creation of "New Villages." Though the Emergency lasted from 1948 to 1960, by the end of 1951, the rebellion was greatly limited due to the resettlement of over 500,000 rural Chinese (the insurgency was mostly along ethnic lines), and regrouping of up to 600,000 estate laborers in these new villages, cutting them off from the rebel forces.[2]

Sir Robert Thompson, who developed and implemented the strategy, later advised the United States and its South Vietnamese allies as they replicated the strategy of strategic hamlets from 1961–1964 during the Vietnam War.[3] For a variety of reasons, resettlement was considerably less successful in Vietnam.

However, a key element of resettlement, as Thompson conceived of it, was a simultaneous effort to "win hearts and minds." Uprooting villagers for strategic purposes was coercive—according to Thompson it needed to be accompanied by efforts to convince people that, first, their lives would improve, and, second, that the insurgency was politically illegitimate. The aspirations of the people have to be addressed by the counterinsurgency.[4]

The *Tatmadaw* failed to achieve either of these necessary adjuncts to their four cuts doctrine, never earning the legitimacy or respect that a more thoughtful policy might have engendered. With the early emergency years of independence behind them and by the mid–1960s fully in control of the government, the military perceived time to be on their side. They thus prosecuted the strategy methodically, moving villagers by force and taking key areas to deny rebels support and supplies. This gradually choked the various insurgent groups, limiting the potential for what they might accomplish.

7. Why Myanmar and Not North Korea? 171

The military also divided the country into black, brown and white zones to reflect insurgent-controlled, partially insurgent-controlled and government controlled areas. In the "black zones," soldiers were essentially given license to kill freely. Forced relocations, forced conscriptions and porterage, even rape as a tool of social control appear to have been common tactics under the four cuts doctrine.

It is incredibly difficult to assess the claims made by actors in these multiple conflicts. Insurgents and their sympathizers are strongly incentivized to portray the Burmese military as wholly evil and disseminate information in that regard through NGO and alternative media networks. The *Tatmadaw*, for its part, tries to frame every single atrocity or act of coercion as anti-regime propaganda.

The weight of evidence to the contrary is hefty, however, and testifies to the ugliness with which the four cuts was implemented. For example, a series of Refugees International focus groups in the early 2000s found 100 percent of respondents had heard of rapes taking place in their home regions, while 75 percent said that they personally knew someone who had been raped.[5]

Testimony on forced labor is bountiful as well. One refugee, We Se, recalls the experience thus: "They told me, 'don't run away. We can shoot you.' And we were afraid. They broke a stick ... they broke my head.... I cannot carry anything because I was very tired." He suffered a severe beating for his fatigue.[6]

Many people fled these pressures, either to refugee camps or when possible to other villages and towns, where they might be able to start over with the help of family. Hundreds of thousands have ended up in refugee camps either in Myanmar or in neighboring Thailand. Camps have changed in size over time, but the Internal Displacement Monitoring Center estimates over 660,000 internally displaced persons as of March 2015.[7] The United Nations estimates 120,000 Myanmar refugees in Thailand as of 2014.[8]

Life is meager and tenuous in refugee camps both in-country and across the border. One Karen refugee, Mary, describes having fled her village when Karen rebels had to pull back from the city of Manerplaw and it fell to the *Tatmadaw* in 1995. She managed to evacuate a large loom along with her five kids and settle in a refugee camp. Along with a few other Karen women, Mary began earning money through weaving and filling orders placed by Oxfam, a UK charity. In April 1996, the *Tatmadaw* crossed the border and burned the camp down.[9]

From the beginning of the four cuts through the 1990s and beyond, one has to conclude, in terms of security and hegemony, the position of the state improved considerably. That rather dry phrasing belies just how disrupted and immiserated were the lives of those living in conflict regions and just how many of them there were. By 1992 there were some 260,000 refugees in Bangladesh, at least 70,000 in Thailand and more in India and China.[10] These numbers don't include Internally Displaced Persons (IDPs). One group estimated that in Shan State alone, just between 1996 and 2000, 300,000 people were forcibly relocated.[11] Another group calculates that between 1996 and 2009 in Eastern Myanmar, some 3,506 villages were destroyed, abandoned or forcibly relocated into communities under the army's control, displacing over 600,000 people.[12]

In the end, this slow squeeze on many armed ethnic groups through the 1980s, accelerating in the 1990s, led many insurgents to conclude their struggles were no longer viable. This was especially true when the government began offering concessions for the leaders of rebel groups to start making money.

New Worries, New Victories

If at the end of the 1988 uprising in the major cities the military were somewhat confused about their lack of support, after the 1990 elections they were both aware of the popular demand for democracy and just how profoundly unpopular they had become. The realization that system change was necessary was beginning to dawn. First, however, they felt they needed more stability. The quick rush to democracy that they'd allowed between 1988 and 1990 wouldn't do. The military leadership could and would accept a more cautious approach to system change, but not before mollifying existing threats to their control. After over two decades, the four cuts doctrine was putting them in a position to win against insurgencies or find accommodation with them.

The massacres of August 1988 had complicated things for them, however. In November 1988 the National Democratic Front (a minority ethnic grouping) joined with Burman groups to form the Democratic Alliance of Burma (DAB). The DAB shares the KNU headquarters at Manerplaw on the Moei river, a tributary of the Salween river which forms part of the boundary with Thailand. The DAB began calling for federalism, believing that it was not feasible for all the various minority groups to form their own independent states and that they should instead aim for a 'genuine' federal union of Burma. As one Kachin leader comments, many people in the outside world have scarcely heard of Burma—let alone the Kachin. The international community would give little sympathy or support to a plethora of Burmese micro-states.[13]

The *Tatmadaw* had to secure hegemony over ethnic armed groups before turning to a democratic reforms to satisfy the Bamar majority.

The End of the Communist Threat

In April 1989, through little skill of its own, the military suddenly found one of Asia's longest communist insurrections over. The Communists still controlled some areas in Shan State after decades of fighting and surviving in large part on the opium trade. The Communist Party of Burma was long-headquartered at Panghsang, a town sitting on the river that divides Myanmar and China. An "all-out mutiny" occurred on April 16 causing the committed, aging ideologues to flee across the river to China, never to return. The rebel troops rapidly took control of caches of weapons and key buildings while symbolically smashing communist icons and burning texts.[14]

China, which had actively financed and provided materiel to the CPB through the 1960s and 1970s, had been trying to avoid such an outcome while getting the old Maoist leadership to abdicate peacefully. The decreasingly ideological People's Republic of China had even offered high-ranking cadres relatively generous retirements in China.[15] Younger cadres were keen to open the border and increase the flow of goods between the two countries, including the drug trade.

The main body of the new leadership formed the United Wa State Army and ended the communist insurgency within days. Within weeks, on May 9, they had agreed on peace terms and signed a treaty with the central government.[16] The biggest non-state army in Burma had agreed to peace in exchange for an extremely high degree of autonomy.[17] Today, centered in Panghsang, Wa is effectively its own country, with an army of 20,000 to 25,000 soldiers. It has its own banks (Wa Pang Bank), uses Chinese currency, and flies its own flags; The Myanmar Union flag can only be seen above a small liaison office and a government-run clinic.[18]

The government of Burma—which changed the name of the country to Myanmar two weeks after this peace treaty—had acceded a huge degree of power to this quasi-independent state. In return, they gained official sovereignty over the territory of the Wa and, conversely, a commitment that the Wa had no territorial ambitions beyond what was agreed in the treaty. A major concession, signed off on by Khin Nyunt, the military intelligence chief at the time, was that the Wa would retain control in the area over production of jade and opium, two extremely lucrative exports.[19]

The Communist territories were split into three groups, with separate armies and leaders. Out of the agreement emerged the United Wa State Army, the Kokang Army (Myanmar National Democratic Alliance Army) and the Mongla Group (National Democratic Alliance Army).

This cessation of hostilities with the former Communists was important for two other reasons. First, it freed up *Tatmadaw* resources to be focused on groups still fighting while providing a model for negotiations.[20] This increased pressure both militarily and politically on insurgent groups.

Second, the 1989 peace treaty created a chain reaction with immediate effect on the allies of the Communists. As a part of the deal, the former Communists had to cease supporting other active insurgent groups: "smaller ethnic armies that had depended on the CPB for arms and ammunition also gave in."[21]

It also appears that as a reward for pacifying their border region, China and Myanmar signed an arms deal in 1990, estimated at between $1 billion and $1.4 billion. China would continue to supply the Wa, Kokang and Mongla armies over the coming years, also, helping maintain the status quo.

Smaller Groups

From 1989, the government began a policy of both offering peace deals *and* fighting with insurgent groups. It sent over 80,000 troops into action against the KNU and various Mon, Kachin and Karenni armed nationalist groups in the NDF coalition in 1989, for example.[22] To borrow a U.S. diplomatic phrase, the *Tatmadaw* was "sharpening the choice" for the rebel groups, saying, in effect, "we have the resources to fight you forever, you can choose that or the peace terms we offer you." Different groups chose different paths.

The Karenni resistance in Karenni State (now called Kayah) was shattered in the mid–1990s. A peace treaty was signed between the SLORC and the Karenni National Progressive Party in 1995. This didn't last long and fighting resumed almost immediately. Sensing weakness, the *Tatmadaw* decided to prosecute their four cuts strategy with even greater aggression, pushing to break the back of Karenni resistance. By 1996, Karenni estimates were that 75,000 villagers were forcibly relocated.[23] Thousands more villagers were also uprooted in the subsequent years to deny the Karenni army access, "altering the human landscape of practically the whole Karenni State in the space of three years."[24] Those that did not wish to attempt life in a *Tatmadaw*-controlled new village fled to refugee camps in Thailand.

At the same time, smaller Karenni groups were persuaded to give up the struggle, isolating the KNPP, which was no longer an effective point of resistance to government forces. By the 2010s, the KNPP and the Karenni Army were estimated to have a fighting force of just 600 men.[25] They can barely operate now. Kayah State was the last area of the country to be opened to foreign travelers, in 2015.

The Pa-O finally gave up in the 1990s. The Red Faction lost CPB support after 1989 and had to sue for peace. The non-communist Pa-O National Organisation came to be trapped in a small, non-viable corner of Shan State. They had to sign a peace treaty with the SLORC in April 1991 and got to keep their arms and operate as a sanctioned militia. They were also given a jade mine concession and could operate tourist hotels at Inle Lake. This caused a final splinter group to form and vow continued struggle, but most had deserted by early 1994. In October 1994, those remnants of the Red Faction signed a cease-fire.[26]

Slightly earlier, the Palaung also had to agree to terms. As the Palaung Women's organization laments:

> First, they cut off communications between the PSLA and the Palaung villagers. They forcibly relocated villagers to sites near towns during the tea-harvesting season. As a result, the villagers could not harvest their tea, and they suffered great difficulties from the loss of income. The PSLA feared the situation might worsen, so they were forced to negotiate with the SLORC to provide relief to the Palaung people. They reached a cease-fire agreement in 1991. Even with the cease-fire agreement, the State Peace and Development Council (SPDC) continue to commit human rights abuses in Palaung land.... The people who facing [sic] the threat of total destruction are the Pa-O army, some Kachin units based in the Shan State and some Shan armed forces made deals with the SLORC. The Palaung State Liberation Army (PSLA) was left surrounded by a very large number of SLORC troops and had no choice so they had to sign a cease-fire agreement as well.

The Palaung communities came under pressure while the four cuts removed the PSLA's capacity to supply themselves or liaise with other groups fighting the Army. They had to surrender.

The Mon resistance was also broken in these years. The first major blow was in 1990, when the New Mon State Party (NMSP) headquarters near Three Pagodas Pass was overrun by government troops. Under pressure from Thailand, the Mon entered ceasefire negotiations with the government in late 1993, finally signing a treaty in June 1995.[27] As with other insurgent groups, cash-earning concessions were given, though not as great as the lucrative extractives and drugs trades further north.

The Karen

Events in 1994 ensured that Karen resistance, weary after a half-century struggle, was broken:

> By the 1990s, it had lost control of most of its once extensive "liberated zones," although the organisation still exerted varying degrees of influence over areas contested with government forces and proxy militias. The decline of the KNU was exacerbated by the defection in late 1994 of several hundred battle-hardened soldiers, who established the government-allied Democratic Karen Buddhist Army (DKBA) and shortly afterwards overran the KNU's long-standing headquarters at Manerplaw.[28]

The splinter group DKBA formed and later another splinter group from the DKBA (and actually another one from that), but they were well beyond the point where they could ever challenge the state again.

This was a major victory for the *Tatmadaw*, who had made a concerted effort in 1992 to take Manerplaw but failed and unilaterally called a ceasefire.[29] By 1994, however, the *Tatmadaw* had gained intelligence regarding a rift between Buddhist soldiers and the leadership of the KNU, which was largely Christian. The *Tatmadaw* mounted an offensive in December 1994, and the new DKBA torched the KNU headquarters a month later. This forced the KNU to retreat to a fallback base, the hills, or over the border to Thailand.[30] Exploiting the diversity of identity politics with the Karen movement itself, the military crippled the Karen insurgency.

A ceasefire wasn't signed until 2012 with the KNU, and sweeping up operations continued well through the 2000s with activist groups complaining about the destruction of homes, displacement of villagers, food security problems, and forced labor.[31]

The DKBA was eventually turned into a Border Guard Force, a semi-autonomous militia, but integrated into government forces. This means of integration of former insurgents was specified in the 2008 constitution. Essentially it is a means of semi-autonomous integration into *Tatmadaw* control. It isn't without controversy or opposition, but several former insurgent groups have signed on to the plan.[32]

Kachin Ceasefire

Sporadic attempts at a ceasefire between the Kachin Independence Organization (KIO) and the government had been made a few times in the past, though they always broke down. Upon the failure of talks in 1981, the *Tatmadaw* doubled down on the four cuts strategy, prosecuting it in an "especially harsh" manner; by the time of the KIO-government ceasefire in 1994, the KIO estimated that one-third of the population of the state was displaced.[33]

As in other areas, the populace tended to suffer as the once-distant central state imposed itself after it had control of an area. Testimony after testimony speaks to suffering from forced labor in mines or construction, rent seeking through informal taxes, and other forms of minor harassment. Starting in 1988, Kachin also saw the large-scale relocation of villagers to new towns in secure areas close to transportation infrastructure.[34]

Not only was there direct and indirect pressure from the *Tatmadaw*, but China ceased supporting the KIO in the late 1980s. Then, when the Communists surrendered, and the Kachin suddenly found themselves quite isolated. The stress must have been huge, compelling one brigade to defect in 1991, form the Kachin Defence Army, and sign a separate peace deal with the government.[35]

"For the KIO," Ashley South writes, "the civil war had become a dead end." They entered into peace negotiations in 1993 and signed a deal on February 24, 1994, though the SLORC government refused to address most of the Organization's political concerns, claiming they were merely an interim government.[36] The KIO had committed to continuing the struggle for their rights in the political arena. The *Tatmadaw* had bound the KIO to whatever version of politics would be allowed in the coming years.

In the end a total of 17 ceasefires were signed between 1989 and 1997.[37] This allowed the *Tatmadaw* "greater control over the country by building up its forces, expanding to bases previously contested borderlands, weakening the armed opposition, and isolating the pro-democracy movement."[38]

Some of these peace deals have broken down in recent years, most significantly with the Kokang group and the Kachin in 2009 and 2011, respectively, even if at the same time progress in pacification was made with the Karen. "Under pressure from the military government, during 2009 to 2010 the most significant non–KNU armed Karen groups, including most elements of the Democratic Karen Buddhist Army (DKBA), were transformed into Border Guard Forces (BGFs) under direct *Tatmadaw* control."[39]

Peaceful periods may have created new traumas for locals on the ground who suddenly faced an environment in which more government soldiers were visible, sometimes continuing legal but dubious activities.[40] However, where and when ceasefires hold, more stability exists, sometimes allowing for better quality of life for many residents of post-conflict areas.

The ceasefires generally have also allowed the military to have more control over resources in areas that previously would have been too volatile to exploit. In Kachin State, deforestation has accelerated following the ceasefire, as government and local groups fill the gap left by a 1998 China-wide band on logging.[41] Mining and other concessions have also gone largely to companies from outside the region.

When the KIO ceasefire broke down in 2011, it was largely due to the Myitsone Dam project. All the ceasefires were to some degree negotiated over resource sharing. Environmental and cultural reasons for opposing the dam are usually given; in fact, it is widely thought that the Kachin leadership simply was not cut in to the profits that the dam would generate. The Myitsone Dam was strategically an egregious error by the regime and evidence that the politics of inclusion still did not and does not motivate *Tatmadaw* decision makers.

Ceasefires also meant the strict delineation of areas of control. Once that took place, the *Tatmadaw* would push right up to the new borders and create infrastructures to support forward bases. When ceasefires broke down the insurgents found themselves trapped like never before. Breakout is certainly off the cards.

Not the Total End

Fighting still persists, unfortunately.

For example, the Palaung State Liberation Front (PSLF) gave up their arms in 2005 after signing a bilateral ceasefire with the SLORC government in 1991. However, when the peace process stalled and there was no follow-up action from the government, the Palaung (Ta'aung) people formed the TNLA and began rearmament.

In late 2016 the TNLA joined forces with the larger Kachin Independence Army and two smaller groups, the Arakan Army and the Myanmar National Democratic Alliance Army (the Kokang group), to form what they call "the Northern Alliance." The alliance was announced just after a coordinated series of attacks on police and military positions in northern Shan State on November 20. Fighting has essentially continued since and the alliance members have struggled against the *Tatmadaw*.

To deal with some of the conflicts that have flared up in recent years, whether the Karen splinter groups in the 2000s, the Kokang since 2009, or the Kachin since 2011, the military seem to have gone back to what they know: the four cuts. Reports in 2011 suggest that they had ordered an official revival of the doctrine.[42]

Some of these groups, particularly the Kachin, can hold out against the *Tatmadaw*—or at least have so far managed to do so. None will be able to challenge the state again.

Naypyidaw

One often overlooked factor in providing the military and state with the stability and power projection is Myanmar's new capital city, Naypyidaw. This city, weird as it is, offers advantages in nation building and pacification. Moving the capital from Yangon shifts the heartland of the country, insulates politicking from the urban centers where unrest might develop, and allows power projection into the hinterlands. If one takes the regime at its word, Brigadier General Kyaw San, the Minister for Information, made explicit the core reason behind moving the capital: it was simply "to ensure more effective administration of nation-building activities."[43]

Construction on Naypyidaw began in 2004, among a cloud of rumor and secrecy, though the regime had been quietly approaching foreign governments and institutions for financial assistance since at least 1998.[44] In 2005, civil servants began moving offices up from Yangon. Also from 2005, the International Labour Organization was releasing reports of forced labor being used in the city's construction. In March 2006, on Armed Forces Day, the capital's de facto inauguration took place and flights began serving the city; two months later the first official envoy was received—Ibrahim Gambari, the UN under secretary-general for political affairs.[45]

Naypyidaw is a strange place, located some 360 kilometers north of Yangon. One can't help but feel the authority and power of the government when you visit. The city is a manicured articulation of a vision for how the 21st century capital of Myanmar should look and function. Naypyidaw's impossibly wide boulevards, tidy roundabouts, organized layout, consistent electricity supply and fast Internet put the city in stark contrast with anywhere else in the country. In that sense it is hopeful: a place the rest of the country can aspire to.

Still, Naypyidaw is an eccentric city and rumors still abound on why it exists in the first place. Speculation was rife that the new capital, whose name means "Capital of Kings," was borne of delusions of grandeur or Than Shwe's dementia; either way, it was criticized as an absurd vanity project, pointless and surreal.[46] Pundits have also asserted that the vast, largely empty capital was moved in order to insulate the government from restive citizens in Yangon. Others have suggested that the capital was moved to distance it from the coast: away from where an amphibious, American invasion might be. Additional rumors spread that it was moved due to superstitious omens. These may all be partly true, but, again, they ignore the nation-building role, both strategic and metaphoric, that the new location can potentially play.

First it should be noted that in the Burmese context, moving the capital city is not an infrequent occurrence. Nicholas Farrelly calculates that the capital has been moved 38 times, with a tenure of only 52 years on average.[47] There have been 14 moves since the capital redeployed from Bagan to Taungoo in 1486.[48] Every move of the capital took place for a mix of strategic, economic and cultural reasons, including when the British Empire decided to move the capital from Mandalay to Rangoon in 1885. Some moves were more salient and more successful than others. The point is this has been a historically common phenomenon.

There is clearly a symbolic element to Naypyidaw. Rangoon was a city built by the British. By the end of the colonial period, the majority of the population of the city was from outside Burma. Its 12th century founding was by a Mon kingdom, but when it truly became a bustling metropolis, it was a foreign, European capital with a downtown built from scratch and designed to efficiently extract wealth from the colony back to the metropole. Moving the capital away from Yangon closed the door on a period of national embarrassment for the Bamar people, as imagined by the military. The move was an expression of independence and marked a new era. The indigenous nature of the capital is reinforced by the installation of massive statues of Burmese conquerors of yore and of Uppatasanti Pagoda, which bears a striking resemblance to Burmese Buddhism's holiest site, Shwedagon Pagoda, in Yangon.[49] It is said to be 12 inches shorter, out of some sort of gesture of respect.

Naypyidaw reimagines where the heartland of the country is located. In the long term this will have an effect on population distribution, encouraging settlement in and around the capital.[50] Industrial and agricultural output from the region is likely to grow. Having the capital in Naypyidaw will help create a core area that is much closer to the ethnic states and regions, binding them together through its political functions. The beating political heart of the country is now located closer to the peripheries of the state and less isolated from potentially restive regions.

Naypyidaw may someday become an alternative economic center to Yangon, linking not only Yangon and Mandalay in an industrial belt but also sitting at an intersection between a current and potentially expanding transportation network that links Thailand and India. The new capital may aid economic efficiency gains by providing an alternative location for rural to urban migration, relieving pressure from Yangon in the medium-term.

There are more concrete strategic effects, also. Naypyidaw is not only the political center, but also now the military center of the country. It therefore allows for greater power projection, and "is an attempt to control and stabilize chronically turbulent regions, particularly in Kayin, Kayah and Shan States."[51] The new location can act as a strategic springboard from which both conventional and asymmetric forces can operate in the surrounding regions, helping impose the hegemony of the state over its own territory. Some would argue the hegemony of the Bamar majority over minority groups is part of that package, also.

In an area of convergence, it was North Koreans, having become master tunnelers following the Korean War, who helped build a vast network of tunnels under Naypyidaw.[52] This serves the military's defensive strategy for the city, again contributing to a sense of stability, security and preparedness for the regime. The military facilities of the capital also form something of a ring around the civilian buildings, which are closer to the center, effectively reducing the size and strength of popular uprisings in the capital," should such instability come to pass.[53] As noted already,

Naypyidaw also insulates the government from the two biggest population centers, allowing the business of politicking to take place away from the madding crowd.

Controlled Transition

In essence, the combination of military victories, ceasefire agreements, and the new capital city by the mid–2000s put the state in a more secure position than it had ever been. The regime was able to address its core security concern—the potential fracture of the union through secession movements, before it turned to address the twin issues of democracy and Aung San Suu Kyi.

This began, publically, with the 2003 proclamation of a seven-step process called the "Road Map to Democracy" or the "Roadmap to Discipline-flourishing Democracy."[54] The seven steps were:

1. Reconvening of the National Convention that has been adjourned since 1996.
2. After the successful holding of the National Convention, step by step implementation of the process necessary for the emergence of a genuine and disciplined democratic system.
3. Drafting of a new constitution in accordance with basic principles and detailed basic principles laid down by the National Convention.
4. Adoption of the constitution through national referendum.
5. Holding of free and fair elections for Pyithu Hluttaws (legislative bodies) according to the new constitution.
6. Convening of Hluttaws attended by Hluttaw members in accordance with the new constitution.
7. Building a modern, developed and democratic nation by the state leaders elected by the Hluttaw; and the government and other central organs formed by the Hluttaw.

Predictably, Myanmar state media covered a slew of massive rallies nationwide of a populace apparently in near-delirium at the prospect of discipline flourishing democracy.[55] Others were more skeptical. People found it hard to see the military as being genuinely interested in democracy and there were many unanswered questions.

Why was there no timeline? (To give the military maximum flexibility and the capacity to respond to changing conditions as they saw fit.) Was holding a National Convention during the process a way to invalidate the 1990 elections once and for all? (Yes.) Would minorities be sufficiently included in the seven steps? (Maybe.) On the latter question, even UN Secretary General Kofi Annan weighed in, criticizing the process.[56]

Importantly, the military had the most control in the earlier stages of the process, leading up to the creation of a new constitution. This would help them enshrine their core interests during latter, potentially more unruly, democratic periods. Thus, the 2008 constitution is a semi-democratic document with which the military are extremely comfortable.

Their comfort inspires criticism from quarters that wish to see a fuller democracy. The constitution creates a bicameral legislature in which military representatives automatically get 56 of 224 seats in the National Assembly (lower house) and 110 seats of 440 in the People's Assembly (upper house). It also gave the military control over the three most powerful ministries: border affairs, home affairs and defense. It allowed the head of the armed forces to unilaterally call a state of emergency and suspend the constitution. Finally, it prevented citizens with foreign relatives from holding the office of President. This meant Aung San Suu Kyi.

All these measures spoke to the degree to which the military envisioned democracy developing in the coming decades. They clearly think of the process as being a slow one.

The 2008 constitution was passed (incredibly) with overwhelming support in a referendum that took place during the mayhem and confusion wreaked by Cyclone Nargis. (Some 98.12 percent of eligible voters took part, according to the government.[57]) The military still needed the NLD and Aung San Suu Kyi's buy-in for the process to have legitimacy.

Many foreigners who have worked with Aung San Suu Kyi suggest that her intractability contributed to the length of the reform process.[58] Having the NLD walk out of the 1995 National Convention might be one example. Once the military made it clear that the 1990 election results would not be honored but some lesser (or perhaps, more "discipline-flourishing") form of democracy would be considered, a more pragmatic person might have sought to find a compromise position. Aung San Suu Kyi stuck to her guns, buoyed by international support, domestic adoration, a strong sense of justice, and an intense stubbornness.

After the 2010 elections, which the military-backed candidate won absent NLD participation, the process has moved forward. The story of how Aung San Suu Kyi, the United States, other foreign stakeholders and the *Tatmadaw* negotiated and compromised to keep the reform agenda moving is a complicated tale for another book. But suffice it to say its peak thus far was in the November 8, 2015, election.

The NLD won handily, taking almost exactly the same percentage of contested seats—just under 80 percent—as it did in 1990. There were few irregularities reported, with foreign and domestic observers broadly acclaiming the vote to be credible and legitimately reflecting the will of the people.[59] Much remains to be done, however.

Thinking of it as an incomplete process is helpful. It is certainly an unfinished transition to democracy, if the norms of the West are being upheld as a gold standard (though recently the tarnish on several democratic systems seems more exposed than ever).

The process has not been a smooth one and since 2016, the year that Aung San Suu Kyi's NLD took the reigns of government, there have seen several black spots. First, there is the renewed fighting in the north of the country. Second, libel and telecommunications laws are being ungenerously interpreted to pressure journalists and critics. Most troubling, the huge minority of Rohingya in Rakhine State are no closer to being given civil rights. Following October 2016 attacks on border outposts in Rakhine, the military enacted a brutal crackdown. Many activists fear something approaching genocide is under way.[60] On issues of free speech and minority rights, Aung San Suu Kyi is clearly not the leader that many had hoped for.

Nonetheless, a measure of democracy has arrived. A measure of freedom of speech has arrived. Foreign investors are back and GDP is growing. How much further the process goes remains to be seen, but it will certainly require the *Tatmadaw* staying comfortable with the security and integrity of the union that they have come to define over the past 70 years.

Just before the election in 2015, Naypyidaw signed a Nationwide Ceasefire Agreement with eight ethnic armies, including three Karen organizations. But some of the largest ethnic armies—including the United Wa State Army and Kachin Independence Army—did not sign. Other groups such as the Ta'ang National Liberation Army (TNLA), Myanmar National Democratic Alliance Army and Arakan Army are still fighting the *Tatmadaw*. Aung San Suu Kyi has (perhaps wastefully) thrown significant political capital behind finding a comprehensive peace deal, calling the process a "21st Century Panglong."[61]

Conclusion
What Now?

The world is faced, in 2017, with countries that pose different challenges to the international community, and to the United States, in particular. In Myanmar, the ethnic cleansing of a Muslim minority in Rakhine State is the primary concern. Continued fighting with armed groups in the North and consolidation of democratic gains are also issues. In North Korea it remains Pyongyang's nuclear weapons and ballistic missiles.

How now can we in the international community encourage positive outcomes in Myanmar and North Korea? These remain two difficult countries creating complex problems for the more powerful countries they are involved with and for international organizations. Myanmar finds itself at the crossroads of China, India and ASEAN. Competition for natural resources, strategic access to ports and river ways, as well as issues related to exportation of drugs, ongoing wars and human rights abuses, such as human trafficking and perhaps even genocide, animate leaders in Naypyidaw and elsewhere. North Korea meanwhile stubbornly refuses to integrate with its neighbors, denies many basic rights to its citizens, and is running nuclear and missile programs that other countries feel increasingly threatened by. What can be done about these issues?

On Myanmar

The most distressing problem is the fate of the Rohingya, in Myanmar's Southwestern Rakhine State. The longsuffering Rohingya, ethnically Bengali and religiously Muslim, have mostly been denied citizenship rights under the 1982 Citizenship Act. This act demands proof of a family's residence in Myanmar through documents that few Rohingya can provide. In response, most of the Bamar majority claim that none of these people qualify as citizens and are instead recent "Bengali migrants." Some may be, but many are not. Resentment of Muslims is rife among much of Myanmar's population.

The Rohingya have suffered particularly since a group of insurgents from this community (and possibly from abroad) attacked and killed Myanmar border guards and police in in October 2016. The reprisals have involved torching villages wholesale, rape and summary executions, according to survivors. Had this horror taken place earlier in the country's democratic transition process, one suspects that the response by the military might have been more restrained given that it would have risked all the engagement and trust-building that began in 2010.

Some 70,000 Rohingya fled to Bangladesh in the wake of the October 2016 attack. The number of deaths among the group was difficult to estimate, but by February 2017 the United Nations guessed it could be higher than one thousand.[1] The numbers of internally displaced people has been even harder to gauge as the townships where the crackdown is taking place have been mostly closed off to NGOs and journalists.

Then, somehow, in August 2017, the situation went from crisis to catastrophe. Militant Rohingya again mounted an attack on at least 20 police stations and an army base, inviting the fury of a well-prepared *Tatmadaw* on the Muslim population at large. The *Tatmadaw* appears to be applying a version of its four cuts doctrine—one that displaces a massive population of Muslims entirely and permanently.

The violence has forced well over 600,000 Rohingya to flee across the border, bringing the number of people who have sought refuge in Bangladesh to over half a million since 2012, when inter-communal violence broke out.[2] Testimonies by refugees and satellite images indicate that hundreds of Rohingya villages have been burned down.[3] Tales of rape have been widespread during this purge.[4]

The international community has been vociferous in their condemnation of these deplorable abuses and has been particularly disappointed in Aung San Suu Kyi's reluctance to criticize the *Tatmadaw* or take a stand against what is going on in Rakhine. The Rohingya issue illustrates how difficult it can be to coordinate international action in Myanmar's post-sanctions environment, however.

When a push took place at the UN Human Rights Council for a commission of inquiry into the Rohingya crisis in early March of 2017, the

European Union at first appeared to block it. EU diplomats stated they "preferred using an existing mechanism that had received good cooperation and access from Myanmar's government, rather than a new approach, and to give more time to the domestic process."[5] Later in the month the European Union did push for a full probe. Still, there is a tension between maintaining relations with Naypyidaw (and protecting the interests of businesses and NGOs) with seeking to pressure Myanmar over human rights issues. It is widely thought that Russia and China are disinterested in censuring Myanmar at the UN Security Council. This is despite widespread concern that Myanmar is engaging in what is essentially genocide of the Rohingya.

As it is, outsiders have little influence over an issue that not only the military but also Aung San Suu Kyi appear little interested in resolving. Too many key actors in Naypyidaw still see ethnic relations as a zero-sum game. If a commission of inquiry or some other UN report officially rebukes Myanmar, we may see some symbolically punitive measures taken, such as fewer invitations to summit meetings or regional fora, but it is difficult to imagine significant sanctions being re-applied.

Moreover, a remarkable alignment has occurred: the international criticism of Aung San Suu Kyi and the military on an issue that most Myanmar people feel strongly about has created broad support for both her *and* the military. Sanctions now would, ironically, give the military back some of the legitimacy they lost in 1988. Narrow, punitive measures on the military could be taken by Western countries, but, even so, it is difficult to see how severing lines of communication and exchange with the men prosecuting wars and violence will solve anything.

Moreover, strong engagement on governance and civil society issues is necessary from the West, despite the diminished leverage the United States and other countries now have. NGOs and government agencies must help Myanmar's government craft an inclusive political and economic environment, improving on corruption and issues of efficiency. They must also continue to support the values of democratic participation and free speech. Certainly, democratization is far from complete.

One emergent problem with the democratic transition has been the increasingly notorious Section 66(d) of the 2013 Telecommunications Act. This has been the main tool for silencing criticism of public figures. The clause allows for three years in prison and a fine for "extorting, coercing, restraining wrongfully, defaming, disturbing, causing undue influence or threatening to any person by using any Telecommunications Network." In practice this means any critical speech on social media is vulnerable to prosecution, and in Myanmar the accused waits in jail while the case is prepared for court.

The examples of its use are varied and genuinely threaten free speech. In February 2017 an NLD member sued a teacher and her husband under Section 66(d) over a Facebook post that was allegedly defamatory toward State Counselor Aung San Suu Kyi. Also in 2017 a popular transgender entertainer, Myo Ko Ko San, was accused of spreading rumors about a high-society individual on her Facebook page. She was arrested and spent several days in jail before it was determined that someone else was responsible for the page. A non-66(d) defamation suit against two Eleven Media executives is ongoing: Eleven had suggested that Yangon Chief Minister Phyo Min Thein had accepted a bribe in exchange for a development concession.

Most dishearteningly, prosecution using the act has increased dramatically under the watch of Aung San Suu Kyi's government. The law was used 38 times in 2016, compared to just seven from 2013 to 2015, according to PEN Myanmar, an activist group.[6] The cases continued to mount in 2017. The international community has to continue to advocate for freer speech while recognizing it is up to political elites who may not see the relative benefits of a more open society.

Another barrier to democratization is that under the 2008 constitution, the *Tatmadaw* continue to control key ministries and automatically have 25 percent of parliamentary seats, giving them veto power over constitutional amendments. Again, the international community no longer has the leverage to pressure for reforms, but it can continue using development aid and capacity building to encourage long-term thinking on how to reduce the military's role in society. This will be an uphill task.

In the region, Indonesia is probably the best example of how this might be carried out and perhaps Jakarta could be engaged to encourage a similar path for Myanmar, given its experience with civilianization of government in the late 1990s and early 2000s. Even the less positive example of neighboring Thailand could be useful: there the military is theoretically apolitical but intervenes with occasional coups to take over the government and enforce stability. Lest I be misunderstood: having periodic military juntas is clearly sub-optimal, but at least it is widely recognized that times of military intervention in politics are abnormal and should not be permanent. The international community has to encourage the *Tatmadaw* to continue the process of democratization.

Another goal of the United States is to sever the military-to-military relationship between Myanmar and the DPRK. In November 2015, five days after the NLD won the Myanmar general election, the U.S. Treasury put the North Korean ambassador to Myanmar, Kim Sok Chol, on the Specially Designated Nationals (SDN) List. The next day, the Pyongyang Koryo Restaurant in Yangon closed amid this uncertainty, denying restaurant goers their dose of mediocre Korean food and music. Kim left soon after. The restaurant reopened, too.

American intelligence officers are reluctant to say (or just don't know) the extent of weapons sales from Pyongyang to Naypyidaw, but they clearly believe some relationship still exists. Washington sees this as relatively simple to resolve and has frequently communicated to the *Tatmadaw* that they could easily purchase weapons from any other supplier and the United States would not object. From the perspective of the United States, Myanmar still has a number of workable options for weapons purchases, including Russia, China, Israel and perhaps even South Korea.

The United States might be able offer the long-term prospect of normalized military-military relations in return, but it can't offer much in the short-term given the ongoing conflicts and the Rohingya issue. The United States will certainly not be able to offer military equipment as a substitute, but it may be able to offer training for the navy or border guard force as an incentive so long as the training could not be used in operations against the ethnic armed groups or Rohingya.

Myanmar-DPRK ties are primarily an issue for U.S. diplomacy and intelligence. Continued democratization is a complex issue that will require positive engagement from governments, development agencies, NGOs and businesses. It will require keeping Myanmar's elites interested in these issues, as well as grassroots education and support.

On North Korea

There are three ways to approach North Korea's nuclear development: war, negotiation and diplomacy, and containment. The latter could and should work in tandem with diplomacy.

Another Korean War would be disastrous. Yet one side or the other miscommunicating their intentions could certainly spark a conflict. With the escalation in Pyongyang's testing schedule, sanctions and aggressive rhetoric between Kim Jong Un and Donald Trump, the conflict between their two countries is approaching an inflection point. In the summer of 2017, Pyongyang suggested that both an atmospheric nuclear test over the Pacific was possible and that a missile test that "enveloped Guam" was in the cards. With unprecedented rhetorical flourishes and insults, the U.S. president promised the destruction of North Korea if Pyongyang continued to threaten the United States.

One could easily imagine a miscalculation under these conditions, especially since Trump and his cabinet members have sent mixed signals on the Korea crisis. One danger is that Washington draws a red line—such as a missile test near Guam—that North Korea thinks they can violate without incurring a military response. After all, the DPRK has a history of brazen actions: they captured a U.S. ship in 1968 as well as shot down a U.S. spy plane in 1969 and a helicopter that strayed across the DMZ in 1994. All of these actions provoked a minimal response. However, the Trump administration's communications are so inconsistent and divergent in tone that the North Koreans could easily misinterpret a hard red line. They might think an unpunished and audacious maneuver is possible, when this time it would provoke a military response.

In turn, the Americans might think they could launch a limited, punitive strike on a site in North Korea, but there is no guarantee that the Koreans would interpret it as such. If they thought some U.S. action was the preliminary phase of a broader action, Pyongyang would likely feel compelled to escalate. North Korea may also misinterpret a "show of force," such as the September 23, 2017, flight up its coastline by U.S. tactical bombers, as an attack, and try to shoot down U.S. planes. This would generate another response in turn.

The general assumption for some time has been that the United States and its allies would win a war against North Korea, but the damage the Korean People's Army could inflict would be so horrific, the cost so high, that such a conflict should be avoided. It would destroy generations of South Korean economic growth and infrastructure building. North Korean missiles targeting U.S. facilities in Yokohama harbor would imperil Tokyo. Capital would flee the region, likely casting China into recession. The Chinese Communist Party, with its legitimacy riding on the back of its economic growth, would face an unprecedented challenge.

If they think all out war is upon them, the North Koreans may also consider sending missiles towards U.S. forces stationed elsewhere in the Asia Pacific. The United States, South Korea and Japan would attempt to intercept any missile launches through overlapping defensive systems, including the THAAD, Aegis and Patriot systems. The allies would also attempt to find and destroy North Korea's nuclear weapons missile systems even before they had time to launch. But if North Korea saw its prize military possessions at risk, it may decide to use them.

This seems suicidal, but such a decision could be made, and made incorrectly, by a leadership under pressure and facing an unclear pattern of escalation. Kim Jong Un might think after an attack or limited exchange, a pause for talks would be possible.

However, if Pyongyang were to use a nuclear weapon, or think it could attack one of South Korea's 24 nuclear power plants with conventional weapons, the U.S. response would also probably be nuclear. The Korean peninsula would be put to the torch, in flame and death. It is difficult to know how a stopping point might emerge as a conflict escalated upwards. There are certainly elements in the U.S. military who feel that if fighting breaks out, it should be "once and for all," not leaving another generation of Americans to patrol the DMZ, nor another generation of North Koreans to grow up with the Kim family determining their lives.

If fighting remains below the threshold of a nuclear exchange, it is unclear how things would unfold in a fluid and dynamic escalation. But very likely in the early minutes of a war, artillery tubes from across the DMZ would begin pounding strategic sites in Seoul, sending people fleeing for the subway. Other tunnel systems dug decades ago under the DMZ would be used to send troops hustling under the border. Two of North Korea's asymmetric advantages could be employed: cyber attacks would hit South Korean institutions connected to infrastructure, government, and banking; a network of spies would also be activated to commit sabotage against institutions and infrastructure in the country.

Meanwhile, young and middle-aged South Korean men would be mobilized from their universities, offices and factories. The R.O.K. military would come under a combined command led by the United States in support of a United Nations Command.

Pyongyang and other North Korean cities would be leveled by air power unseen since the Gulf War. Cruise missiles would be unleashed from ships, while constant sorties of heavy bombers would stream in from Guam, Okinawa and further afield, dropping wave after wave of ordnance on North Korea's crumbling infrastructure. North Koreans would flee underground if they can find a way. Those who could not fit in Pyongyang's subway systems or basements would attempt to escape the city, though highways would be controlled by the Korean People's Army. With every passing day, the superiority of South Korean and American hardware would come to bear on North Korean tanks and other field weapons systems.

South Korea's military expects chemical and biological weapons. Such weapons could create confusion and civilian losses, while slowing troops on the battlefield as they tried to move North. These weapons would also allow Pyongyang a degree of deniability not possible with, say, a nuclear explosion.

Ultimately, the costs of such a conflict would be immense, especially in terms of human life, and have only increased as the weaponry on both sides grows more potent. It is the primary reason why war has not broken out since the armistice was signed in 1953.

If war is basically a non-option, attempting to contain and deter the North Korean threat becomes the only option. "Containment," in this sense, is a mix of sanctions and intelligence work that attempts to make it hard for North Korea to procure material that support its state and military. It also seeks to prevent the export of weapons, particularly weapons of mass destruction. Finally, it includes a military deterrence.

Extended deterrence is a Cold War concept whereby America's enemies are made aware that invasion of or serious harm to the Untied States or its allies would be met with overwhelming, indeed nuclear, force. The capacity to inflict massive damage on the North is continually calibrated and communicated to ensure the tense co-existence on the peninsula continues, perhaps indefinitely, or at least until a miscalculation takes place.

In a way, Pyongyang finds this acceptable, though its whole nuclear policy has sought to shift the balance. During the Cold War, the United States and Soviet Union's mutual deterrence postures led to the concept of Mutually Assured Destruction, which kept the two superpowers in check. Pyongyang now wants this: to credibly be able to inflict a nuclear strike on the U.S. homeland and be treated with the respect that such a capacity inevitably confers. Consequently, the United States and its allies need to make sure Pyongyang is deterred from military action or other provocations.

This leaves negotiation as the third way to approach North Korea's nuclear development (in combination with deterrence). Yet this too has failed. Politically in the United States (or anywhere with a democratic system) it is very hard to construct an agreement with a loathed enemy that can withstand the political pressures of skeptics in Washington, not to mention the capitals of U.S. allies. As of late 2017, President Obama's 2015

Iran deal is under tremendous pressure. President Clinton's 1994 Agreed Framework with the DPRK also crumbled under Republican opposition to it.

It would be harder now than ever before to successfully negotiate a compromise because North Korea has shown no willingness at all to discuss denuclearization since 2012, if not earlier. Its nuclear weapons appear to be completely off the table. At the same time, thus far, the United States has been unable to accept negotiations wherein a freeze, monitoring, and no new production is the best-case outcome. It would be a deflating admission of two decades of U.S. failures; an admission that the United States had lost.

And yet, the United States *has* lost. Pyongyang is a nuclear power. This basket case of repression, this failed, minuscule economy has developed nuclear weapons and can put objects into space. Both of these are remarkable achievements, putting the country into an elite club. North Korea sees its nuclear weapons as its only safeguard.

As for North Korea's other driver of its pariah status, human rights abuses of its own citizens, again, there are few good options. Cataloging and gathering evidence is crucial to someday be able to have as complete an accounting as possible and help with the social construction of a unified Korea.

However, applying pressure to Pyongyang on these grounds is currently counterproductive. As it is, the last several years have seen South Korea, the United States, and the United Nations more interested in taking Pyongyang to task for its wretched prisons, capricious justice system, and other restrictions on speech, association and communication. Key aspects of the North Korean Human Rights Law, passed in 2016 by South Korea's parliament, deal with punishment for perpetrators. Eight months after the UN Commission of Inquiry into human rights in North Korea published its findings and specifically named Kim Jong Un responsible, the UN General Assembly voted to refer the Democratic People's Republic of Korea to the International Criminal Court in the Hague. Thus far, these moves have produced a predictably stubborn response from Pyongyang.

Here, we might learn from Myanmar. Activists looking for transition in the 2000s were generally not interested in talking about justice in a punitive sense. There may exist cultural or religious explanations for the acceptance of the sins of a brutal, unforgiving regime, but the tactical ones are more interesting. Simply, many realized that pushing for justice would scare the generals and delay the potential for transition. Advocating for the recognition and granting of rights is another matter, and this is where efforts focused. In this way, the fixation on responsibility for and eventual punishment of the abuses that take place in North Korea is probably a mistake if the goal is to encourage an eventual transition or more open version of that society. This is, of course, emotionally unsatisfying.

Regardless, if negotiations can lead to a freeze in Pyongyang's missile and nuclear testing in return for some kind of economic engagement, we will eventually see a country that is more connected to the outside world, through trade and investment. A gradual transformation of its society may take place, not dissimilar to what has taken place in China, as market forces come to exert a deeper influence over the daily lives of North Koreans. More interaction with the outside world *will* affect DPRK society. This will take time and the results will be uneven. In the long run, however, this is the only realistic road towards a North Korea that is less unjust, aggressive and threatening.

North Korea's weapons development is putting it on a collision course with Washington, while Myanmar has joined the global economy and given its citizens unprecedented freedoms. Much work remains to be done to consolidate Myanmar's democracy, and the country's treatment of the Rohingya is distressing. However, there is still reason to hope and to be pleased at what has been accomplished in the past seven years.

With North Korea, it remains harder to be optimistic. President Donald Trump sees himself as a dealmaker, yet resolving the seven-decade standoff with Pyongyang is a challenge that has eluded his predecessors. Perhaps his unconventional style leads to a breakthrough. Yet failing to understand and address the complex, overlapping interests on the Korean peninsula could equally lead to disaster.

In the medium term, North Korea will also have to be less belligerent in rhetoric and action if a compromise is to be found. Some kind of agreement between the United States and the DPRK that recognizes that for the coming decades U.S. troops are not going anywhere—hard for Pyongyang—and that North Korean nukes are not disappearing—hard for Washington—seems like the only realistic goal. Language that includes a vague acknowledgement that neither side is satisfied and must continue to review and dialogue would be useful.

Unwinding some sanctions for behavior changes by North Korea in ways that encourage the continuing marketization of the North Korean economy will be necessary. Ultimately, the process of economic change will alter the way ordinary and elite North Koreans think about their place in the world. In the long run this will profoundly change their society.

The United States needs to reassure and cooperate closely with Seoul on everything related to its security and the safety of its citizens. After all, if North Korea really were to attack the U.S. homeland, it means the alliance demands South Koreans fight and die defending America. Hitherto, it has been the other way around. The alliance matters more than ever. The United States also needs to keep defending the pillars of liberal democracy—individual rights, freedom of speech and political participation—and making the case to people in Northeast Asia, including and especially North Koreans, that this is the best way to organize societies in the 21st century.

Chapter Notes

Introduction

1. ILO Asia—Pacific Working Paper Series, *ASEAN Community 2015: Managing Integration for Better Jobs and Shared Prosperity in Myanmar*, February 2015, 19.
2. "CIA World Factbook *North Korea*," https://www.cia.gov/library/publications/the-world-factbook/geos/print/country/countrypdf_kn.pdf.
3. Megha Rajagopalan, "Lighter Traffic, Little Sign of Customs Crackdown at North Korea Border," Reuters, March 3, 2016, http://www.reuters.com/article/us-northkorea-nuclear-border-idUSKCN0W511L.
4. David Mathieson, "Burma's Forgotten Prisoners," *Human Rights Watch*, September 2009, 35.
5. David Hawk, "North Korea's Hidden Gulag: Interpreting Reports of Changes in the Prison Camps," *Human Rights in North Korea*, 2013, 33.
6. Lee Chae-In, *A Troubled Peace: U.S. Policy and the Two Koreas* (Baltimore: Johns Hopkins University Press, 2006), 221.
7. Hazel J. Land, *Fear and Sanctuary: Burmese Refugees in Thailand* (Ithaca, NY: SEAP, 2002), 38–45.
8. Bruce Bechtol, Jr., "Maintaining a Rogue Military: North Korea's Military Capabilities and Strategy at the End of the Kim Jong-il Era," *International Journal of Korean Studies* 16, no. 1 (Spring 2012): 164–165.
9. Article 3, Republic of Korea Constitution.
10. Lim Jae-Chon, *Leader Symbols and Personality Cult in North Korea: The Leader State* (London: Routledge, 2015), 51–95.
11. "World Bank International Tourism Data, 2016," http://data.worldbank.org/indicator/ST.INT.ARVL?locations=MM.
12. "Witness to Transformation," https://piie.com/blogs/north-korea-witness-transformation.
13. Nat Kretchun and Jane Kim, "A Quiet Opening: North Koreans in a Changing Media Environment," *Intermedia*, 2012, 8.

Chapter 1

1. Interestingly, sweeping the highway is something that happens in Naypyidaw, the Myanmar military regime's showpiece city. Naypyidaw will be discussed in Chapter 7.
2. Kim Yangson, 김양선 *Hanguk Gidokgyo Haebang 10-nyeon Sa* 한국기독교 해방 10년사 ("Korean Christianity liberation 10 year history") [Seoul: Yaesu Gyojang Rohui, Jonggyo Gyoyukbu, 1956], 160.
3. New terminals began operation in 2016 and 2017. They are a *major* upgrade but are still cheap, short term solutions.
4. U Khin Win, *A Century of Rice Improvement in Burma* (Manila: International Rice Research Institute, 1991), 7.
5. Ramon Hawley Myers and Mark R. Peattie, *The Japanese Colonial Empire, 1895–1945* (Princeton, NJ: Princeton University Press, 1984), 487.
6. Thant Myint-U, *The Making of Modern Burma* (Cambridge: Cambridge University Press, 2001), 18.
7. Rajiv Bhatia, *India–Myanmar Relations: Changing Contours* (London: Taylor and Francis, 2015), 70.
8. See James Scott, *The Art of Not Being Governed: An Anarchist History of Upland Southeast Asia* (New Haven: Yale University Press, 2009).
9. Robert H. Taylor, "British Policy Towards Myanmar and the Creation of the Burma Problem," in *Myanmar: State, Society*

and Ethnicity, eds. N. Ganesan and Kyaw Yin Hlaing (Singapore: ISEAS, 2007), 75–76.
10. Harry Ignatius Marshall, *The Karen People of Burma* (Bangkok: White Lotus, 2007), 298. [Reprint of 1922 edition].
11. *Ibid.*
12. Michael Gravers, "Spiritual Politics, Political Religion, and Religious Freedom In Burma," *The Review of Faith & International Affairs* 11:2 (2013): 46–54.
13. J.J. Snodgrass, *Narrative of the Burmese War* (New Delhi: Lancer, 1952), 142.
14. Marshall, *The Karen*, 306.
15. San C. Po, *Burma and the Karens* (Bangkok: White Lotus, 2001), 66. [Reprint of 1928 edition].
16. *Ibid.*, 68
17. Jafar Suryomenggolo, *Organising under the Revolution: Unions and the State in Java, 1945–48* (Singapore: NUS Press, 2013), 41–42.
18. Robert H. Taylor, *The State in Burma* (London: Hurst, 2009), 100.
19. Ola Hanson, *The Kachins: Their Customs and Traditions* (Cambridge: Cambridge University Press, 1913), preface. [2012 reprint].
20. Mandy Sadan, *Being and Becoming Kachin* (Oxford: Oxford University Press, 2013), 24.
21. Edmund Leach, *Political Systems of Highland Burma: A Study of Kachin Social Structure* (London: Athlone, 1954), 2.
22. Victor B. Leiberman, "Ethnic Politics in Eighteenth Century Burma," *Modern Asian Studies* 12:3 (1978): 457.
23. Susan H. Williams, *Social Difference and Constitutionalism in Pan-Asia* (Cambridge: Cambridge University Press, 2014), 155.
24. Chao Tzang Yawnghwe, *The Shan of Burma: Memoirs of a Shan Exile* (Singapore: ISEAS, 2010), 13.
25. Sadan, *Being and Becoming Kachin*, 122.
26. "OECD Development Pathways Multi-Dimensional Review of Myanmar, Volume 1," *OECD*, 2013, 172.
27. Mya Than, "The Ethnic Chinese in Myanmar and Their Identity," in *Ethnic Chinese as Southeast Asians*, ed. Leo Suryadinata (Singapore: ISEAS, 1997), 116.
28. Tin Maung Maung Than, "Some Aspects of Indians in Rangoon," in *Indian Communities in Southeast Asia*, eds. K.S. Sandhu and A. Mani (Singapore: ISEAS, 2006), 258.
29. Stephen L. Keck, *British Burma in the New Century 1895–1918* (London: Palgrave Macmillan, 2015), 145, 146.
30. S.C.M. Paine, *The Sino-Japanese War of 1894–1895: Perceptions, Power, and Primacy* (Cambridge: Cambridge University Press, 2006), 45.
31. Ian Nish, *The Anglo-Japanese Alliance: The Diplomacy of Two Island Empires 1984–1907* (London: Bloomsbury, 2012), 1.
32. Kim Ji-Jung "The War and U.S.-Korea Relations," in *The Russo-Japanese War in Global Perspective: World War Zero*, vol. 2, eds. David Wolff, et al. (Leiden: Brill, 2007), 478.
33. Martina Deuchler, *The Confucian Transformation of Korea: A Study of Society and Ideology* (Cambridge, MA: Harvard University Press, 1992), 13–14.
34. Bruce Cumings, "Japanese Colonialism in Korea: A Comparative Perspective," Asia/Pacific Research Center: Stanford University, 1997. http://iis-db.stanford.edu/pubs/10061/Cumings.etc.pdf.
35. "WTO Country Profile: Republic of Korea," WTO, http://stat.wto.org/CountryProfile/WSDBCountryPFView.aspx?Country=KR&Language=F.
36. Sonia Ryang, *Koreans in Japan: Critical Voices from the Margin* (London: Routledge, 2000), 2.
37. Leslie Glass, *The Changing of Kings: Memories of Burma, 1934–1949* (London: Peter Owen, 1985), 138.
38. *Being and Becoming Kachin*, 258.
39. Daniel D. Gray, "Myanmar's Ethnic Karen Minority Remember World War II Hero," Associated Press, August 15, 2015, http://www.sandiegouniontribune.com/news/2015/aug/15/myanmars-karen-remember-world-war-ii-hero/.
40. Tzang Yawnghwe, *The Shan of Burma*, 80.
41. *Ibid.*, 81.
42. "My Hero Aung San," *The Guardian*, April 29, 2011, http://www.theguardian.com/books/2011/apr/30/my-hero-aung-san-suu-kyi.
43. Paul H. Kratoska, "The Karen of Burma Under Japanese Rule," in *Southeast Asian Minorities in the Wartime Japanese Empire*, ed. Paul H. Kratoska (London: Routledge Curzon, 2002), 24.
44. *Ibid.*
45. *Ibid.*, 37.
46. Gustaaf Houtman, *Mental Culture in Burmese Crisis Politics: Aung San Suu Kyi and the National League for Democracy* (Tokyo: ILCAA, 1999), 249.
47. Angelene Naw, *Aung San and the Struggle for Burmese Independence* (Bangkok: Silkworm, 2001), 63.
48. Christopher Alan Bayly and Timothy

Norman Harper, *Forgotten Armies: The Fall of British Asia, 1941–1945* (Cambridge, MA: Harvard University Press, 2005), 13.
    49. U Ba Than, *The Roots of the Revolution: A Brief History of the Defence Services of the Union of Burma and the Ideals for Which They Stand* (Rangoon: Director of Information, 1962), 46.
    50. Houtman, *Mental Culture in Burmese Crisis Politics*, 250.
    51. Robert H. Taylor, *Ne Win: A Political Biography* (Singapore: ISEAS, 2015), 60.
    52. Don Oberdorfer, *The Two Koreas: A Contemporary History* (New York: Basic, 2014), 5.
    53. Hugh Deane, *The Korean War* (London: China, 1999), 149.
    54. See R. Dingman, "Atomic Diplomacy during the Korean War," *International Security* 3, Issue 13 (Winter 1988–1999): 50–91.
    55. Wada Haruki, *The Korean War: An International History* (New York: Rowman and Littlefield, 2014), 287.
    56. Bruce Cumings, *Korea's Place in the Sun: A Modern History* (New York: W. W. Norton, 1997), 238.
    57. Naw, *Aung San and the Struggle for Burmese Independence*, 139.
    58. *Ibid.*, 67
    59. Robert H. Taylor, *Dr. Maung Maung: Gentleman, Scholar, Patriot* (Singapore: ISEAS, 2008), 197.
    60. Martin John Smith, *Burma: Insurgency and the Politics of Ethnicity* (London: Zed, 1991), 78.
    61. Bertil Lintner, "The Shans and the Shan State of Burma," *Contemporary Southeast Asia* 5, no. 4 (March 1984):409–420.
    62. N. Ganesen, *Bilateral Legacies in East and Southeast Asia* (Singapore: ISEAS, 2015), 125.
    63. See Kathryn Weathersby, "Soviet Aims in Korea and the Origins of the Korean War, 1945–1950: New Evidence from Russian Archives," Woodrow Wilson International Center for Scholars: Cold War International History Project Working Paper No. 8, November 1993.

Chapter 2

1. Mary P. Callahan, *Making Enemies: War and State Building in Burma* (Ithaca, NY: Cornell University Press, 2003), 114–115.
    2. Martin Smith, *Burma: Insurgency and the Politics of Ethnicity* (London: Zed, 1991), 119.
    3. Smith, *Burma: Insurgency*, 111, 116.
    4. John H. Badgley, "Burmese Communist Schisms," *Peasant Rebellion and Communist Revolution in Asia*, eds. John H. Badgley and John Wilson Lewis (Palo Alto: Stanford University Press, 1974), 153.
    5. There is some disagreement about how to refer to the new main faction in English. See Helen S. Castelli, *Reviewed Work(s): The Rise and Fall of the Communist Party of Burma (CPB)* by Bertil Lintner, *Crossroads: An Interdisciplinary Journal of Southeast Asian Studies* 6, no. 2 (1991): 133.
    6. Smith, *Burma: Insurgency*, 67.
    7. Virginia Thompson, "Burma's Communists," *Far Eastern Survey* 17, no. 9, (1948): 104.
    8. Bertil Lintner, *The Rise and Fall of the Communist Party of Burma (CPB)* (Ithica, NY: Cornell University Press, 1990), 11.
    9. "Communist Influence in Burma," CIA Report, ORE 86–49, January 11, 1950, 1.
    10. *Ibid.*, 7.
    11. Jack Fong, *Revolution as Development: The Karen Self-Determination Struggle Against Ethnocracy (1949–2004)* (New York: Brownwalker, 2008), 99.
    12. Karen National Union Website, http://karennationalunion.net/index.php/burma/about-the-knu/objectives.
    13. Bertil Linter, *Burma in Revolt: Opium and Insurgency since 1948* (Chiang Mai: Silkworm, 1999), 83.
    14. Moshe Yegar, *Between Integration and Secession: The Muslim Communities of the Southern Philippines, Southern Thailand, and Western Burma/Myanmar* (New York: Roman & Littlefield, 2002), 33–34.
    15. *Ibid.*, 37.
    16. "Rohingya/Bengali: A Snapshot of Community in 1960s," *The Network for International Protection of Refugees*, August 2015. www.netipr.org/policy/node/ 50.
    17. Smith, *Insurgency*, 219.
    18. Linter *Rise and Fall*, 26.
    19. Richard Butwell, *U Nu of Burma* (Palo Alto: Stanford University Press, 1969), 99.
    20. Some scholars may dislike that characterization, pointing to complex ceremonies and integration with Buddhism as evidence of sophistication or to Western religious practices as equally superstitious. If the word "superstition" is to have any meaning, nat propitiation must be included it that term, however.
    21. Linter, *Burma in Revolt*, 167–168.
    22. Smith, *Insurgency*, 169.
    23. Bertil Linter, "The CIA's First Secret War: Americans Helped Stage Raids into

China from Burma," *Far Eastern Economic Review*, 16 September 1993.
24. Callahan, *Making Enemies*, 155.
25. Frank Trager, "Burma and China," *Journal of Southeast Asian History* 5, no. 1 (1964): 43.
26. Maung Aung Myoe, *In the Name of Pauk-Phaw: Myanmar's China Policy Since 1948* (Singapore: ISEAS, 2011), 39.
27. Joseph Camilleri, *Southeast Asia in China's Foreign Policy* (Singapore: ISEAS, 1975), 22.
28. "Burmese Rioting Hits Mao Support," Associated Press, June 27, 1967.
29. Hongwei Fan, "China–Burma Geopolitical Relations in the Cold War," *Journal of Current Southeast Asian Affairs* 31, no. 1 (2012): 8.
30. Linter, *Burma in Revolt*, 249.
31. Ashley South, *Burma's Longest War: Anatomy of the Karen Conflict* (Amsterdam: Transnational Institute, 2011), 8.
32. Jack Fong, *Revolution as Development: The Karen Self-Determination Struggle Against Ethnocracy (1949–2004)* (New York: Brownwalker, 2008), 107.
33. *Ibid.*, 14.
34. "About the Karenni," Karenni Independence through Education Website, http://www.karenni.org/about_the_karenni.php.
35. Bibhu Prasad Routray, "Myanmar's National Reconciliation: An Audit of Insurgencies and Ceasefires," *IPCS Special Report* No. 138, March 2013, 2.
36. Martin Smith, "Ethnic Groups in Burma: Development, Democracy and Human Rights," *Anti-Slavery International Report* No. 8 (1994): 37.
37. Russ Christensen and Sann Kyaw, *The Pa-O: Rebels and Refugees* (Chiang Mai: Silkworm, 2006), 22–23.
38. *Ibid.*, 28.
39. *Ibid.*, 30–31.
40. Sein Win, *The Split Story* (Rangoon: Guardian, 1959), 2.
41. Matthew Foley, *Post-Colonial Transition, Aid and The Cold War in Southeast Asia: Britain, the United States and Burma, 1948–1962* (PhD. Diss., University of Nottingham, 2007), 273.
42. "Interview with Colonial Chit Myiang," *Burma Debate* 4, no. 3 (1997): 19.
43. Richard Butwell, *U Nu of Burma* (Palo Alto: Stanford University Press, 1969), 116.
44. Mary P. Callahan, "Building an Army," *Burma Debate* 4, no. 3 (1997): 9.
45. Maung Maung Myoe, *Building the Tatmadaw: Myanmar Armed Forces Since 1948* (Singapore: ISEAS, 2009), 54–55.
46. David I. Steinberg, *Burma/Myanmar: What Everyone Needs to Know* (Oxford: Oxford University Press, 2009), 55.
47. Lucian Pye, "The Army in Burmese Politics," *The Role of the Military in Underdeveloped Countries*, ed. John Asher Johnson (Princeton: Princeton University Press, 2015), 232–233.
48. Richard Butwell, "The Four Failures of U Nu's Second Premiership," *Asian Survey* 2, no. 1 (1962), 6.
49. Marine La Raw, "On the Continuing Relevance of E.R. Leach's 'Political Systems of Highland Burma' to Kachin Studies," *Social Dynamics in the Highlands of Southeast Asia: Reconsidering Political Systems of Highland Burma by E.R. Leach*, eds. François Robinne and Mandy Sadan (Leiden: Brill, 2007), 32.
50. Richard Allen, "Recent Developments in Burma (Address Given to Royal Asiatic Society July 22, 1964)," *Journal of The Royal Central Asian Society* 52:1, 6–19 (1965): 12.
51. Bertil Linter, "The Shans and the Shan State of Burma," *Contemporary Southeast Asia* 5, no. 4 (1984): 415.
52. Josef Silverstein, "Politics in the Shan State: The Question of Secession from the Union of Burma," *The Journal of Asian Studies* 18, no. 1 (1958), 57.
53. Matthew Foley, *The Cold War and National Assertion in Southeast Asia: Britain, the United States and Burma, 1948–1962* (London: Routledge, 2009), 151.
54. Letter to the Editor, "In Burma, 'Bloodless' Coup Began Violent Era," *New York Times*, August 13, 1988. http://www.nytimes.com/1988/08/13/opinion/l-in-burma-bloodless-coup-began-violent-era-570888.html.
55. Smith, *Ethnic Groups in Burma*, 25.
56. Robert A. Holmes, "Burmese Domestic Policy: The Politics of Burmanization," *Asian Survey* 7, no. 3 (March 1967): 189.
57. Carolyn Wakeman and San San Tin, *No Time for Dreams: Living in Burma Under Military Rule* (New York: Rowman & Littlefield, 2009), 17.
58. *Ibid.*
59. "Burma/Karens (1948-present) Timeline," University of Central Arkansas Political Science Website, http://uca.edu/politicalscience/dadm-project/asiapacific-region/burmakarens-1948-present/.
60. Smith, *Ethnic Groups in Burma*, 186.
61. Linter, *The Shans*, 416.
62. Robert B. Maule, "The Opium Question in the Federated Shan States, 1931–36: British Policy Discussions and Scandal," *Jour-

nal of Southeast Asian Studies 23, no. 1 (1992), 15.

63. Linter, *The Shans*, 418.

64. Harish Chandola, "The Politics of Opium," *Economic and Political Weekly*, June 5, 1976, http://www.epw.in/journal/1976/23/our-correspondent-columns/thailand-politics-opium.html.

65. Smith, *Insurgency*, 191.

66. Peter Trager, "Burma—1968—A New Beginning," *Asian Survey* 9, no. 2, A Survey of Asia in 1968: Part II, February 1969, 107.

67. Peter Trager, "Burma—1967—A Better Ending than Beginning in Asian Survey," *Asian Survey* 8, no. 2, A Survey of Asia in 1967: Part II, February 1968, 114.

68. *Ibid*.

69. Bertil Lintner, "Insurgencies Among Mons and Karens," *Economic and Political Weekly* 16, no. 16 (1981): 703.

70. "The Summary Background of Rakhaing Nation and Arakan Liberation Party," *Arakan Liberation Party (ALP) Official Webpage*, http://www.arakanalp.com/?page_id=6.

71. Martin Smith, *State of Strife: The Dynamics of Ethnic Conflict in Burma* (Singapore: ISEAS, 2007), 14.

72. Anthony R. Walker, "The Divisions Of The Lahu People," *Journal of Siam Society* 62, Part 2. (1974): 253–255.

73. Kyaw Yin Hlaing, "Reconsidering the Failure of the Burma Socialist Programme Party Government to Eradicate Internal Economic Impediments," *South East Asia Research* 11, no. 1, (March 2003): 9–10.

74. Author interviews, October 2016.

75. Holmes, *Burmese Domestic Policy*, 192.

76. Robert H. Taylor, *The State in Myanmar* (Singapore: NUS Press), 351.

77. David Steinberg, *Burma/Myanmar: What Everyone Needs to Know* (Oxford: Oxford University Press, 2009), 67.

78. Koichi Fujita, "Agriculture and Rural Development Strategy in Myanmar: With a Focus on the Rice Sector," *The Myanmar Economy: Its Past, Present and Prospects*, ed. Konosuke Odaka (New York: Springer, 2015), 106.

79. Taylor, *The State in Myanmar*, 378.

80. Holmes, *Burmese Domestic Policy*, 189.

81. Peter John Perry, *Myanmar (Burma) Since 1962: The Failure of Development* (London: Routledge, 2007), 91.

82. Raja Segaran Arumugam, "Burma: Political Unrest and Economic Stagnation," *Southeast Asian Affairs* ISEAS (1976), 173–174.

83. Donald M. Seekins, *Burma and Japan Since 1940: From "Co-Prosperity" to "Quiet Dialogue"* (Copenhagen: NIAS, 2007), 78.

84. Koichi Fujita, "Agriculture and Rural Development Strategy in Myanmar," *The Myanmar Economy: Its Past, Present and Prospects*, ed. Konosuke Odaka (Tokyo: Springer, 2016), 107.

85. E.A. Brown, "Burma Facts, 1989," *Christian Science Monitor*, May 8, 1989, http://www.csmonitor.com/1989/0518/d1tburm.html#.

86. Suh Dae Sook, *Kim Il Sung: The North Korean Leader* (New York: Columbia University Press, 1988), 219–220.

87. Kim Il Sung *Our People's Army Is an Army of the Working Class, an Army of the Revolution; Class and Political Education Should Be Continuously Strengthened* speech delivered to People's Army Unit Cadres above the Level of Deputy Regimental Commander for Political Affairs and the Officials of the Local Party and Government Organs, February 8, 1963.

88. Adrian Buzo, *The Guerilla Dynasty* (Boulder: Westview, 1999), 68.

89. *Korea in the 20th Century: 100 Significant Events* (Pyongyang: Foreign Languages Publishing House, 2002), 179.

90. *Ibid.*, 180.

91. Jo Song Hun조성훈, "Dae-nam Dobal Sa" 대남도발사 ["A history of provocations of South Korea'] (Paju, South Korea: Baeknyun Dongan, 2015), 23.

92. Buzo, *Guerilla Dynasty*, 58.

93. Cumings, Bruce, *The Origins of the Korean War, Volume II, The Roaring of the Cataract, 1947–1950* (Princeton: Princeton University Press, 1990), 473–474.

94. B.C. Koh, "Inter-Korean Relations: Seoul's Perspective," *Asian Survey* 20, no. 11 (November 1980): 1109–1110.

95. Kim Il Sung 김일성 *Jogugtongil wibeul silhyonhagi wihayo hyukmyung ryokryangeul baekbangeuro ganghwa haja* 조국통일위업을 실현하기 위하여 혁명력량을 백방으로 강화하자 ["Let's strengthen by all means the revolutionary power to realize the feat of the unification of the fatherland"] In *Nam Choson Hyokmyong kwa Joguk tongilae daehayeo* 남조선혁명과 조국통일에 대하여 ("On South Korea's revolution and unification of the fatherland") (Pyongyang: Choson Rodongdang Chulpansa, 1969), 264.

96. Mitchell Lerner, *"Mostly Propaganda in Nature:" Kim Il Sung, the Juche Ideology, and the Second Korean War* (Washington, D.C.: Woodrow Wilson International Center for Scholars, 2010), 1.

97. Daniel P. Bolger, *Scenes from an Unfinished War: Low-Intensity Conflict-Korea, 1966–1969* (Combat Studies Institute, U.S. Army Command and General Staff College,

1991), 18. Available at Korean War Veterans Association website, www.kwva.org.

98. Jo, *A History of Provocations*, 30.

99. Goh Yoo-hwan 고유환 *Rodong Sinmun tong hae bon bukhan byeonghwa* 로도신문을 통해 본 북한 변화 ["Seeing change in North Korea through Rodong Shinmin'] (Seoul: Sonin, 2006), 68, 69.

100. Kim Jong Il 김정일 *Widaehan Suryongui Dokchangjokin Gunsasasang-e Daehayo* 위대한 수령의 독창적인 군사사상에 대하여 ["On the creative military thought of the Great Leader'] (Pyongyang: Korean Worker's Party Publishing, 2002), 4.

101. *Ibid.*, 12.

102. *Ibid.*, 27–28.

103. Rodong Sinmun *Jajusongul Onghohaja* August 12, 1966 in Bukhan 1945–1988 (Seoul: Dong-a Ilbo, 1989), (로도신문 자주성을 옹호하자 in 북한 1945–1988, 서울 동아일보사, 1988), 244, 246.

104. "Signing of a Protocol Agreement for North Korea to Send a Number of Pilots to Fight the American Imperialists During the War of Destruction Against North Vietnam, September 30, 1966," *History and Public Policy Program Digital Archive, Vietnam Ministry of Defense Central Archives, Central Military Party Committee Collection*, File No. 433. Obtained and translated for NKIDP by Merle Pribbenow. http://digitalarchive.wilsoncenter.org/document/113926.

105. Bernd Schaefer, "Communist Vanguard Contest in East Asia during the 1960s and 1970s in Dynamics of the Cold War," in *Asia: Ideology, Identity, and Culture*, eds. Tuong Vu and Wasana Wongsurawat (New York: Macmillan, 2009), 117.

106. Bernd Schaefer, "North Korean 'Adventurism' and China's Long Shadow, 1966–72," Working Paper No. 44, Cold War International History Project (October 2004), 10–11.

107. Daniel P. Bolger, *Scenes from an Unfinished War: Low-Intensity Conflict-Korea, 1966–1969* (Combat Studies Institute, U.S. Army Command and General Staff College, 1991). Available at Korean War Veterans Association, www.kwva.org, 4–5.

108. Kathryn Weathersby, "Dependence and Mistrust: North Korea's Relations with Moscow and the Evolution of Juche," Working Paper 08–08, U.S.-Korea Institute, SAIS, August 2008, 13, 14.

109. "The July 4 South-North Joint Communique," ROK Ministry of Unification: Major Agreements, http://eng.unikorea.go.kr/content.do?cmsid=1889&mode=view&page=8&cid=32113.

110. Jae Kyu Park, "A Critique on 'The Democratic Confederal Republic of Koryo,'" *Journal of East and West Studies* 12:1 (1983): 13–25.

111. Manwoo Lee, "Korean Reconciliation: Combining Two Track Diplomacy," *Korean Reunification: New Perspectives and Approaches*, eds. Tae-Hwan Kwak, Chonghan Kim, and Hong Nack Kim (Seoul: Kyungnam University Press, 1984), 3.

112. Donald S. Zagoria and Young Kun Kim, "North Korea and the Major Powers," *Asian Survey* 15, no. 12 (December 1975), 1020.

113. William Chapman, "North Korean Leader's Son Blamed for Rangoon Bombing," *The Washington Post*, December 3, 1983, https://www.washingtonpost.com/archive/politics/1983/12/03/north-korean-leaders-son-blamed-for-rangoon-bombing/ddec34cc-9c12-4fc6-bf75-36057091aa4e/?utm_term=.137c1dc5d020.

114. Lee Man-woo, "Is North Korea Changing Course," *Asian Perspective* 9, no. 1 (Spring-Summer 1985): 3.

115. "State Department Cable 366371," Origin INR-10, Digital National Security Archive, December 28, 1983.

116. Yoon Tae-young, "Terrorism and Crisis Management: The Rangoon Bombing Incident of 1983," *Global Economic Review* 30:4 (2001), 115.

117. Young Whan Kihl, "North Korea in 1983: Transforming 'The Hermit Kingdom'?" *Asian Survey* 24, no. 1, A Survey of Asia in 1983, Part I (January 1984), 109.

118. Seo Bo-hyeok 서보혁, Lee Chang-hee 이창희 and Cha Sung-ju 차승주 *Orae Doen Mirae? 1970 Nyundae Bukhan-ae Jae Jomyeong* 오래된 미래? 1970년대 북한의 재조명 ["An old future? 1970s North Korea in a new light'] (Seoul: Seonin, 2015), 59–60.

119. Hamm Taik-young, *Arming the Two Koreas* (London: Routledge, 1999), 89.

120. Kang Myung-Kyu, "Industrial Management and Reforms in North Korea," eds. Stanislaw Gomulka, Yong-Chool Ha, and Cae-One Kim, *Economic Reforms in the Socialist World* (New York: M.E. Sharpe, 2002), 202.

121. "China-DPRK Bilateral Relations—Before 1990s of the 20th Century," Embassy of the People's Republic of China in the DPRK, http://kp.china-embassy.org/eng/zcgx/sbgx/90ndzq/.

122. Eric Yong-Joong Lee, "Development of North Korea's Legal Regime Governing Foreign Business Cooperation: A Revisit under the New Socialist Constitution of 1998," *Northwestern Journal of International Law & Business* 21, no. 1 (2000): 203.

123. This author has heard this excuse for

poor economic performance in North Korea many times.
124. Selig Harrison, "North Korea in Transition," *Korean Challenges and American Policy*, ed. Ilpyong J. Kim (New York: Paragon, 1991), 318.
125. Yonhap News Agency, *North Korea Handbook* (Armonk, NY: M.E. Sharpe, 2003), 320.
126. Ian Jeffries, *North Korea: A Guide to Economic and Political Developments* (London: Routledge, 2003), 447.
127. Stephan Haggard and Marcus Noland, *Famine in North Korea: Markets, Aid, and Reform* (New York: Columbia University Press, 2007), 11.

Chapter 3

1. Victoria Armour-Hileman, *Singing to the Dead: A Missioner's Life Among Refugees from Burma* (Athens: University of Georgia Press, 2002), 204.
2. Kim Kwang Il, et al., *Anecdotes of Kim Il Sung's Life* (Pyongyang: Foreign Languages Publishing House, n.d.), 65.
3. Nick Eberstadt, *The End of North Korea* (Washington, D.C.: AEI, 1999), 35.
4. Nicholas Eberstadt, "North Korea's 'Epic Economic Fail' in International Perspective," Asan Institute (November 2015): 8.
5. Marcus Noland, Sherman Robinson and Tao Wang, "Famine in North Korea: Causes and Cures, *Economic Development and Cultural Change* 49, no. 4 (July 2001): 746.
6. Stephen Haggard and Marcus Noland, *Famine in North Korea: Markets, Aid, and Reform* (New York: Columbia University Press, 2009), 76.
7. Walter C. Clemens, "North Korea's Quest for Nuclear Weapons: New Historical Evidence," *Journal of East Asian Studies* 10, no. 1 (2010): 129.
8. *Ibid.*, 131–133, 144–145.
9. Vladimir Orlov, "Russia's Nonproliferation Policy and the Situation in East Asia," *Nautilus*, March 5, 2001, http://nautilus.org/nuke-policy/russias-nonproliferation-policy-and-the-situation-in-east-asia-2/.
10. Wade L. Huntley, Mitsuru Kurosawa, and Kazumi Mizumoto, *Nuclear Disarmament in the Twenty-first Century* (Hiroshima: Hiroshima Peace Institute, 2004), 96.
11. "Disarmament Diplomacy with North Korea," *IISS Strategic Dossier* (2011): 5–7.
12. Victor Gilinsky, *Nuclear Blackmail: The 1994 U.S.-Democratic People's Republic of Korea Agreed Framework on North Korea's Nuclear Program* (Palo Alto: Hooever Institution, 1997): 6.
13. Michael Mazarr, *North Korea and the Bomb: A Case Study in Nonproliferation* (Basingstoke: Macmillan, 1997): 85–86.
14. *Ibid.*, 121.
15. Joel S. Wit, Daniel B. Poneman, and Robert L. Gallucci, *Going Critical: The First North Korean Nuclear Crisis* (Washington, D.C.: Brookings Institution, 2004), 92.
16. Mazarr, *North Korea and the Bomb*, 163.
17. Ramon Pacheco Pardo, *North Korea–U.S. Relations Under Kim Jong II: The Quest for Normalization?* (New York: Routledge, 2014), 26.
18. Bruce Cumings, *North Korea: Another Country* (New York: New, 2003), 64.
19. Gilensky, *Nuclear Blackmail*, 10–11.
20. Chuck Downs, *Over the Line: North Korea's Negotiating Strategy* (Washington, D.C.: AEI, 1999): 261.
21. Wit, et al., *Going Critical*, 252–53.
22. Mike Chinoy, *Meltdown* (New York: St. Martin's Griffin, 2008), 8.
23. Various conversations by author with U.S. officials, 2010.
24. Leon Sigal, "North Korea Is No Iraq: Pyongyang's Negotiating Strategy," *Arms Control Today* 32, no. 10 (December 2002): 11.
25. Mitchell B. Reiss and Robert L. Gallucci, "Dead to Rights," *Foreign Affairs* 84, no. 2 (March-April 2005): 142–145.
26. Michael Laufer, "A.Q. Khan Nuclear Chronology," Carnegie Endowment, September 7, 2005, http://carnegieendowment.org/2005/09/07/a.-q.-khan-nuclear-chronology.
27. Rebecca MacKinnon, "S. Korean Leader Sorry for Summit Scandal," CNN, February 14, 2003, http://edition.cnn.com/2003/WORLD/asiapcf/east/02/13/kim.scandal/.
28. Chinoy, *Meltdown*, 19.
29. "Secretary Albright's Visit to North Korea," Arms Control Association Press Conference, October 20, 2000, https://www.armscontrol.org/node/2513.
30. Chinoy, *Meltdown*, 29.
31. PBS *Frontline* Interview with Madeline Albright, 2003, http://www.pbs.org/wgbh/pages/frontline/shows/kim/interviews/albright.html.
32. Wendy Sherman, "Talking to the North Koreans," *New York Times*, March 7, 2001, http://www.nytimes.com/2001/03/07/opinion/talking-to-the-north-koreans.html.
33. Jo Seung-hoo, "U.S.-ROK Relations: The Political-Diplomatic Dimension," in *The*

United States and the Korean Peninsula in the 21st Century, eds. Tae-Hwan Kwak and Seung-Ho Joo (Aldershot: Ashgate, 2006), 41.

34. James A. Kelly, "Assistant Secretary of State for East Asian and Pacific Affairs Remarks at the Woodrow Wilson Center," U.S. Department of State, December 11, 2002, https://2001-2009.state.gov/p/eap/rls/rm/2002/15875.htm.

35. Leon Sigal, "Hand In Hand For Korea: A Peace Process and Denuclearization," *Asian Perspective* 32, no. 2 (2008), 10.

36. "Chronology of U.S.–North Korean Nuclear and Missile Diplomacy," Arms Control Association, https://www.armscontrol.org/factsheets/D.P.R.K.chron.

37. Kim Yong-ho, *North Korean Foreign Policy* (Plymouth: Lexington, 2011), 121.

38. "Joint Statement of the Fourth Round of the Six-Party Talks Beijing 19 September 2005," https://www.state.gov/p/eap/regional/c15455.htm.

39. Xin Chen, "Introduction: The Six Party Talks and Challenges to Multilateralism," in *Whither the Six-Party Talks*, ed. Yongjin Zhang (Auckland: New Zealand Asia Institute, 2006), 3.

40. Kim Yong-ho, *North Korean Foreign Policy*, 127–128.

41. Paul Kerr, "North Korea Talks Stalled by Banking Dispute," *Arms Control Today* 37, no. 3 (April 2007): 25–26.

42. Stephen Haggard and Marcus Noland, "North Korea in 2007: Shuffling in from the Cold," *Asian Survey* 48, no. 1 (2008): 108.

43. *Ibid.*, 109.

44. Glenn Kessler, "New Data Found On North Korea's Nuclear Capacity," *Washington Post*, June 21, 2008, http://www.washingtonpost.com/wp-dyn/content/article/2008/06/20/AR2008062002499.html.

45. Glenn Kessler, "Message to U.S. Preceded Nuclear Declaration by North Korea," *Washington Post*, July 2, 2008, http://www.washingtonpost.com/wp-dyn/content/article/2008/07/01/AR2008070102847.html.

46. Siegfried Hecker, "A Return Trip to North Korea's Yongbyon Nuclear Complex," NAPSNet Special Reports (November 22, 2010), http://nautilus.org/napsnet/napsnet-special-reports/a-return-trip-to-north-koreas-yongbyon-nuclear-complex/.

47. Geoffrey Lewis, "Progressive Pragmatism or Cynicism in Confronting North Korea?" 38 North, May 1, 2012, http://38north.org/2012/05/jlewis050212/.

48. Ankit Panda, "A Great Leap to Nowhere: Remembering the U.S.–North Korea 'Leap Day' Deal," *The Diplomat*, February 29, 2016, http://thediplomat.com/2016/02/a-great-leap-to-nowhere-remembering-the-us-north-korea-leap-day-deal/.

49. Scott Snyder, "U.S. Policy Toward North Korea," Council on Foreign Relations, January 23, 2013, http://www.cfr.org/north-korea/us-policy-toward-north-korea/p29962.

50. Mitchell B. Reiss, *North Korea: Getting to Maybe* in *Double Trouble: Iran and North Korea as Challenges to International Security* (Westport, CT: Praeger, 2008), 108.

51. "Bukhan Gaejeong Heonbeobseo haek Boyuguk Myeong Si" 북한 개정 헌법서 핵 보유국 명시 ["North Korea in revised consitution clearly claims it is a nuclear state"] *Hankyoreh* 한겨레, May 30, 2012, http://www.hani.co.kr/arti/politics/defense/535439.html.

52. John B. Haseman, "Burma in 1987: Change in the Air?" *Asian Survey* 28, no. 2, A Survey of Asia in 1987, Part II (February 1988): 224.

53. United Nations Committee for Development Policy Development Policy and Analysis Division Department of Economic and Social Affairs, "List of Least Developed Countries (as of May 2016)," http://www.un.org/en/development/desa/policy/cdp/ldc/ldc_list.pdf.

54. Stefan Colligen, "Human Rights and Economy in Burma," in *Burma: Political Economy Under Military Rule*, ed. Robert Taylor (London: Hurst, 2001), 89.

55. Moe Maka, "The Death of a Student—Ko Phone Maw—March 13th 1988 in Rangoon, Burma," Moe Maka, April 10, 2011, http://eng.moemaka.net/2011/04/the-death-of-a-student-ko-phone-maw-march-13th-1988-in-rangoon-burma/.

56. Aung Zaw, *The Face of Resistance: Aung San Suu Kyi and Burma's Fight for Freedom* (Chiang Mai: Silkworm, 2013), 4.

57. Wa Lone, "Red Bridge Burns Bright for Student Activists," *Myanmar Times*, April 8, 2014, http://www.mmtimes.com/index.php/national-news/10110-red-bridge-burns-bright-for-student-activists.html.

58. Htun Khaing, "Shedding New Light on 88," *Frontier Myanmar*, August 8, 2016, http://frontiermyanmar.net/en/shedding-new-light-on-88.

59. Josef Silverstein, "Civil War and Rebellion in Burma," *Journal of Southeast Asian Studies* 21, no. 1 (March 1990): 124.

60. *Ibid.*

61. Yeni, "Twenty Years of Marking Time," *The Irrawaddy*, August, 2008, http://www2.irrawaddy.com/article.php?art_id=13772.

62. Seth Mydans, "Uprising in Burma: The Old Regime Under Siege," *The New York*

Times, August 12, 1988, http://www.nytimes.com/1988/08/12/world/uprising-in-burma-the-old-regime-under-siege.html.
 63. Burma Watcher, "Burma in 1988: There Came a Whirlwind," *Asian Survey* 29, no. 2, A Survey of Asia in 1988, Part II (February 1989): 177.
 64. Author interview, December 2016.
 65. *Ibid.*
 66. *Ibid.*
 67. A full English text of Aung San Suu Kyi's speech can be found archived at burmalibrary.org/docs3/Shwedagon-ocr.doc
 68. *Human Rights in Burma (Myanmar)*, (New York: Human Rights Watch, 1990), 3.
 69. Kyaw Zwa Moe "From the Archive: The Heroic Medics of the 8888 Uprising," *The Irrawaddy*, September 19, 2016.
 70. Watcher, "Burma in 1988," 179.
 71. Watcher, "Burma in 1988," 180
 72. James F. Guyot and John Badgley, "Myanmar in 1989: Tatmadaw V," *Asian Survey* 30, no. 2, A Survey of Asia in 1989, Part II (February 1990): 189.
 73. Jesper Bengtsson, *Aung San Suu Kyi: A Biography* (Washington, D.C.: Potomac, 2012), 86–88.
 74. Lowell Dittmer, *Burma or Myanmar? The Struggle for National Identity* (New York: World Scientific, 2010), 11.
 75. Bengtsson, *Aung San Suu Kyi*, 93.
 76. Steven Erlanger, "Burmese Ban Top Opposition Candidate," *The New York Times*, January 18, 1990, http://www.nytimes.com/1990/01/18/world/burmese-ban-top-opposition-candidate.html.
 77. James F. Guyot, "1990: The Unconsummated Election," *Asian Survey* 31, no. 2, A Survey of Asia in 1990, Part II (February 1991): 205, 209.
 78. San Yamin Aung, "NLD Candidates Await Latest Appeal on Coco Islands Access," *The Irrawaddy*, October 12, 2015, http://www.irrawaddy.com/election/news/nld-candidates-await-latest-appeal-on-coco-islands-access.
 79. Times Staff and Wire Reports, "World in Brief: Myanmar: Opposition Gains, Standoff Continues," *Los Angeles Times*, May 31, 1990, http://articles.latimes.com/1990–05–31/news/mn-937_1_standoff-continues.
 80. Bertil Lintner, "Democracy as Practiced by the Burmese Generals: Myanmar: Today's Elections, First in 28 Years, Won't Empower an Oppressed People—But They Will Fatten the Treasury by Bringing Back Foreign Investors," *Los Angeles Times*, May 27, 1990, http://articles.latimes.com/1990–05–27/opinion/op-103_1_general-elections.

 81. Guyot, *1990*, 209–211.
 82. Nay Htun Naing, "When the Promise of 1990 Election Was Nullified," *Eleven Media*, May 11, 2015, http://www.elevenmyanmar.com/opinion/when-promise-1990-election-was-nullified.
 83. Wai Moe, "The Opposition's Generation Gap," *The Irrawaddy*, June 25, 2004, http://www2.irrawaddy.com/opinion_story.php?art_id=3586.
 84. Kyaw Yin Hlaing, "Aung San Suu Kyi of Myanmar: A Review of the Lady's Biographies," *Contemporary Southeast Asia* 29, no. 2 (2007): 362, 374.
 85. Bertil Lintner, *Aung San Suu Kyi and Burma's Struggle for Democracy* (Chiang Mai: Silkworm, 2011), 99.
 86. *Ibid.*, 78.
 87. Anthony Spaeth, "Setting Free 'the Lady,'" *Time*, July 24, 1995, http://content.time.com/time/magazine/article/0,9171,983201,00.html.
 88. Bertil Linter, "Access to Information: The Case of Burma," *Asia Pacific Media Series* (1997): 7, http://www.asiapacificms.com/papers/pdf/burma_access_to_information.pdf.
 89. "Committee Representing the People's Parliament [CRPP]," *The Irrawaddy*, January 1, 2003, http://www2.irrawaddy.com/research_show.php?art_id=448.
 90. Kyaw Yin Hlaing, "Myanmar in 2003: Frustration and Despair?" *Asian Survey* 44, no. 1 (January/February 2004): 88.
 91. *Preliminary Report of The Ad Hoc Commission on Depayin Massacre (Burma)*, July 4, 2003.
 92. Paul Harris, "An Opinion on the Depayin Massacre," *Article 2*, December 7, 2003, http://alrc.asia/article2/2003/12/an-opinion-on-the-depayin-massacre/.
 93. "Burma Leaders Double Fuel Prices," *BBC*, August 15, 2007, http://news.bbc.co.uk/2/hi/asia-pacific/6947251.stm.
 94. David Steinberg, "Globalization, Dissent, and Orthodoxy: Burma/Myanmar and the Saffron Revolution," *Georgetown Journal of International Affairs* 9, no. 2 (Summer/Fall 2008): 54.
 95. "Q&A: Protests in Burma," BBC, October 2, 2007, http://news.bbc.co.uk/2/hi/asia-pacific/7010202.stm.
 96. Mridul Chowdhury, "The Role of the Internet in Burma's Saffron Revolution," *Internet & Democracy Case Study Series: Berkman Center Research Publication* no. 2008–08 (September 2008): 4.
 97. Benedict Rogers, *Than Shwe: Unmasking Burma's Tyrant* (Chiang Mai: Silkworm, 2010), 177–178.

98. Author interview, May 2016.
99. Saw Yan Naing, "Information on Dead, Arrested, Missing is Hard to Find," *The Irrawaddy*, October 2, 2007, http://www2.irrawaddy.com/article.php?art_id=8850&Submit=Submit.
100. Stephen McCarthy, "Overturning the Alms Bowl: The Price of Survival and the Consequences for Political Legitimacy in Burma," *Australian Journal of International Affairs* 62, no. 3 (2008): 301–303.
101. Andrew Selth, "Even Paranoids Have Enemies: Cyclone Nargis and Myanmar's Fears of Invasion," *Contemporary Southeast Asia* 30, no. 3 (December 2008), 380–382.
102. Samuel Blythe, "Myanmar's Junta Fears U.S. Invasion," *Asia Times Online*, April 28, 2006, http://www.atimes.com/atimes/Southeast_Asia/HD28Ae03.html.
103. Donald M. Seekins, "Myanmar in 2008: Hardship, Compounded," *Asian Survey* 49, no. 1 (January/February 2009): 167–168.
104. "First U.S. Aid Plane Lands in Burma," BBC, May 12, 2008, http://news.bbc.co.uk/2/hi/asia-pacific/7395364.stm.
105. "Response to Cyclone in Myanmar 'Unacceptably Slow'—Ban Ki-Moon," U.N. News Centre, May 12, 2008 http://www.un.org/apps/news/story.asp?NewsID=26634#.WEjEzWR96L1.
106. Ian MacKinnon, "Burma to Let in All Cyclone Nargis Aid Workers," *The Guardian*, May 23, 2008, https://www.theguardian.com/world/2008/may/23/cyclonenargis.burma.
107. Emma Larkin, *No Bad News for the King* (New York: Penguin, 2011): 29–31.
108. Author interview, August 2016.
109. Tin Maung Maung Than, "Myanmar in 2008: Weathering the Storm," *Southeast Asian Affairs* (2009): 204.
110. "Burma: Chronology of Aung San Suu Kyi's Detention," *Human Rights Watch*, November 13, 2010, https://www.hrw.org/news/2010/11/13/burma-chronology-aung-san-suu-kyis-detention.

Chapter 4

1. Robert Cox, "Gramsci, Hegemony, and International Relations: An Essay in Method," *Millennium: Journal of International Studies* 12, no. 2 (1983): 128.
2. Benedict Anderson, *Imagined Communities: Reflections on the Origin and Spread of Nationalism*, rev. and extended. ed. (London: Verso, 1991), 6–7.
3. Josef Silverstein, "The Evolution and Salience of Burma's National Political Culture," in *Burma: Prospects for a Democratic Future*, ed. Robert I. Rotberg (Washington, D.C., and Cambridge, MA: Brookings Institution and World Peace Foundation, 1998), 14.
4. Nicholas Tarling, *The Cambridge History of Southeast Asia: Volume 1, from Early Times to c. 1800* (Cambridge: Cambridge University Press, 1993), 267.
5. Donald Baker, "Rhetoric, Ritual, and Political Legitimacy: Justifying Yi Seonggye's Ascension to the Throne," *Korea Journal* 53, no. 4 (Winter 2013), 141–167.
6. Martin Smith, *Burma: Insurgency and the Politics of Ethnicity* (London: Zed, 1991), 180.
7. Richard Allen, "Recent Developments in Burma—Address to the Royal Central Asian Society on July 22, 1964," *Journal of the Royal Central Asian Society*, 52:1, 6–19 (1965): 11.
8. Juliane Schober, "Colonial Knowledge and Buddhist Education in Burma," in *Buddhism, Power and Political Order*, ed. Ian Harris (London: Routledge, 2007), 66.
9. Author interview, March 2015.
10. Robert H. Taylor, *General Ne Win: A Political Biography* (Singapore: ISEAS, 2015), 260–261.
11. Ibid., 262.
12. Revolutionary Council, *Burmese Way to Socialism*, http://www.ibiblio.org/obl/docs/The_Burmese_Way_to_Socialism.htm.
13. Author interview, May, 2016
14. Mya Maung, *The Burma Road to Poverty* (New York: Praeger, 1991), 120, 121.
15. Ibid., 126–127.
16. David Steinberg, *Burma/Myanmar: What Everyone Needs to Know* (Oxford: Oxford University Press, 2009), 66.
17. Allen. "Recent Developments in Burma," 12.
18. Win Min, "Burma: A Historic Force, Forcefully Met," in *Student Activism in Asia: Between Protest and Powerlessness*, eds. Meredith L. Weiss and Edward Aspinall (Minneapolis: University of Minnesota Press, 2012), 181–184.
19. Donald M. Seekins, *State and Society in Modern Rangoon* (London: Routledge, 2011), 127–129
20. Mary P. Callahan, *Making Enemies: War and State Building in Burma* (Ithaca: Cornell University Press, 2003), 208.
21. Anonymous audience member at May 15–17, 2015, Myanmar-United States Friendship Association (MUSFA) Diversity Conference, Mandalay.

22. *Who Is the Drug King of the Golden Triangle?* Directed by Ludo Poppe (UK: Journeyman Pictures, 1994), https://www.youtube.com/watch?v=ji2S_cGFPqc.
23. Rewata Dhamma, *Buddhism, Human Rights and Justice In Burma* (speech, Church Center for the UN, New York, November 1989), http://www.burmalibrary.org/docs08/Rewata_Dhamma-Buddhism_Human_Rights_and_Justice_in_Burma.pdf.
24. Kim Il Sung, *On eliminating dogmatism and formalism and establishing Juche in ideological work* (Pyongyang: Foreign Languages Publishing House, 1973), 1. Available online at https://www.marxists.org/archive/kim-il-sung/1955/12/28.htm.
25. Erik Van Ree, "The Limits of Juche: North Korea's Dependence on Soviet Industrial Aid, 1953–76," *Journal of Communist Studies* 5:1 (1989), 52.
26. Andrei Lankov, *Crisis in North Korea: The Failure of De-Stalinization, 1956* (Honolulu: University of Hawaii Press, 2004), 41.
27. Kim Seok Hyang *The Juche Ideology of North Korea: Sociopolitical Roots of Ideological Change* (Athens: University of Georgia Press, 1993), 28.
28. Jae-Cheon Lim, *Kim Jong-il's Leadership of North Korea* (London: Routledge, 2008), 90–91.
29. Kim Jong Il, *Socialism Is a Science* (Pyongyang, 1994). Available at http://www.korea-dpr.info/lib/106.pdf.
30. Kim Jong Il, *On the Juche Idea* (Pyongyang: Pyongyang Foreign Languages Publishing House, 1982), 75.
31. Pong Paik, *Kim Il Sung: Premier of the Democratic People's Republic of Korea* (New York: Guardian, 1970), 590.
32. *Ibid.*, 3
33. Jae-Jung Suh, "Making Sense of North Korea: Juche as an Institution," in *Origins of North Korea's Juche Colonialism, War, and Development*, eds. Jae-Jung Suh and Chaejong So (Lanham, MD: Rowman & Littlefield, 2103), 17.
34. See, for example, the DPRK's third and fourth nuclear tests in 2013 and 2016, Pyongyang declaring a 200-mile economic and fishing exclusion zone in the Yellow Sea in 1977 or Pyongyang's purge of pro-Chinese officials in 1956.
35. From *The Propaganda Game*, directed by Alvaro Longoria (documentary, Spain, 2015).
36. In conversation, September, 2012. This individual appeared a little more cynical by 2017, for what it's worth.
37. "Juche Iron Production System Established," KCNA, October 7, 2010.
38. Kim Seok Hyang, *The Juche ideology of North Korea*, 120.
39. This author has seen/heard all of these.
40. "Jung-Guk Nae Wa Ju-Min 100 Myeong-E-Ge Gyeong-Je Sa-Jeong-P-Ssa-Hoe Hyeon-Si-Re"中국 내 北 주민 100명에게 경제 사정.사회 현실에 대해 인터뷰했더…. ["We interviewed 100 northerners living in China about the economic situation and current society"], *Choson Ilbo* 朝鮮日報July 8, 2014, http://thestory.chosun.com/site/data/html_dir/2014/07/08/2014070800866.html.
41. Christopher Green, "Chosun Ilbo Surveys 100 North Koreans," SinoNK, July 18, 2014, http://sinonk.com/2014/07/28/chosun-ilbo-surveys-100-north-koreans/.
42. Choe Won-gi최 원 기 "tal-ppuk-jjadeul, e-bu-kan bong-geon-si-dae-ro hu-toe-e" 탈북자들, "북한 봉건시대로 후퇴"["Defectors: North Korea has Regressed to the Feudal Era"] July 8, 2010, VOA, http://www.voakorea.com/content/north-korea-98012094/1334887.html.
43. In conversation, June 2011.
44. Mina Yoon, "Who do North Koreans Think Started the Korean War?" NKNews, January 8, 2014, https://www.nknews.org/2014/01/who-do-north-koreans-think-started-the-korean-war/.
45. "North Korea Human Rights Conference," Heritage Foundation, April 2015, https://www.youtube.com/watch?v=C-2HbYHFjf4.
46. Jeyup S. Kwaak, "North Korean Escapees Say They Perceive Solid Support for Dictator," *Wall Street Journal*, August 26, 2015, http://www.wsj.com/articles/north-korean-escapees-report-solid-support-for-dictator-kim-1440568866.
47. Burma Watcher, "Burma in 1988: There Came a Whirlwind," *Asian Survey* 29, no. 2, A Survey of Asia in 1988: Part II (February 1989), 174- 180.
48. Christina Fink, *Living Silence: Burma Under Military Rule* (London: Zed, 2001), 63.

Chapter 5

1. Christopher Hitchens, "Worse Than 1984," *Slate*, May 2, 2005, http://www.slate.com/articles/news_and_politics/fighting_words/2005/05/worse_than_1984.html.
2. *The Propaganda Game*, directed by Álvaro Longoria (documentary, Spain, 2015).
3. David I. Steinberg, *Burma: The State*

of Myanmar (Washington, D.C.: Georgetown University Press, 2001), 26.

4. Seol Song Ah, "In Russia, North Korean Laborers Risk Death for a Chance to Earn Cash," *Daily NK*, June 27, 2016, http://www.dailynk.com/english/read.php?cataId=nk02500&num=14010.

5. "Profile of Internal Displacement: Myanmar," Norwegian Refugee Council/Global IDP Project, 2005; "The Rohingya Crisis," European Civil and Humanitarian Aid Operations Report, 2017, http://ec.europa.eu/echo/files/aid/countries/factsheets/rohingya_en.pdf; "Myanmar: IDP Sites in Kachin and Northern Shan States (September 2017)," Reliefweb Map, October 2017 https://reliefweb.int/map/myanmar/myanmar-idp-sites-kachin-and-northern-shan-states-september-2017.

6. Marc Simms, "United Wa State Army," *Human Security Centre, Security and Defence*, issue 3, no. 7 (2014).

7. "Replacing Opium in Kokang and Wa Special Regions, Shan State, Myanmar," The Joint Kokang-Wa Humanitarian Needs Assessment Team, 2003, 7–9.

8. Andrei Lankov, *North of the DMZ* (Jefferson, NC: McFarland, 2007), 181–184.

9. Author interview, March 2017.

10. Yonhap News Agency, *North Korea Handbook* (London: M.E. Sharpe, 2003), 410.

11. Article 157, 1974 Constitution of the Socialist Republic of Burma.

12. Jennifer Leehey, "Message in a Bottle: A Gallery of Social/Political Cartoons from Burma," *Southeast Asian Journal of Social Science* 25, no. 1 (1997): 152–153.

13. Bertil Linter, "Access to Information: The Case of Burma," *Asia Pacific Media Series* (1997): 7–8, http://www.asiapacificms.com/papers/pdf/burma_access_to_information.pdf.

14. "Attacks on the Press 2009: Burma," Committee to Protect Journalists, 2009, https://www.cpj.org/2010/02/attacks-on-the-press-2009-burma.php.

15. Htet Aung Kyaw, "No Press Freedoms Yet," *The Irrawaddy*, December 16, 2002, http://www2.irrawaddy.com/print_article.php?art_id=2174.

16. A. Lin Neumann, "Special Report: Burma Under Pressure," Committee to Protect Journalists, 2002, https://cpj.org/reports/2002/02/burma-feb02.php.

17. Leheey, "Message in a Bottle," 154.

18. Saw Yan Naing, "'Sandwich Reporting' Keeps the Censors Guessing," *The Irrawaddy*, August 12, 2010, http://www.burmanet.org/news/2010/08/12/irrawaddy-sandwich-reporting-keeps-the-censors-guessing-%E2%80%93-saw-yan-naing/.

19. Helen Pidd, "Burma Ends Advance Press Censorship," *The Guardian*, August 20, 2012, http://www.theguardian.com/world/2012/aug/20/burma-ends-advance-press-censorship.

20. Andray Abrahamian, "Article 66(d): A Menace to Myanmar's Democracy," *The Lowy Interpreter*, August 1, 2017, https://www.lowyinstitute.org/the-interpreter/article-66d-menace-myanmar-s-democracy.

21. Min Zin, "Keeping the Pulse of Burmese Airwaves," *The Irrawaddy*, November 2002, http://www2.irrawaddy.com/article.php?art_id=2784.

22. Author interview, May 2015.

23. Stephan Haggard and Marcus Noland, *Famine in North Korea: Markets, Aid, and Reform* (New York: Columbia University Press, 2007), 280.

24. Koh Jung-Sik, *Is North Korea Really Changing?* (Seoul: Institute for Unification Education, 2014), 43.

25. Kim Seong Hwan, "30–40% of NK Thought to be Tuning into Pirate Radio: How Do We Reach More?" *Daily NK*, September 14, 2015, http://www.dailynk.com/english/read.php?cataId=nk00100&num=13460.

26. Lankov, *North of the DMZ*, 59.

27. Author interview, March, 2016

28. Author interviews, March, 2016

29. "Man Arrested for Allegedly Contacting Foreign Radio Stations," BBC Monitoring Media [London] Burma, February 15, 2002.

30. "Analysis: New Media Challenges Old-Style Repression in Burma," BBC Monitoring Media [London], October 9, 2007.

31. Author interview, March 2016.

32. Shelly Culbertson, "Foreign Radio Stations Most Popular Source of News in Myanmar," Associated Press, July 31, 2003, http://jacksonville.com/tu-online/apnews/stories/073103/D7SK9E000.html.

33. "Myo Thein on BBC Burmese Service's Impact on Burma," BBC TV, September 2, 2010. https://www.youtube.com/watch?v=3Ty7rOu6PQo.

34. "The Internet in Burma (1998–2009)," *Mizzima News*, December 24, 2009.

35. Email interview with Martyn Williams, editor of *North Korea Tech*, April 2016.

36. Discussion with author, 2015.

37. Kojo Boakye, Nigel Scott, and Claire Smyth, "Mobiles for Development," UNICEF (October 2010): 21, http://www.unicef.org/cbsc/files/Mobiles4DeReport.pdf.

38. Htoo Thant, "Mobile Penetration Reaches Half the Country," *Myanmar Times*,

June 2, 2015, http://www.mmtimes.com/index.php/business/technology/14815-mobile-penetration-reaches-half-the-country.html.

39. Catherine Trautwein, "Myanmar Named Fourth-Fastest-Growing Mobile Market in the World by Ericsson," *Myanmar Times*, November 20, 2015, http://www.mmtimes.com/index.php/business/technology/17727-myanmar-named-fourth-fastest-growing-mobile-market-in-the-world-by-ericsson.html.

40. James Pearson, "North Korea's Black Market Becoming the New Normal," Reuters, October 29, 2015, http://www.reuters.com/article/us-northkorea-change-insight-idUSKCN0SN00320151029.

41. Interview with author, January 2016.

42. Pearson, "North Korea's Black Market."

43. Emma Larkin, *No Bad News for the King* (London: Penguin, 2010), 52–53.

44. Interview with author, October 2016.

45. Renaud Egreteau and Larry Jagan, *Soldiers and Diplomacy in Burma* (Singapore: Singapore National University Press, 2013), 198.

46. Andrew Selth, *Burma's Intelligence Apparatus* (Canberra: ANU Press, 1997): 19.

47. Hla Oo, "Martyrs' Mausoleum Bombing Video (Rangoon—1983)," June 2011, http://hlaoo1980.blogspot.com/2011/06/martyrs-mausoleum-bombing-video-rangoon.html.

48. Interview with author, March 2017.

49. Robert Collins, *Pyongyang Republic* (Washington, D.C.: HRNK, 2016): 120.

50. Ken E. Gause, *Coercion, Control, Surveillance, and Punishment* (Washington, D.C.: HRNK, 2012): 18.

51. Email interview with Curtis Melvin, March 2017

52. David Hawk, *Hidden Gulag* (Washington, D.C.: HRNK, 2012): 17.

53. *Ibid.*, 36.

54. Gause, *Coercion, Control, Surveillance, and Punishment*, 58.

55. Jang Jin-sung, *Dear Leader* (New York: Simon & Schuster, 2013): 315–317.

56. Jae Young Kim, "Why Did We Never Complain? We Didn't Even Know How To," *NK News*, November 5, 2012, https://www.nknews.org/2012/11/why-did-we-never-complain-some-of-us-didnt-even-know-how-to/.

57. Ji-Min Kang, "Neighborhood Watch: Inside North Korea's Secret Police System," *NK News*, February 26, 2014, https://www.nknews.org/2014/02/neighborhood-watch-inside-north-koreas-secret-service-system/.

58. Lee Seok Young, "Pyongyang Seeing Tighter Inspections," *Daily NK*, August 24, 2011, http://www.dailynk.com/english/read.php?cataId=nk01500&num=8094.

59. Andrei Lankov, *The Real North Korea: Life and Politics in the Failed Stalinist Utopia* (Oxford: Oxford University Press, 2013): 50.

60. Matthew Bugher, "Midnight Intrusions," Fortify Rights (March 2015), 17, http://www.fortifyrights.org/downloads/FR_Midnight_Intrusions_March_2015.pdf.

61. Bugher, "Midnight Intrusions."

62. Author interview with political activist, March 2016.

63. There are some strategic flaws in the report, assuming the authors' strategy is to encourage systemic change. The most serious flaw was naming Kim Jong Un personally responsible and recommending sending criminals to the International Criminal Court. This only serves to reinforce to the next generation of elites that any opening to the outside world and reform is too risky.

64. Report of the commission of inquiry on human rights in the Democratic People's Republic of Korea, 2014, Section 4, Clause 259, 7.

65. Report of the commission of inquiry on human rights in the Democratic People's Republic of Korea, 2014, 7–8.

66. Report of the commission of inquiry on human rights in the Democratic People's Republic of Korea, 2014, Section 4, Clause 239, 7.

67. Robert Taylor, *General Ne Win: A Political Biography* (Singapore: ISEAS, 2015): 15.

68. Hla Oo, "1974 U Thant Uprising—A First Hand Account," *New Mandala*, July 23, 2008, http://asiapacific.anu.edu.au/newmandala/2008/07/23/1974-u-thant-uprising-a-first-hand-account/.

69. Ei Thae Thae Naing, "Yangon University Set to Reopen," *Myanmar Times*, July 31, 2013, http://www.mmtimes.com/index.php/national-news/7654-yangon-university-set-to-reopen.html.

70. Elliott Prasse-Freeman, "Power, Civil Society, and an Inchoate Politics of the Daily in Burma/Myanmar," *The Journal of Asian Studies* 71, no. 2 (2012): 382.

71. *Ibid.*, 384.

72. "Democratic Voice of Burma 88 Students' Open Heart Campaign Ends," *BurmaNet News*, March 5, 2007, http://www.burmanet.org/news/2007/03/05/democratic-voice-of-burma-88-students%E2%80%99-open-heart-campaign-ends/.

73. Daniel Tudor and James Pearson, *North*

Korea Confidential (Singapore: Tuttle, 2015): 112.
74. Interview with Bo Kyi, *LinkAsia*, Link TV, March 16, 2012, https://www.youtube.com/watch?v=MrXEvN1N7mc.
75. Larkin, *No Bad News for the King*, 2010.
76. Author interview, June 2016.
77. Ma Thanegi, *Nor Iron Bars a Cage* (Hong Kong: ThingsAsian, 2013), 54.
78. *Ibid.*, 63.
79. Swe Win, "Exclusive—Abuse and Corruption Exposed in Myanmar's Prison Labour Camps," Reuters, September 1, 2016, http://uk.reuters.com/article/uk-myanmar-prisons-idUKKCN1175FQ.
80. Renaud Egreteau and Larry Jagan, *Soldiers and Diplomacy in Burma* (Singapore: National University of Singapore Press, 2013): 230.
81. Andrei Lankov, "Mathematics—a la North Korea," *Korea Times*, August 8, 2011, http://www.koreatimes.co.kr/www/news/nation/2011/08/113_93651.html.
82. *Under the Sun*, directed by Vitaly Mansky (documentary, Russia, 2015).
83. Interview with school teacher Daw Nyu Nyu, July 2016.
84. Interview, July 2016.
85. Kim Yoo-sung, "College Life in North Korea: It's Like the Military," *NK News*, February 10, 2016, https://www.nknews.org/2016/02/college-life-in-north-korea-its-like-the-military/.
86. Korea and the World Podcast, Episode 56—Hyeonseo Lee, http://www.koreaandtheworld.org/.
87. The 2009 currency reform was one such occasion.

Chapter 6

1. Gary Clyde Hufbauer, Jeffrey J. Schott, Kimberly Ann Elliott, and Barbara Oegg, *Economic Sanctions Reconsidered* (Washington, D.C.: Peterson Institute for International Economics, 2007), 62.
2. *Ibid.*, 13.
3. *Ibid.*, 5.
4. *Ibid.*, 6.
5. Richard Haass, *Economic Sanctions and American Diplomacy* (New York: Council on Foreign Relations, 1998), 206.
6. Daniel W. Drezner, "Bargaining, Enforcement, and Multilateral Sanctions: When Is Cooperation Counterproductive?" *International Organization* 54, 1 (2000): 75.
7. *Ibid.*, 73.
8. *Ibid.*, 98.

9. Nikolay Marinov, "Do Economic Sanctions Destabilize Country Leaders?" *American Journal of Political Science* 49, no. 3 (2005): 566.
10. Hufbauer, et al., *Economic Sanctions Reconsidered*, 159.
11. Sanctions can and do occur between allies. Indeed, the threat of sanctions loomed over U.S.-South Korea relations in the early 1970s, as Seoul pursued both nuclear weapons and passed an undemocratic constitution.
12. See Daniel W. Drezner, *The Sanctions Paradox: Economic Statecraft and International Relations* (Cambridge: Cambridge University Press, 1999).
13. Emma Ashford, "Not-So-Smart Sanctions: The Failure of Western Restrictions Against Russia," *Foreign Affairs*, January/February 2016, 116.
14. Sylvanus Kwaku Afesorgbor and Renuka Mahadevan, "The Impact of Economic Sanctions on Income Inequality of Target States," *World Development* 83 (July 2016).
15. Robert W. McGee, "The Ethics of Economic Sanctions," *Economic Affairs* 23, no. 4 (2003), 43.
16. David Steinberg, "Burma-Myanmar: The U.S.–Burmese Relationship and Its Vicissitudes," in *Short of the Goal: U.S. Policy and Poorly Performing States*, eds. Nancy Birdsall, Milan Vaishnav, and Robert L. Ayres (Washington, D.C.: Center for Global Development, 2006), 225.
17. Michael F. Martin, "U.S. Sanctions on Burma," *Congressional Research Service Report* (2012): 12.
18. The GSP is a non-reciprocal, duty-free tariff plan for certain products imported from designated developing countries. The decision to grant GSP is dependent on several factors, including maintaining certain standards for workers' rights, reducing or eliminating barriers to trade in services and protecting intellectual property rights. Not having a communist government helps, also.
19. Steven Erlanger, "Clinton Approves New U.S. Sanctions Against Burmese," *New York Times*, April 22, 1997, http://www.nytimes.com/1997/04/22/world/clinton-approves-new-us-sanctions-against-burmese.html.
20. *Ibid.*
21. "Treasury Department Designates Burma and Two Burmese Banks to Be of 'Primary Money Laundering Concern' and Announces Proposed Countermeasures Under Section 311 of the USA PATRIOT Act," *Department of the Treasury Office of Public Affairs* (2003), 3, https://www.treasury.gov/

resource-center/terrorist-illicit-finance/Terrorist-Finance-Tracking/Documents/js1014attachment.pdf.

22. "Jade: Myanmar's 'Big State Secret,'" *Global Witness Report* (October 2016): 6.

23. *Ibid.*, 38.

24. "Singapore Denies Money Laundering Myanmar Leaders: TV," Reuters, October 5, 2007.

25. "Total Impact: The Human Rights, Environmental, and Financial Impacts of Total and Chevron's Yadana Gas Project in Military-Ruled Burma September," Earth Rights International (2009), 43.

26. "Myanmar-Singapore Bilateral Trade Reaches $1.86 Bln," *Xinhua*, June 30, 2010, http://en.people.cn/90001/90778/90858/90863/7047513.html.

27. Mohammed Ahmedullah, "Not-So-Selective Sanctions," *Bulletin of the Atomic Scientists* (November/December 2003), 12.

28. Kudo Toshihiro, "The Impact of U.S. Sanctions on the Myanmar Garment Industry," *Asian Survey* 48, Issue 6 (2008): 1008.

29. *Ibid.*, 1009.

30. *Ibid.*, 1017.

31. Thihan Myo Nyun, "Feeling Good or Doing Good: Inefficacy of the U.S. Unilateral Sanctions Against the Military Government of Burma/Myanmar," *Washington University Global Studies Law Review* 7, Issue 3 (2008): 484.

32. *Ibid.*, 490.

33. David I. Steinberg, "Myanmar and the United States, Closing and Opening Doors: An Idiosyncratic Analysis," *Social Research* 82, no. 2 (2015), 433.

34. Bertil Lintner, "China Behind Myanmar's Course Shift," *Asia Times*, October 19, 2011, http://www.atimes.com/atimes/Southeast_Asia/MJ19Ae03.html.

35. "Myanmar Trade, Exports and Imports," *Economy Watch*, March 17, 2010, http://www.economywatch.com/world_economy/myanmar/export-import.html.

36. Thihan, *Feeling Good or Doing Good*, 490.

37. Author interview, June, 2016.

38. Author interview, March, 2016.

39. Toshihiro Kudo, "Myanmar and Japan: How Close Friends Became Estranged," Institute of Developing Economies, IDE Discussion Paper no. 118 (August 2007), 13.

40. Ian Storey, "Burma's Relations with China: Neither Puppet nor Pawn," *Jamestown Foundation China Brief* 7, Issue: 3 (2007), https://jamestown.org/program/burmas-relations-with-china-neither-puppet-nor-pawn-4/.

41. Maung Aung Myoe, *In the Name of Pauk-Phaw: Myanmar's China Policy Since 1948* (Singapore: ISEAS, 2010),153, 158.

42. Grant Peck, "Arms Easy to Buy for Myanmar Junta," Associated Press, October 12, 2007, http://www.washingtonpost.com/wp-dyn/content/article/2007/10/12/AR2007101201310_pf.html.

43. Stockholm International Peace Research Institute Trade Registers, http://armstrade.sipri.org/armstrade/page/trade_register.php.

44. Tin Maung Maung Than, *Myanmar and China: A Special Relationship?* In ISEAS Southeast Asian Affairs (Singapore: ISEAS, 2003), 204.

45. *Ibid.*

46. Kevin Woods, "China in Burma: A Multi-Scalar Political Economy Analysis," in *Chinese Encounters in Southeast Asia*, eds. Pál Nyíri and Danielle Tan (Seattle: University of Washington Press, 2016), 237.

47. Narayanan Ganesan, "Myanmar-China Relations: Interlocking Interests but Independent Output," *Japanese Journal of Political Science* 12, no. 1 (2011): 96.

48. David I. Steinberg, "Aung San Suu Kyi's Sanctions Conundrum," *Nikkei Asian Review*, April 25, 2016, http://asia.nikkei.com/Viewpoints/Viewpoints/David-I.-Steinberg-Aung-San-Suu-Kyi-s-sanctions-conundrum.

49. "Myanmar Is Not Afraid of U.S. Sanctions: Suu Kyi," *Eleven Myanmar*, May 23, 2016, http://www.elevenmyanmar.com/politics/myanmar-not-afraid-us-sanctions-suu-kyi.

50. "Chronology of U.S.-North Korean Nuclear and Missile Diplomacy," Arms Control Association, https://www.armscontrol.org/factsheets/dprkchron.

51. Video of the March 19, 1994, exchange was leaked. It is a available here: https://www.youtube.com/watch?v=oBxEFajdfrg.

52. Walter C. Clemens, *Getting to Yes in Korea* (London: Routledge, 2016), 124.

53. "Notices, September 20, 2005," Federal Register—p. 55214, https://www.fincen.gov/statutes_regs/patriot/pdf/finding_banco.pdf.

54. Jay Solomon and Neil King, Jr., "How U.S. Used a Bank to Punish North Korea," *Wall Street Journal*, April 12, 2007.

55. Bruce Klingner, "Debunking Six Myths About North Korean Sanctions," *CSIS The Korea Chair Platform*, December 19, 2014, https://www.csis.org/analysis/debunking-six-myths-about-north-korean-sanctions.

56. "Security Council Condemns Nuclear Test by Democratic People's Republic of Korea,

Unanimously Adopting Resolution 1718 (2006)," United Nations Security Council Archive, October 14, 2006, http://www.un.org/press/en/2006/sc8853.doc.htm.

57. Marcus Noland, "The (Non-) Impact of UN Sanctions on North Korea," East-West Center Working Papers, Economics Series, No. 98 (January 2009), 63–64.

58. "Security Council, Acting Unanimously, Condemns in Strongest Terms Democratic People's Republic of Korea Nuclear Test, Toughens Sanctions," *United Nations Security Council Archive*, June 12, 2009, http://www.un.org/press/en/2009/sc9679.doc.htm.

59. "Security Council Strengthens Sanctions on Democratic People's Republic of Korea, in Response to 12 February Nuclear Test," United Nations Security Council Archive, March 7, 2013, http://www.un.org/press/en/2013/sc10934.doc.htm.

60. "North Korea Sanctions," United States Government Accountability Office, Report to the Chairman, Committee on Foreign Relations, U.S. Senate, May, 2015, 19.

61. Executive orders were issued in 2008, 2010 and 2012 that all imposed restrictions on North Korea.

62. "The Mining Industry of North Korea," *NAPSNet Special Reports*, August 4, 2011, http://nautilus.org/napsnet/napsnet-special-reports/the-mining-industry-of-north-korea/.

63. Statistics on the North Korean economy are notoriously poor. The DPRK stopped publishing statistics in the 1960s. And while Chinese customs *should* give an accurate representation of trade, much that is given as aid, barter, smuggled at the ground level or even with state-to-state approval and is missed.

64. Choe Jang-ho and Choe Yu-jeong최장호, 최유정 "2015 nyeon bukhan ui daejung muyeok bunseok" 2015년 북한의 대중 무역 분석 ["North Korea's China Trade in 2015"], World Economy Today, Korea Institute for International Policy 16, no. 16, 2016, 4.

65. Kim Jeong-u김정우 "Bukhan dae jungguk suchul 1wi pummok 'seoktan', suip 1wi-hapseong Pilamentusa jikmul"북한 대중국 수출 1위 품목 '석탄', 수입 1위 '합성 필라멘트사 직물') ["North Korea's no. 1 export to China is coal; no. 1 import is 'synthetic filament-yarn textiles'"], Voice of America, February 4, 2016.

66. Kim Deok-hyun, "China's Imports of N. Korean Goods Fall 12.6 pct in May," *Yonhap News*, June 22, 2016, http://english.yonhapnews.co.kr/national/2016/06/22/26/0301000000AEN20160622010200315F.html.

67. "China Coal Imports from North Korea Dip 35 Percent as Sanctions Bite," Reuters, May 23, 2016.

68. Leo Byrne "North Korean Coal, Iron Exports Increase Again in June," NKNews Pro, July 25, 2016. https://www.nknews.org/pro/north-korean-coal-iron-exports-increase-again-in-june/.

69. Clyde Russell "China Buys Record North Korean Coal as Sanctions Ignored: Russell," Reuters, September 26, 2016. http://www.reuters.com/article/us-column-russell-coal-china-idUSKCN11W0CO.

70. Marcus Noland, "Analysis of UNSCR 2321 Sanctions on North Korea," Peterson Institute for International Affairs Blogs—Witness to Transformation, November 30, 2016, https://piie.com/blogs/north-korea-witness-transformation/analysis-unscr-2321-sanctions-north-korea.

71. Syed Zain Al-Mahmood and Alastair Gale, "North Korean with $1.4 Million in Gold Stopped in Bangladesh," *Wall Street Journal*, March 7, 2015.

72. U.S. Mission to the "UN Fact Sheet: Resolution 2375 (2017) Strengthening Sanctions on North Korea," September 11, 2017, https://usun.state.gov/remarks/7969.

73. The law largely took shape last year in response to findings by the 2014 UN Commission of Inquiry on Human Rights in the DPRK. See "H.R.757—North Korea Sanctions and Policy Enhancement Act of 2016," U.S. Congress, February 18, 2016, https://www.congress.gov/bill/114th-congress/house-bill/757.

74. "Treasury Takes Actions to Further Restrict North Korea's Access to the U.S. Financial System," U.S. Treasury Press Release, June 1, 2016. https://www.treasury.gov/press-center/press-releases/Pages/jl0471.aspx

75. Bruce Klingner, "Time to Go Beyond Incremental North Korean Sanctions," 38 North-U.S.-Korea Institute at SAIS, April 29, 2014, http://38north.org/2014/04/bklingner042914/.

76. We have a clearer view of how this worked in Iran. The U.S. Treasury designated Iran as a primary money laundering concern over its nuclear program in 2011. Banks were then unwilling to touch Iran and an entire industry of informal "exchangers" sprang up, handling nearly all international transactions for Iranian businesspeople. Most of these exchangers were based in Dubai and were tolerated by the United Arab Emirates (U.A.E.) and by extension the United States, which needs the alliance with the U.A.E. to remain smooth in a tricky region. It works like this:

let's say you wanted to buy a $10,000 Persian carpet. You'd wire the money to an "exchanger" in Dubai. He'd call his counterpart in Tehran and say, "I've got the dollars here. You can put 10 grand worth of Iranian rial into the rug merchant's account." Then the rug merchant sends you the carpet. So trade with Iran wasn't completely stopped, but it certainly hurt the economy: The carpet merchant has to pay for the exchanger's services, often 3 percent to 5 percent in the case of Dubai. Moreover, bigger transactions, say perhaps in the millions of dollars, were still difficult. Larger deals had to be spaced out over time or through several exchangers, taking time and adding fees. The commissions taken by Chinese financiers for facilitating DPRK transactions will be higher. Common estimates are 5 percent to 15 percent.

77. Mark Manyin, "CRS Insight: The Shutdown of the Joint North/South Korean Kaesong Industrial Complex," Congressional Research Service Report, February 11, 2016 https://www.fas.org/sgp/crs/row/IN10442.pdf.

78. "Inter-Korean Trade Hits Record High in 2015 Despite Shaky Ties," *Yonhap News* January 21, 2016, http://english.yonhapnews.co.kr/northkorea/2016/01/21/0401000000AEN20160121001500320.html.

79. Leo Byrne, "Trade figures Between Two Koreas Drop by over 99 Percent," *NKNews*, June 15, 2016, https://www.nknews.org/2016/06/trade-figures-between-two-koreas-drop-by-over-99-percent/.

80. Lee Yong Suk, "Countering Sanctions: The Unequal Geographic Impact of Economic Sanctions in North Korea," Freeman Spogli Institute of International Studies Working Paper, No. 519, August 2014, 11.

81. *Ibid.*, 16.

82. *Ibid.*, 2.

83. John S. Park, "The Key to the North Korean Targeted Sanctions Puzzle," *The Washington Quarterly*, Fall 2014, 208–209.

84. *Ibid.*, 210

85. Author experience. The best coffee in Pyongyang, for those who are interested, is at the Pyongyang Hotel, owned by the pro–North association of Koreans in Japan. The prices aren't too crazy, either.

86. 2015 북한 대외무역 동향 *2015 Bukhan Daewae Muyeok Monghyang* ["2015 trends in North Korea external trade"], KOTRA Report, 2016, 1.

87. *Ibid.*, 8.

88. *Ibid.*

89. *Ibid.*, 9.

90. Lim Jae-Cheon, *Kim Jong-il's Leadership of North Korea* (London: Routledge, 2009), 127.

91. Shane Smith, "North Korea's Evolving Nuclear Strategy," U.S.-Korea Institute at SAIS Nuclear Futures Series, August 2015, 16.

92. "Report on Plenary Meeting of WPK Central Committee," KCNA, March 31, 2013.

93. "North Korea Amends the Constitution," IFES NK Briefs No. 16–06–06, June 6, 2012.

94. "Challenges Ahead in Dealing with North Korea's Nuclear Ambitions," East-West Center, U.S. Asia Pacific Council Washington Report, November 2009, 3, http://www.eastwestcenter.org/fileadmin/resources/washington/cha1109.pdf.

Chapter 7

1. Author interview, August 2016.
2. Karl Hack, "The Malayan Emergency as Counter-Insurgency Paradigm," *Journal of Strategic Studies* 32, 3 (2009): 4.
3. Spencer C. Tucker, "The Encyclopedia of the Vietnam War: A Political, Social, and Military History" (Santa Barbara: ABC-CLIO, 2011), 1070.
4. Robert Thompson, "Defeating Communist Insurgency: Experiences from Malaya and Vietnam," (New York: Frederick A. Praeger, 1966), 70.
5. Testimony by Veronika A. Martin (advocate, Refugees International) to the Senate Committee on Foreign Relations Subcommittee on East Asian and Pacific Affairs, June 18, 2003, https://www.foreign.senate.gov/imo/media/doc/MartinTestimony030618.pdf.
6. Interview with We Se, *From Burma to New York: The Stories of Burmese Refugees*, multimedia project, www. http://fromburmatonewyork.com/.
7. Internal Displacement Monitoring Center, "Myanmar IDP Figure Analysis," http://www.internal-displacement.org/south-and-south-east-asia/myanmar/figures-analysis.
8. "U.S. Wraps Up Group Resettlement for Myanmar Refugees in Thailand," UNCHR, January 19, 2014, http://www.unhcr.org/en-us/news/latest/2014/1/52e90f8f6/wraps-group-resettlement-myanmar-refugees-thailand.html.
9. "Thailand: Burma Hits Refugees," *Off Our Backs* 26, no. 2 (February 1996): 7.
10. John Bray, "Ethnic Minorities and the Future of Burma," *The World Today* 48, no. 8/9 (1992): 144.

11. Heather Rae, "Internal Displacement in Eastern Burma," *Forced Migration Review* 28 (2007).
12. Thierry Falise, "On the Run: In Burma's Jungle Hell," *World Policy Journal* 27, no. 1 (2010): 58.
13. Bray, *Ethnic Minorities*, 146.
14. Bertil Linter and Michael Black, *Merchants of Madness: The Methamphetamine Explosion in the Golden Triangle* (Chiang Mai: Silkworm, 2009), 17.
15. *Ibid.*, 20.
16. "United Wa State Army," Myanmar Peace Monitor, http://www.mmpeacemonitor.org/component/content/article/57-stakeholders/169-uwsa.
17. A smaller group of former Communists centered in Kokang followed shortly thereafter.
18. Bertil Linter, *Great Game East* (New Haven: Yale University Press, 2015), 172.
19. "Lords of Jade," *Global Witness Report*, December 3, 2015, 9–10.
20. Mary Callahan, *Political Authority in Burma's Ethnic Minority States* (Washington, DC: East-West Center, 2007), 13.
21. *Ibid.*, 173
22. Martin Smith, "Ethnic Groups in Burma: Development, Democracy and Human Rights," *Anti-Slavery International Report*, 1994, 29.
23. See Burma Human Rights Yearbook 1996, Human Rights Documentation Unit, 1997.
24. Karl Grundy-Warr, "The Karenni: a Troubled People and a Destroyed State," *IBRU Boundary and Security Bulletin*, Autumn 1998, 83.
25. "Summary: Karenni National Progressive Party," Myanmar Peace Monitor, http://www.mmpeacemonitor.org/stakeholders/armed-ethnic-groups/160-knpp.
26. Russ Christensen and Sann Kyaw, *The Pa-O: Rebels and Refugees* (Chiang Mai: Silkworm, 2006), 22–23, 37–38.
27. Ashley South, "Mon Nationalist Movements: Insurgency, Ceasefires and Political Struggle," conference paper published by the Mon Unity League (Bangkok: January 2008): 14.
28. South, *Burma's Longest War*, 8.
29. David Steinberg, "Myanmar in 1992: Plus Ca Change…?" *Asian Survey* 33, no. 2, A Survey of Asia in 1992: Part II (February 1993): 176.
30. Mary P. Callahan, "Burma in 1995: Looking Beyond the Release of Aung San Suu Kyi," *Asian* Survey 36, no. 2, A Survey of Asia in 1995: Part II (February 1996): 163.
31. David Eubank, "Under Attack: A Way of Life," *Forced Migration Review*, FMR Report 30, April 2008, http://www.fmreview.org/sites/fmr/files/FMRdownloads/en/FMRpdfs/FMR30/10–11.pdf.
32. "Border Guard Force Scheme," Myanmar Peace Monitor, http://www.mmpeacemonitor.org/background/border-guard-force.
33. Ashley South, *Ethnic Politics in Burma: States of Conflict* (London: Routledge, 2008), 152.
34. "Difficult Lives: Interviews in Kachin State," Project Maje Interview, September 1991, http://www.projectmaje.org/pdf/dif_live.pdf.
35. Ashley South, *Mon Nationalism and Civil War in Burma: The Golden Sheldrake* (London: Routledge, 2013), 166.
36. *Ibid.*, 167.
37. Zaw Oo and Win Min, *Assessing Burma's Ceasefire Accords* (Singapore: ISEAS, 2007), xi.
38. *Ibid.*, xii.
39. Ashley South, *Burma's Longest War: Anatomy of the Karen Conflict* (Amsterdam: Transnational Institute, 2011), 4.
40. Karin Dean, "Struggle Over Space in Myanmar: Expanding State Territoriality After the Kachin Ceasefire," in *Autonomy and Armed Separatism in South and Southeast Asia*, ed. Michelle Ann Miller (Singapore: ISEAS, 2012), 130.
41. *Ibid.*, 124.
42. Wai Moe, "Naypyidaw Orders New 'Four Cuts' Campaign," *Irrawaddy*, March 4, 2011, http://www2.irrawaddy.com/article.php?art_id=20880.
43. Quoted in Maung Aung Myoe, "The Road to Naypyitaw: Making Sense of the Myanmar Government's Decision to Move its Capital," Asia Research Institute Working Paper Series No. 79, National University of Singapore (2006): 3.
44. Clive Parker, "Naypyidaw: A Dusty Work in Progress," *Irrawaddy Magazine* October 2006, http://www2.irrawaddy.com/article.php?art_id=6427.
45. *Ibid.*
46. Matt Kennard and Claire Provost, "Burma's Bizarre Capital: A Super-Sized Slice of Post-Apocalypse Suburbia," *The Guardian*, March 19, 2015, https://www.theguardian.com/cities/2015/mar/19/burmas-capital-naypyidaw-post-apocalypse-suburbia-highways-wifi.
47. Comments by Nicholas Farrelly during "Naypyitaw: A Home for Myanmar's Unexpected Democracy," conference at East-West Center, Washington, D.C., September

6, 2013, http://publicinternationallawand-policygroup.org/wp-content/uploads/2013/09/PILPG-Event-Review-Naypyitaw-A-Home-for-Myanmars-Unexpected-Democracy.pdf.

48. Dulyapak Preecharushh, *Naypyidaw: The New Capital of Burma* (Bangkok: White Lotus, 2009), 46.

49. Donald M. Seekins, *State and Society in Modern Rangoon* (London: Routledge, 2009), 5.

50. Preecharushh, *Naypyidaw*, 75.

51. Preecharushh, *Naypyidaw*, 58.

52. Bertil Lintner, "Tunnels, Guns and Kimchi: North Korea's Quest for Dollars—Part I North Korea Digs Tunnels for Burma's Brutal, Secretive Regime," *YaleGlobal*, June 9, 2009, http://yaleglobal.yale.edu/content/NK-quest-for-dollars-part1.

53. Dulyapak Preecharushh, "Myanmar's New Capital City of Naypyidaw," in *Engineering Earth: The Impacts of Megaengineering Projects*, ed. Stanley D. Brunn (New York: Springer, 2011), 1029.

54. This echoed sentiments expressed at the last National Convention, in 1993. Those ideas were put on ice for a decade, it appears.

55. Various reports on mass rallies in support of the 7-point roadmap from the state-owned *The New Light of Myanmar* newspaper. Archived at http://www.ibiblio.org/obl/docs/rallies-etc..htm.

56. Kwa Zwa Moe, "Annan Criticizes Road Map," *The Irrawaddy*, November 12, 2003, http://www2.irrawaddy.com/article.php?art_id=1345.

57. Lu Thit, "Do Not Make the Goal of Democracy Far Away from the People," *The New Light of Myanmar*, July 3, 2008, translation at http://www.burmanet.org/news/2008/07/31/the-new-light-of-myanmar-do-not-make-the-goal-of-democracy-far-away-from-the-people-%E2%80%93-lu-thit/.

58. Various interviews, 2016.

59. "Myanmar's 2015 landmark elections explained," BBC News, Dec. 3, 2015, http://www.bbc.com/news/world-asia-33547036.

60. Penny Green, "Countdown to Annihilation: Genocide in Myanmar," International State Crime Initiative, School of Law, Queen Mary University, London, October 2015, http://statecrime.org/data/2015/10/ISCI-Rohingya-Report-PUBLISHED-VERSION.pdf.

61. Ye Htut, "21st Century Panglong and New Challenges," *Myanmar Times*, May 23, 2017, https://www.mmtimes.com/national-news/26095-21st-century-panglong-and-new-challenges.html.

Conclusion

1. "Exclusive: More than 1,000 Feared Killed in Myanmar Army Crackdown on Rohingya—U.N. officials," Reuters, February 9, 2017, http://www.reuters.com/article/us-myanmar-rohingya-idUSKBN15N1TJ.

2. Volker Türk, *Statement to the 68th Session of the Executive Committee of the High Commissioner's Programme* October 5, 2017, http://www.unhcr.org/en-us/admin/dipstatements/59d4b99d10/statement-68th-session-executive-committee-high-commissioners-programme.html.

3. Sergio Peçanha and Jeremy White, "Satellite Images Show More Than 200 Rohingya Villages Burned in Myanmar," *New York Times*, September 18, 2017, https://www.nytimes.com/interactive/2017/09/18/world/asia/rohingya-villages.html?_r=0.

4. Simon Lewis and Tommy Wilkes, "U.N. Medics See Evidence of Rape in Myanmar Army 'Cleansing' Campaign," Reuters, September 24, 2017.

5. Reuters "Myanmar Set to Dodge Full U.N. Probe on Rohingya Abuse," March 9, 2017, http://uk.reuters.com/article/uk-myanmar-rohingya-un-idUKKBN16G03Q.

6. VOA, "Activists: Defamation Cases Surge in Myanmar," January 2, 2017, http://www.voanews.com/a/activists-say-defamation-cases-surge-in-myanmar/3659806.html.

Bibliography

Books and Journal Articles

Afesorgbor, Sylvanus Kwaku, and Renuka Mahadevan. "The Impact of Economic Sanctions on Income Inequality of Target States." *World Development* 83 July (2016).

Ahmedullah, Mohammed. "Not-So-Selective Sanctions." *Bulletin of the Atomic Scientists*, November/December 2003.

Allen, Richard. "Recent Developments in Burma (Address Given to Royal Asiatic Society July 22, 1964)." *Journal of the Royal Central Asian Society* 52:1 (1965), 6–19.

Anderson, Benedict. *Imagined Communities: Reflections on the Origin and Spread of Nationalism*, rev. and extended ed. London: Verso, 1991.

Armour-Hileman, Victoria. *Singing to the Dead: A Missioner's Life Among Refugees from Burma*. Athens: University of Georgia Press, 2002.

Arumugam, Raja Segaran. "Burma: Political Unrest and Economic Stagnation." *Southeast Asian Affairs*, 1976.

Ashford, Emma. "Not-So-Smart Sanctions: The Failure of Western Restrictions Against Russia." *Foreign Affairs*, January/February 2016.

Aung Zaw. *The Face of Resistance: Aung San Suu Kyi and Burma's Fight for Freedom*. Chiang Mai: Silkworm, 2013.

Badgley, John H. "Burmese Communist Schisms." In *Peasant Rebellion and Communist Revolution in Asia*, edited by John H. Badgley and John Wilson Lewis. Palo Alto, CA: Stanford University Press, 1974.

Baker, Donald. "Rhetoric, Ritual and Political Legitimacy: Justifying Yi Seong-gye's Ascension to the Throne." *Korea Journal* 53, no. 4 (Winter 2013).

Bayly, Christopher Alan, and Timothy Norman Harper. *Forgotten Armies: The Fall of British Asia, 1941–1945*. Cambridge, MA: Harvard University Press, 2005.

Bechtol, Bruce, Jr. "Maintaining a Rogue Military: North Korea's Military Capabilities and Strategy at the End of the Kim Jong-il Era." *International Journal of Korean Studies* 16, no. 1 (Spring 2012).

Bengtsson, Jesper. *Aung San Suu Kyi: A Biography*. Washington, D.C.: Potomac, 2012.

Bhatia, Rajiv. *India—Myanmar Relations: Changing Contours*. London: Taylor and Francis, 2015.

Bolger, Daniel P. *Scenes from an Unfinished War: Low-Intensity Conflict-Korea, 1966–1969*. Combat Studies Institute, U.S. Army Command and General Staff College, 1991.

Bray, John. "Ethnic Minorities and the Future of Burma." *The World Today* 48, no. 8/9 (1992).

Brown, E.A. "Burma Facts, 1989." *Christian Science Monitor*, May 8, 1989. http://www.csmonitor.com/1989/0518/d1tburm.html#.

Burma Watcher. "Burma in 1988: There Came a Whirlwind." *Asian Survey* 29, no. 2, A Survey of Asia in 1988, Part II (February 1989).
Butwell, Richard. "The Four Failures of U Nu's Second Premiership." *Asian Survey* 2, no. 1 (1962).
Butwell, Richard. *U Nu of Burma*. Palo Alto, CA: Stanford University Press, 1969.
Buzo, Adrian. *The Guerilla Dynasty*. Boulder, CO: Westview, 1999.
Callahan, Mary P. "Building an Army." *Burma Debate* 4, no. 3 (1997).
Callahan, Mary P. "Burma in 1995: Looking Beyond the Release of Aung San Suu Kyi." *Asian Survey* 36, no. 2, A Survey of Asia in 1995, Part II (February 1996).
Callahan, Mary P. *Making Enemies: War and State Building in Burma*. Ithaca: Cornell University Press, 2003.
Callahan, Mary. *Political Authority in Burma's Ethnic Minority States*. Washington, D.C.: East-West Center, 2007.
Camilleri, Joseph. *Southeast Asia in China's Foreign Policy*. Singapore: ISEAS, 1975.
Castelli, Helen S. "Reviewed Work(s): The Rise and Fall of the Communist Party of Burma (CPB) by Bertil Lintner." *Crossroads: An Interdisciplinary Journal of Southeast Asian Studies* 6, no. 2 (1991).
Chandola, Harish. "The Politics of Opium." *Economic and Political Weekly*, June 5, 1976. http://www.epw.in/journal/1976/23/our-correspondent-columns/thailand-politics-opium.html.
Chinoy, Mike. *Meltdown*. New York: St. Martin's Griffin, 2008.
Choe Jang-ho and Choe Yu-jeong. 최장호, 최유정. "2015 nyeon bukhan ui daejung muyeok bunseok 2015" 년 북한의 대중 무역 분석[North Korea's China trade in 2015]. *World Economy Today*, Korea Institute for International Policy 16, no. 16 (2016).
Chao Tzang Yawnghwe. *The Shan of Burma: Memoirs of a Shan Exile*. Singapore: ISEAS, 2010.
Chowdhury, Mridul. "The Role of the Internet in Burma's Saffron Revolution." Internet & Democracy Case Study Series: Berkman Center Research Publication No. 2008–08 (September 2008).
Christensen, Russ, and Sann Kyaw. *The Pa-O: Rebels and Refugees*. Chiang Mai: Silkworm, 2006.
Clemens, Walter C. *Getting to Yes in Korea*. London: Routledge, 2016.
Clemens, Walter C. "North Korea's Quest for Nuclear Weapons: New Historical Evidence." *Journal of East Asian Studies* 10, no. 1 (2010).
Colligen, Stefan. "Human Rights and Economy in Burma." In *Burma: Political Economy Under Military Rule*, edited by Robert Taylor. London: Hurst, 2001.
Collins, Robert. *Pyongyang Republic*. Washington, D.C.: Committee for Human Rights in North Korea, 2016.
Cox, Robert. "Gramsci, Hegemony and International Relations: An Essay in Method." *Millennium: Journal of International Studies* 12, no. 2 (1983).
Cumings, Bruce. "Japanese Colonialism in Korea: A Comparative Perspective." Asia/Pacific Research Center: Stanford University, 1997. http://iis-db.stanford.edu/pubs/10061/Cumings.etc.pdf.
Cumings, Bruce. *Korea's Place in the Sun: A Modern History*. New York: W. W. Norton, 1997.
Cumings, Bruce. *North Korea: Another Country*. New York: New, 2003.
Dean, Karin. "Struggle Over Space in Myanmar: Expanding State Territoriality After the Kachin Ceasefire." In *Autonomy and Armed Separatism in South and Southeast Asia*, edited by Michelle Ann Miller. Singapore: ISEAS, 2012.
Deane, Hugh. *The Korean War*. London: China, 1999.
Deuchler, Martina. *The Confucian Transformation of Korea: A Study of Society and Ideology*. Cambridge, MA: Harvard University Press, 1992.
Dingman, R. "Atomic Diplomacy during the Korean War." *International Security* 3, issue 13 (Winter 1988–1999).

Dittmer, Lowell. *Burma Or Myanmar? The Struggle for National Identity*. New York: World Scientific, 2010.
Downs, Chuck. *Over the Line: North Korea's Negotiating Strategy*. Washington, D.C.: AEI, 1999.
Drezner, Daniel W. "Bargaining, Enforcement, and Multilateral Sanctions: When Is Cooperation Counterproductive?" *International Organization* 54, 1 (2000).
Drezner, Daniel W. *The Sanctions Paradox: Economic Statecraft and International Relations*. Cambridge: Cambridge University Press, 1999.
Eberstadt, Nicholas. "North Korea's 'Epic Economic Fail' in International Perspective." Asan Institute Report, November 2015.
Eberstadt, Nick. *The End of North Korea*. Washington, D.C.: AEI, 1999.
Egreteau, Renaud, and Larry Jagan. *Soldiers and Diplomacy in Burma*. Singapore: Singapore National University Press, 2013.
Falise, Thierry. "On the Run: In Burma's Jungle Hell." *World Policy Journal* 27, no. 1 (2010).
Fink, Christina. *Living Silence: Burma Under Military Rule*. London: Zed, 2001.
Foley, Matthew. *Post-Colonial Transition, Aid and the Cold War in Southeast Asia: Britain, the United States and Burma, 1948–1962*. PhD Diss., University of Nottingham, 2007.
Fong, Jack. *Revolution as Development: The Karen Self-Determination Struggle Against Ethnocracy (1949–2004)*. New York: Brownwalker, 2008.
Fujita Koichi. "Agriculture and Rural Development Strategy in Myanmar: With a Focus on the Rice Sector." *The Myanmar Economy: Its Past, Present and Prospects*. Edited by Konosuke Odaka. Springer: New York, 2015.
Ganesen, N. *Bilateral Legacies in East and Southeast Asia*. Singapore: ISEAS, 2015.
Ganesan, Narayanan. "Myanmar-China Relations: Interlocking Interests but Independent Output." *Japanese Journal of Political Science* 12, no. 1 (2011).
Gause, Ken E. *Coercion, Control, Surveillance, and Punishment*. Washington, D.C.: Committee for Human Rights in North Korea, 2012.
Geldenhuys, Deon. *Deviant Conduct in World Politics*. New York: Palgrave Macmillan, 2004.
Gilinsky, Victor. *Nuclear Blackmail: The 1994 U.S.-Democratic People's Republic of Korea Agreed Framework on North Korea's Nuclear Program*. Palo Alto, CA: Hoover Institution, 1997.
Glass, Leslie. *The Changing of Kings: Memories of Burma, 1934–1949*. London: Peter Owen, 1985.
Goh Yoo-hwan 고유환. *Rodong Sinmun tong hae bon bukhan byeonghwa* 로도신문을 통해 본 북한 변화 *Seeing Change in North Korea Through Rodong Shinmin*. Seoul: Sonin, 2006.
Gravers, Michael. "Spiritual Politics, Political Religion, and Religious Freedom In Burma." *The Review of Faith & International Affairs* 11:2 (2013).
Green, Christopher. "Chosun Ilbo Surveys 100 North Koreans." SinoNK, July 18, 2014. http://sinonk.com/2014/07/28/chosun-ilbo-surveys-100-north-koreans/.
Grundy-Warr, Karl. "The Karenni: A Troubled People and a Destroyed State." *IBRU Boundary and Security Bulletin*, Autumn 1998.
Guyot, James F. "1990: The Unconsummated Election." *Asian Survey* 31, no. 2, A Survey of Asia in 1990, Part II (February 1991).
Guyot, James F., and John Badgley. "Myanmar in 1989: Tatmadaw V." *Asian Survey* 30, no. 2, A Survey of Asia in 1989, Part II (February 1990).
Haass, Richard. *Economic Sanctions and American Diplomacy*. New York: Council on Foreign Relations, 1998.
Hack, Karl. "The Malayan Emergency as Counter-Insurgency Paradigm." *Journal of Strategic Studies*, 32:3 (2009).
Haggard, Stephan, and Marcus Noland. *Famine in North Korea: Markets, Aid, and Reform*. New York: Columbia University Press, 2007.

Haggard, Stephen, and Marcus Noland. "North Korea in 2007: Shuffling in from the Cold." *Asian Survey* 48, no. 1 (2008).
Hamm Taik-young. *Arming the Two Koreas*. London: Routledge, 1999.
Hanson, Ola. *The Kachins: Their Customs and Traditions*. Cambridge: Cambridge University Press, 1913 (2012 reprint).
Harris, Paul. "An Opinion on the Depayin Massacre." *Article 2*, December 7, 2003. http://alrc.asia/article2/2003/12/an-opinion-on-the-depayin-massacre/.
Harrison, Selig. "North Korea in Transition." *Korean Challenges and American Policy*, edited by Ilpyong J. Kim. New York: Paragon, 1991.
Haruki, Wada. *The Korean War: An International History*. New York: Rowman and Littlefield, 2014.
Haseman, John B. "Burma in 1987: Change in the Air?" *Asian Survey* 28, no. 2, A Survey of Asia in 1987, Part II (February 1988).
Hawk, David. *Hidden Gulag*. Washington, D.C.: The Committee for Human Rights in North Korea, 2012.
Hawk, David. *North Korea's Hidden Gulag: Interpreting Reports of Changes in the Prison Camps*. Washington, D.C.: The Committee for Human Rights in North Korea, 2013.
Hecker, Siegfried. "A Return Trip to North Korea's Yongbyon Nuclear Complex." NAPSNet Special Reports, November 22, 2010. http://nautilus.org/napsnet/napsnet-special-reports/a-return-trip-to-north-koreas-yongbyon-nuclear-complex/.
Holmes, Robert A. "Burmese Domestic Policy: The Politics of Burmanization." *Asian Survey* 7, no. 3 (March 1967).
Hongwei Fan. "China–Burma Geopolitical Relations in the Cold War." *Journal of Current Southeast Asian Affairs* 31:1 (2012).
Houtman, Gustaaf. *Mental Culture in Burmese Crisis Politics: Aung San Suu Kyi and the National League for Democracy*. Tokyo: ILCAA, 1999.
Hufbauer, Gary Clyde, Jeffrey J. Schott, Kimberly Ann Elliott and Barbara Oegg. *Economic Sanctions Reconsidered*. Washington, D.C.: Peterson Institute for International Economics, 2007.
Huntley, Wade L., Mitsuru Kurosawa and Kazumi Mizumoto. *Nuclear Disarmament in the Twenty-First Century*. Hiroshima: Hiroshima Peace Institute, 2004.
ILO Asia—Pacific Working Paper Series. *ASEAN Community 2015: Managing Integration for Better Jobs and Shared Prosperity in Myanmar*. February 2015.
Jae Kyu Park. "A Critique on 'The Democratic Confederal Republic of Koryo.'" *Journal of East and West Studies*, 12:1 (1983), 13–25.
Jang Jin-sung. *Dear Leader*. New York: Simon & Schuster, 2013.
Jeffries, Ian. *North Korea: A Guide to Economic and Political Developments*. London: Routledge, 2003.
Jo Seung-hoo. "US-ROK Relations: The Political-Diplomatic Dimension." In *The United States and the Korean Peninsula in the 21st Century*, edited by Tae-Hwan Kwak and Seung-Ho Joo. Aldershot: Ashgate, 2006.
Jo Song Hun. 조성훈. "Dae-nam Dobal Sa" 대남도발사 [A history of provocations of South Korea]. Paju, South Korea: Baeknyun Dongan, 2015.
Kang Myung-Kyu. "Industrial Management and Reforms in North Korea." In *Economic Reforms in the Socialist World*, edited by Stanislaw Gomulka, Yong-Chool Ha and Cae-One Kim. New York: M.E. Sharpe, 2002.
Keck, Stephen L. *British Burma in the New Century, 1895–1918*. London: Palgrave MacMillan, 2015.
Kelly, James A. "Assistant Secretary of State for East Asian and Pacific Affairs, Remarks at the Woodrow Wilson Center." U.S. Department of State, December 11, 2002. https://2001-2009.state.gov/p/eap/rls/rm/2002/15875.htm.
Kerr, Paul. "North Korea Talks Stalled by Banking Dispute." *Arms Control Today* 37, no. 3 (April 2007).

Kim Il Sung. 김일성. *Jogugktongil wibeul silhyonhagi wihayo hyukmyung ryokryangeul baekbangeuro ganghwa haja.* 조국통일위업을 실현하기 위하여 혁명력량을 백방으로 강화하자 ["Let's strengthen by all means the revolutionary power to realize the feat of the unification of the fatherland"]. In *Nam Choson Hyokmyong kwa Joguk tongilae daehayeo.* 남조선혁명과 조국통일에 대하여 ["On South Korea's revolution and unification of the fatherland"]. Pyongyang: Choson Rodongdang Chulpansa, 1969.

Kim Il Sung. *On Eliminating Dogmatism and Formalism and Establishing Juche in Ideological Work.* Pyongyang: Foreign Languages Publishing House, 1973.

Kim Ji-Jung. "The War and U.S.-Korea Relations." *The Russo-Japanese War in Global Perspective: World War Zero*, vol. 2, edited by David Wolff and John W. Steinberg. Leiden: Brill, 2007.

Kim Jong Il. 김정일 *Widaehan Suryongui Dokchangjokin Gunsasasang-e Daehayo* 위대한 수령의 독창적인 군사사상에 대하여 ["On the creative military thought of the great leader"]. Pyongyang: Korean Worker's Party, 2002.

Kim Jong Il. *On the Juche Idea.* Pyongyang: Pyongyang Foreign Languages Publishing House, 1982.

Kim Jong Il. *Socialism Is a Science.* Pyongyang, 1994. http://www.korea-dpr.info/lib/106.pdf.

Kim Kwang Il, et al. *Anecdotes of Kim Il Sung's Life.* Pyongyang: Foreign Languages Publishing House, n.d.

Kim Seok Hyang. *The Juche Ideology of North Korea: Sociopolitical Roots of Ideological Change.* Athens: University of Georgia Press, 1993.

Kim Yangson. 김양선. *Hanguk Gidokgyo Haebang 10-nyeon Sa* 한국기독교 해방 10년사 ["Korean Christianity liberation 10 year history"]. Seoul: Yaesu Gyojang Rohui, Jonggyo Gyoyukbu, 1956.

Kim Yong-ho. *North Korean Foreign Policy.* Plymouth: Lexington, 2011.

Klingner, Bruce. "Debunking Six Myths About North Korean Sanctions." CSIS: The Korea Chair Platform, December 19, 2014. https://www.csis.org/analysis/debunking-six-myths-about-north-korean-sanctions.

Klingner, Bruce. "Time to Go Beyond Incremental North Korean Sanctions." 38 North-U.S.–Korea Institute at SAIS, April 29, 2014. http://38north.org/2014/04/bklingner042914/.

Koh Jung-Sik. *Is North Korea Really Changing?* Seoul: Institute for Unification Education, 2014.

Kratoska, Paul H. "The Karen of Burma Under Japanese Rule." In *Southeast Asian Minorities in the Wartime Japanese Empire*, edited by Paul H. Kratoska. London: Routledge Curzon, 2002.

Kudo Toshihiro. "The Impact of U.S. Sanctions on the Myanmar Garment Industry." *Asian Survey* 48, issue 6 (2008).

Kudo Toshihiro. "Myanmar and Japan: How Close Friends Became Estranged." Institute of Developing Economies, IDE Discussion Paper no. 118 (August 2007).

Kyaw Yin Hlaing. "Aung San Suu Kyi of Myanmar: A Review of the Lady's Biographies." *Contemporary Southeast Asia* 29, no. 2 (2007).

Kyaw Yin Hlaing. "Myanmar in 2003: Frustration and Despair?" *Asian Survey* 44, no. 1 (January/February 2004).

Kyaw Yin Hlaing. "Reconsidering the Failure of the Burma Socialist Programme Party Government to Eradicate Internal Economic Impediments." *South East Asia Research* 11, no. 1 (March 2003).

Land, Hazel J. *Fear and Sanctuary: Burmese Refugees in Thailand.* Ithaca, NY: SEAP, 2002.

Lankov, Andrei. *Crisis in North Korea: The Failure of De-Stalinization, 1956.* Honolulu: University of Hawaii Press, 2004.

Lankov, Andrei. *North of the DMZ.* Jefferson, NC: McFarland, 2007.

Lankov, Andrei. *The Real North Korea: Life and Politics in the Failed Stalinist Utopia.* Oxford: Oxford University Press, 2013.
La Raw, Marine. "On the Continuing Relevance of E.R. Leach's 'Political Systems of Highland Burma' to Kachin Studies." *Social Dynamics in the Highlands of Southeast Asia: Reconsidering Political Systems of Highland Burma* by E.R. Leach, edited by François Robinne and Mandy Sadan. Leiden: Brill, 2007.
Larkin, Emma. *No Bad News for the King.* New York: Penguin, 2011.1
Leach, Edmund. *Political Systems of Highland Burma: A Study of Kachin Social Structure.* London: Athlone, 1954.
Lee Chae-In. *A Toubled Peace: U.S. Policy and the Two Koreas.* Baltimore: Johns Hopkins University Press, 2006.
Lee Eric Yong-Joong. "Development of North Korea's Legal Regime Governing Foreign Business Cooperation: A Revisit under the New Socialist Constitution of 1998." *Northwestern Journal of International Law & Business* 21, no. 1 (2000).
Lee Man-woo. "Is North Korea Changing Course." *Asian Perspective* 9, no. 1 (Spring-Summer 1985).
Lee Manwoo. "Korean Reconciliation: Combining Two Track Diplomacy." In *Korean Reunification: New Perspectives and Approaches*, edited by Tae-Hwan Kwak, Chong-han Kim, and Hong Nack Kim. Seoul: Kyungnam University Press, 1984.
Lee, Yong Suk. "Countering Sanctions: The Unequal Geographic Impact of Economic Sanctions in North Korea." *Freeman Spogli Institute of International Studies Working Paper*, no. 519 (August 2014).
Leehey, Jennifer. "Message in a Bottle: A Gallery of Social/Political Cartoons from Burma." *Southeast Asian Journal of Social Science* 25, no. 1 (1997).
Leiberman, Victor B. "Ethnic Politics in Eighteenth Century Burma." *Modern Asian Studies* 12:3 (1978).
Lerner, Mitchell *"Mostly Propaganda in Nature": Kim Il Sung, the Juche Ideology, and the Second Korean War.* Washington, D.C.: Woodrow Wilson International Center for Scholars, 2010.
Lewis, Geoffrey. "Progressive Pragmatism or Cynicism in Confronting North Korea?" 38 North, May 1, 2012. http://38north.org/2012/05/jlewis050212/.
Lim Jae-Cheon. *Kim Jong-il's Leadership of North Korea.* London: Routledge, 2009.
Lim Jae-Chon. *Leader Symbols and Personality Cult in North Korea: The Leader State.* London: Routledge, 2015.
Linter, Bertil. "Access to Information: The Case of Burma." *Asia Pacific Media Series* (1997). http://www.asiapacificms.com/papers/pdf/burma_access_to_information.pdf.
Lintner, Bertil. *Aung San Suu Kyi and Burma's Struggle for Democracy.* Chiang Mai: Silkworm, 2011.
Linter, Bertil. *Burma in Revolt: Opium and Insurgency since 1948.* Chiang Mai: Silkworm, 1999.
Linter, Bertil. "The CIA's First Secret War: Americans Helped Stage Raids into China from Burma." *Far Eastern Economic Review*, 16 September 1993.
Linter, Bertil. *Great Game East.* New Haven: Yale University Press, 2015.
Lintner, Bertil. "Insurgencies Among Mons and Karens." *Economic and Political Weekly* 16, no. 16 (1981).
Lintner, Bertil. *The Rise and Fall of the Communist Party of Burma (CPB).* Ithaca, NY: Cornell University Press, 1990.
Lintner, Bertil. "The Shans and the Shan State of Burma." *Contemporary Southeast Asia* 5, no. 4 (March 1984).
Lintner, Bertil. "Tunnels, Guns and Kimchi: North Korea's Quest for Dollars—Part I: North Korea Digs Tunnels for Burma's Brutal, Secretive Regime." YaleGlobal, June 9, 2009. http://yaleglobal.yale.edu/content/NK-quest-for-dollars-part1.

Linter, Bertil, and Michael Black. *Merchants of Madness: The Methamphetamine Explosion in the Golden Triangle.* Chiang Mai: Silkworm, 2009.
Litwak, Robert. *Rogue States and U.S. Foreign Policy: Containment After the Cold War.* Baltimore: Johns Hopkins University Press, 2000.
Ma Thanegi. *Nor Iron Bars a Cage.* Hong Kong: ThingsAsian, 2013.
Maule, Robert B. "The Opium Question in the Federated Shan States, 1931–36: British Policy Discussions and Scandal." *Journal of Southeast Asian Studies* 23, no. 1 (1992).
Maung Aung Myoe. *In the Name of Pauk-Phaw: Myanmar's China Policy Since 1948.* Singapore: ISEAS, 2011.
Maung Aung Myoe. "The Road to Naypyitaw: Making Sense of the Myanmar Government's Decision to Move its Capital." Asia Research Institute Working Paper Series 79, National University of Singapore (2006).
Marinov, Nikolay. "Do Economic Sanctions Destabilize Country Leaders?" *American Journal of Political Science* 49, no. 3 (2005).
Marshall, Harry Ignatius. *The Karen People of Burma.* Bangkok: White Lotus, 2007. Reprint of 1922 edition.
McCarthy, Stephen. "Overturning the Alms Bowl: The Price of Survival and the Consequences for Political Legitimacy in Burma." *Australian Journal of International Affairs* 62, no. 3 (2008).
McGee, Robert W. "The Ethics of Economic Sanctions." *Economic Affairs* 23:4 (2003).
Mya Maung. *The Burma Road to Poverty.* New York: Praeger, 1991.
Mya Than. "The Ethnic Chinese in Myanmar and Their Identity." In *Ethnic Chinese as Southeast Asians,* edited by Leo Suryadinata. Singapore: ISEAS, 1997.
Myers, Ramon Hawley, and Mark R. Peattie. *The Japanese Colonial Empire, 1895–1945.* Princeton, NJ: Princeton University Press, 1984.
Naw, Angelene. *Aung San and the Struggle for Burmese Independence.* Bangkok: Silkworm, 2001.
Nish. Ian. *The Anglo-Japanese Alliance: The Diplomacy of Two Island Empires, 1984–1907.* London: Bloomsbury, 2012.
Noland, Marcus. "The (Non-)Impact of UN Sanctions on North Korea." East-West Center Working Papers, Economics Series, no. 98 (January 2009).
Noland, Marcus, Sherman Robinson and Tao Wang. "Famine in North Korea: Causes and Cures." *Economic Development and Cultural Change* 49, no. 4 (July 2001).
Oberdorfer, Don. *The Two Koreas: A Contemporary History.* New York: Basic, 2014.
Orlov, Vladimir. "Russia's Nonproliferation Policy and the Situation in East Asia." Nautilus, March 05, 2001. http://nautilus.org/nuke-policy/russias-nonproliferation-policy-and-the-situation-in-east-asia-2/.
Paik Pong. *Kim Il Sung: Premier of the Democratic People's Republic of Korea.* New York: Guardian, 1970.
Paine, S.C.M. *The Sino-Japanese War of 1894–1895: Perceptions, Power, and Primacy.* Cambridge: Cambridge University Press, 2006.
Panda, Ankit. "A Great Leap to Nowhere: Remembering the US-North Korea 'Leap Day' Deal." *The Diplomat,* February 29, 2016. http://thediplomat.com/2016/02/a-great-leap-to-nowhere-remembering-the-us-north-korea-leap-day-deal/.
Pardo, Ramon Pacheco. *North Korea—U.S. Relations Under Kim Jong Il: The Quest for Normalization?* New York: Routledge, 2014.
Park, John S. "The Key to the North Korean Targeted Sanctions Puzzle." *The Washington Quarterly,* Fall 2014.
Parker, Clive. "Naypyidaw: A Dusty Work in Progress." *Irrawaddy Magazine,* October 2006. http://www2.irrawaddy.com/article.php?art_id=6427.
Perry, Peter John. *Myanmar (Burma) Since 1962: The Failure of Development.* London: Routledge, 2007.

Prasse-Freeman, Elliott. "Power, Civil Society, and an Inchoate Politics of the Daily in Burma/Myanmar." *The Journal of Asian Studies* 71, no. 2 (2012).
Preecharushh, Dulyapak. "Myanmar's New Capital City of Naypyidaw." In *Engineering Earth: The Impacts of Megaengineering Projects*, edited by Stanley D. Brunn. New York: Springer, 2011.
Preecharushh, Dulyapak. *Naypyidaw: The New Capital of Burma*. Bangkok: White Lotus, 2009.
Pye, Lucian. "The Army in Burmese Politics." In *The Role of the Military in Underdeveloped Countries*, edited by John Asher Johnson. Princeton, NJ: Princeton University Press, 2015.
Rae, Heather. "Internal Displacement in Eastern Burma." *Forced Migration Review* 28 (2007).
Reiss, Mitchell B. "North Korea: Getting to Maybe." In *Double Trouble: Iran and North Korea as Challenges to International Security*, edited by Patrick M. Cronin. Westport, CT: Praeger, 2008.
Reiss, Mitchell B., and Robert L. Gallucci. "Dead to Rights." *Foreign Affairs* 84, no. 2 (March-April 2005).
Rogers, Benedict. *Than Shwe: Unmasking Burma's Tyrant*. Chiang Mai: Silkworm, 2010.
Routray, Bibhu Prasad. "Myanmar's National Reconciliation: An Audit of Insurgencies and Ceasefires." *IPCS Special Report* no. 138, March 2013.
Ryang, Sonia. *Koreans in Japan: Critical Voices from the Margin*. London: Routledge, 2000.
Sadan, Mandy. *Being and Becoming Kachin*. Oxford: Oxford University Press, 2013.
San C. Po. *Burma and the Karens*. Bangkok: White Lotus, 2001. Reprint of 1928 edition.
Schaefer, Bernd. "Communist Vanguard Contest in East Asia during the 1960s and 1970s in Dynamics of the Cold War." In *Asia: Ideology, Identity, and Culture*, edited by Tuong Vu and Wasana Wongsurawat. New York: Macmillan, 2009.
Schaefer, Bernd. "North Korean 'Adventurism' and China's Long Shadow, 1966–72." Working Paper No. 44, Cold War International History Project, October 2004.
Schober, Juliane. "Colonial Knowledge and Buddhist Education in Burma." In *Buddhism, Power and Political Order,* edited by Ian Harris. London: Routledge, 2007.
Scott, James. *The Art of Not Being Governed: An Anarchist History of Upland Southeast Asia*. New Haven: Yale University Press, 2009.
Seekins, Donald M. *Burma and Japan Since 1940: From "Co-Prosperity" to "Quiet Dialogue."* Copenhagen: NIAS, 2007.
Seekins, Donald M. "Myanmar in 2008: Hardship, Compounded." *Asian Survey* 49, no. 1 (January/February 2009).
Seekins, Donald M. *State and Society in Modern Rangoon*. London: Routledge, 2011.
Sein Win. *The Split Story*. Rangoon: Guardian, 1959.
Selth, Andrew. *Burma's Intelligence Apparatus*. Canberra: ANU Press, 1997.
Selth, Andrew. "Even Paranoids Have Enemies: Cyclone Nargis and Myanmar's Fears of Invasion." *Contemporary Southeast Asia* 30, no. 3 (December 2008).
Seo Bo-hyeok, 서보혁, Lee Chang-hee 이창희and Cha Sung-ju. 차승주. *Orae Doen Mirae? 1970 Nyundae Bukhan-ae Jae Jomyeong* 오래된 미래? 1970년대 북한의 재조명 ["An old future? 1970s North Korea in a new light"). Seoul: Seonin, 2015.
Sigal, Leon. "Hand in Hand for Korea: A Peace Process and Denuclearization." *Asian Perspective* 32, no. 2 (2008).
Sigal, Leon. "North Korea Is No Iraq: Pyongyang's Negotiating Strategy." *Arms Control Today* 32, no. 10 (December 2002).
Silverstein, Josef. "Civil War and Rebellion in Burma." *Journal of Southeast Asian Studies* 21, no. 1 (March 1990).
Silverstein, Josef. "The Evolution and Salience of Burma's National Political Culture." In *Burma: Prospects for a Democratic Future*, edited by Robert I. Rotberg. Washington, D.C., and Cambridge, MA: Brookings Institution and World Peace Foundation, 1998.

Silverstein, Josef. "Politics in the Shan State: The Question of Secession from the Union of Burma." *Journal of Asian Studies* 18, no. 1 (1958).
Simms, Marc. "United Wa State Army." *Human Security Centre, Security and Defence* 7, issue 3, (2014).
Smith, Martin. *Burma: Insurgency and the Politics of Ethnicity.* London: Zed, 1991.
Smith, Martin. "Ethnic Groups in Burma: Development, Democracy and Human Rights." Anti-Slavery International Report No. 8 (1994).
Smith, Martin. *State of Strife: The Dynamics of Ethnic Conflict in Burma.* Singapore: ISEAS, 2007.
Smith, Shane. *North Korea's Evolving Nuclear Strategy.* US-Korea Institute at SAIS Nuclear Futures Series, August 2015.
Snodgrass, J.J. *Narrative of the Burmese War.* New Delhi: Lancer, 1952.
Snyder, Scott. "U.S. Policy Toward North Korea." Council on Foreign Relations, January 23, 2013. http://www.cfr.org/north-korea/us-policy-toward-north-korea/p29962.
South, Ashley. *Burma's Longest War: Anatomy of the Karen Conflict.* Amsterdam: Transnational Institute, 2011.
South, Ashley. *Ethnic Politics in Burma: States of Conflict.* London: Routledge, 2008.
South, Ashley. *Mon Nationalism and Civil War in Burma: The Golden Sheldrake.* London: Routledge, 2013.
South, Ashley. *Mon Nationalist Movements: Insurgency, Ceasefires and Political Struggle.* Conference paper published by the Mon Unity League. Bangkok: January 2008.
Steinberg, David. "Burma-Myanmar: The U.S.-Burmese Relationship and Its Vicissitudes." In *Short of the Goal: U.S. Policy and Poorly Performing States*, edited by Nancy Birdsall, Milan Vaishnav, and Robert L. Ayres. Washington, D.C.: Center for Global Development, 2006.
Steinberg, David I. *Burma/Myanmar: What Everyone Needs to Know.* Oxford: Oxford University Press, 2009.
Steinberg, David I. *Burma: The State of Myanmar.* Washington, D.C.: Georgetown University Press, 2001.
Steinberg, David. "Globalization, Dissent, and Orthodoxy: Burma/Myanmar and the Saffron Revolution." *Georgetown Journal of International Affairs* 9, no. 2 (Summer/Fall 2008).
Steinberg, David I. "Myanmar and the United States, Closing and Opening Doors: An Idiosyncratic Analysis." *Social Research* 82, no. 2 (2015).
Steinberg, David. "Myanmar in 1992: Plus Ca Change...?" *Asian Survey* 33, no. 2, A Survey of Asia in 1992, Part II (February 1993).
Storey, Ian. "Burma's Relations with China: Neither Puppet nor Pawn." *Jamestown Foundation China Brief* 7, issue 3 (2007). https://jamestown.org/program/burmas-relations-with-china-neither-puppet-nor-pawn-4/.
Suh Dae Sook. *Kim Il Sung: The North Korean Leader.* New York: Columbia University Press, 1988.
Suh Jae-Jung. "Making Sense of North Korea: Juche as an Institution." In *Origins of North Korea's Juche Colonialism, War, and Development*, edited by Jae-Jung Suh and Chaejong So. Lanham, MD: Rowman & Littlefield, 2013.
Suryomenggolo, Jafar. *Organising under the Revolution: Unions and the State in Java, 1945–48.* Singapore: NUS, 2013.
Tarling, Nicholas. *The Cambridge History of Southeast Asia: Volume 1, from Early Times to c. 1800.* Cambridge: Cambridge University Press, 1993.
Taylor Robert H. "British Policy Towards Myanmar and the Creation of the Burma Problem." In *Myanmar: State, Society and Ethnicity*, edited by E. Ganesan and Kyaw Yin Hlaing. Singapore: ISEAS, 2007.
Taylor, Robert H. *Dr Maung Maung: Gentleman, Scholar, Patriot.* Singapore: ISEAS, 2008.

Taylor, Robert H. *Ne Win: A Political Biography.* Singapore: ISEAS, 2015.
Taylor, Robert H. *The State in Burma.* London: Hurst, 2009.
Thant Myint-U. *The Making of Modern Burma.* Cambridge: Cambridge University Press, 2001.
Thihan Myo Nyun. "Feeling Good or Doing Good: Inefficacy of the U.S. Unilateral Sanctions Against the Military Government of Burma/Myanmar." *Washington University Global Studies Law Review* 7, issue 3 (2008).
Thompson, Robert. *Defeating Communist Insurgency: Experiences from Malaya and Vietnam.* New York: Frederick A. Praeger, 1966.
Thompson, Virginia. "Burma's Communists." *Far Eastern Survey* 17, no. 9 (1948).
Tin Than Maung Maung. "Myanmar in 2008: Weathering the Storm." *Southeast Asian Affairs* (2009).
Tin Than Maung Maung. "Some Aspects of Indians in Rangoon." In *Indian Communities in Southeast Asia.* Edited by K.S. Sandhu and A. Mani. Singapore: ISEAS, 2006.
Tin Than Maung Maung. "Myanmar and China: A Special Relationship?" *ISEAS Southeast Asian Affairs.* Singapore: ISEAS, 2003
Trager, Frank. "Burma and China." *Journal of Southeast Asian History* 5, no. 1 (1964).
Trager, Peter. "Burma—1967—A Better Ending Than Beginning." *Asian Survey* 8, no. 2, A Survey of Asia in 1967, Part II (February 1968).
Trager, Peter. "Burma—1968—A New Beginning." *Asian Survey* 9, no. 2, A Survey of Asia in 1968, Part II (February 1969).
Tucker, Spencer C. *The Encyclopedia of the Vietnam War: A Political, Social, and Military History.* Santa Barbara: ABC-CLIO, 2011.
Tudor, Daniel, and James Pearson. *North Korea Confidential.* Singapore: Tuttle, 2015.
U Ba Than. *The Roots of the Revolution: A Brief History of the Defence Services of the Union of Burma and the Ideals for which They Stand.* Rangoon: Director of Information, 1962.
U Khin Win. *A Century of Rice Improvement in Burma.* Manila: International Rice Research Institute, 1991.
Van Ree, Erik. "The Limits of Juche: North Korea's Dependence on Soviet Industrial Aid, 1953–76." *Journal of Communist Studies* 5:1 (1989).
Wakeman, Carolyn, and San San Tin. *No Time for Dreams: Living in Burma Under Military Rule.* New York: Rowman & Littlefield, 2009.
Walker, Anthony R. "The Divisions of the Lahu People." *Journal of Siam Society* 62, Part 2 (1974).
Weathersby, Kathryn. "Dependence and Mistrust: North Korea's Relations with Moscow and the Evolution of Juche." Working Paper 08–08, U.S.-Korea Institute, SAIS, August 2008.
Weathersby, Kathryn. "Soviet Aims in Korea and the Origins of the Korean War, 1945–1950: New Evidence from Russian Archives." Woodrow Wilson International Center for Scholars, Cold War International History Project, Working Paper No. 8, November 1993.
Williams, Susan H. *Social Difference and Constitutionalism in Pan-Asia.* Cambridge: Cambridge University Press, 2014.
Win Min. "Burma: A Historic Force, Forcefully Met." In *Student Activism in Asia: Between Protest and Powerlessness* Weiss, edited by Meredith L. Weiss and Edward Aspinall. Minneapolis: University of Minnesota Press, 2012.
Wit, Joel S., Daniel B. Poneman and Robert L. Gallucci. *Going Critical: The First North Korean Nuclear Crisis.* Washington, D.C.: Brookings Institution, 2004.
Woods, Kevin. "China in Burma: A Multi-Scalar Political Economy Analysis." In *Chinese Encounters in Southeast Asia,* edited by Pál Nyíri and Danielle Tan. Seattle: University of Washington Press, 2016.
Xin Chen. "Introduction: The Six Party Talks and Challenges to Multilateralism." In

Whither the Six-Party Talks, edited by Yongjin Zhang. Auckland: New Zealand Asia Institute, 2006.
Yegar, Moshe. *Between Integration and Secession: The Muslim Communities of the Southern Philippines, Southern Thailand, and Western Burma/Myanmar*. New York: Roman & Littlefield, 2002.
Yonhap News Agency. *North Korea Handbook*. Armonk, NY: M.E. Sharpe, 2003.
Yonhap News Agency. *North Korea Handbook*. London: M.E. Sharpe, 2003.
Yoon Tae-young. "Terrorism and Crisis Management: The Rangoon Bombing Incident of 1983." *Global Economic Review* 30:4 (2001).
Young Whan Kihl. "North Korea in 1983: Transforming "The Hermit Kingdom"?" *Asian Survey* 24, no. 1, A Survey of Asia in 1983, Part I (January 1984).
Zagoria, Donald S., and Young Kun Kim. "North Korea and the Major Powers." *Asian Survey* 15, no. 12 (December 1975).
Zaw Oo and Win Min. *Assessing Burma's Ceasefire Accords*. Singapore: ISEAS, 2007.

Newspapers, Reports, Blogs, Statements and Other Media

"Analysis: New Media Challenges Old-Style Repression in Burma." BBC Monitoring Media [London], October 9, 2007.
Arakan Liberation Party (ALP) Official Webpage. "The Summary Background of Rakhaing Nation and Arakan Liberation Party." http://www.arakanalp.com/?page_id=6.
Arms Control Association. "Chronology of U.S.-North Korean Nuclear and Missile Diplomacy." https://www.armscontrol.org/factsheets/DPRKchron.
Arms Control Association. "Secretary Albright's Visit to North Korea." October 20, 2000. https://www.armscontrol.org/node/2513.
BBC TV. "Myo Thein on BBC Burmese Service's Impact on Burma." (Duration 8:10). Recorded September 2, 2010. https://www.youtube.com/watch?v=3Ty7rOu6PQo.
Blythe, Samuel. "Myanmar's Junta Fears U.S. Invasion." Asia Times Online, April 28, 2006. http://www.atimes.com/atimes/Southeast_Asia/HD28Ae03.html.
Boakye, Kojo. Nigel Scott, and Claire Smyth. "Mobiles for Development: Summary Report." UNICEF, November 2010. https://www.unicef.org/cbsc/files/Summary Mobiles4Dev_Report.pdf.
"Border Guard Force Scheme." Myanmar Peace Monitor. http://www.mmpeacemonitor.org/background/border-guard-force.
Bugher, Matthew. "Midnight Intrusions." Fortify Rights, March 2015. http://www.fortifyrights.org/downloads/FR_Midnight_Intrusions_March_2015.pdf.
"Bukhan gaejeong heonbeobseo haek boyuguk myeong si" 북한 개정 헌법서 핵 보유국 명시 [North Korea in revised constitution clearly claims it is a nuclear state]. *Hankyoreh* 한겨레, May 30, 2012. http://www.hani.co.kr/arti/politics/defense/535439.html.
"Burma: Chronology of Aung San Suu Kyi's Detention." Human Rights Watch, November 13, 2010. https://www.hrw.org/news/2010/11/13/burma-chronology-aung-san-suu-kyis-detention.
"Burma Leaders Double Fuel Prices." *BBC*, August 15, 2007. http://news.bbc.co.uk/2/hi/asia-pacific/6947251.stm.
"Burmese Rioting Hits Mao Support." Associated Press, June 27, 1967.
Byrne, Leo. "North Korean Coal, Iron Exports Increase Again in June." NK Pro, July 25, 2016. https://www.nknews.org/pro/north-korean-coal-iron-exports-increase-again-in-june/.
Byrne, Leo. "Trade Figures Between Two Koreas Drop by Over 99 Percent." NKNews, June 15, 2016. https://www.nknews.org/2016/06/trade-figures-between-two-koreas-drop-by-over-99-percent/.

Central Intelligence Agency. "Communist Influence in Burma." ORE 86–49, January 11, 1950.

"Challenges Ahead In Dealing With North Korea's Nuclear Ambitions." East-West Center, U.S. Asia Pacific Council Washington Report, November 2009. http://www.eastwestcenter.org/fileadmin/resources/washington/cha1109.pdf

Chapman, William. "North Korean Leader's Son Blamed for Rangoon Bombing." *The Washington Post*, December 3, 1983, https://www.washingtonpost.com/archive/politics/1983/12/03/north-korean-leaders-son-blamed-for-rangoon-bombing/ddec34cc-9c12-4fc6-bf75-36057091aa4e/?utm_term=.137c1dc5d020.

Choe, Won-gi.최원기. "tal-ppuk-jja-deul, e-bu-kan bong-geon-si-dae-ro hu-toe-e." 탈북자들, "북한 봉건시대로 후퇴 ["Defectors: North Korea has regressed to the feudal era"]. VOA, July 8, 2010. http://www.voakorea.com/content/north-korea-98012094/1334887.html.

Committee to Protect Journalists. "Attacks on the Press 2009: Burma." 2010. https://www.cpj.org/2010/02/attacks-on-the-press-2009-burma.php.

Culbertson, Shelly. "Foreign Radio Stations Most Popular Source of News in Myanmar." Associated Press, July 31, 2003. http://jacksonville.com/tu-online/apnews/stories/073103/D7SK9E000.html.

"Democratic Voice of Burma 88 Students' Open Heart Campaign Ends." BurmaNet News, March 5, 2007. http://www.burmanet.org/news/2007/03/05/democratic-voice-of-burma-88-students%E2%80%99-open-heart-campaign-ends/.

Department of the Treasury, Office of Public Affairs. Treasury Department Designates Burma and Two Burmese Banks to Be of "Primary Money Laundering Concern" and Announces Proposed Countermeasures Under Section 311 of the USA Patriot Act. November 19, 2003.

Dhamma, Rewata. "Buddhism, Human Rights and Justice in Burma." Speech, Church Center for the UN, New York, November 1989. http://www.burmalibrary.org/docs08/Rewata_Dhamma-Buddhism_Human_Rights_and_Justice_in_Burma.pdf.

"Difficult Lives: Interviews in Kachin State." *Project Maje Interview*, September 1991. http://www.projectmaje.org/pdf/dif_live.pdf.

Earth Rights International. "Total Impact: The Human Rights, Environmental, and Financial Impacts of Total and Chevron's Yadana Gas Project in Military-Ruled Burma." September 2009. https://www.earthrights.org/sites/default/files/publications/total-impact.pdf.

Ei Thae Thae Naing. "Yangon University Set to Reopen." *Myanmar Times*, July 31, 2013. http://www.mmtimes.com/index.php/national-news/7654-yangon-university-set-to-reopen.html.

Embassy of the People's Republic of China in the DPRK. "China-DPRK Bilateral Relations—Before 1990s of the 20th Century." http://kp.china-embassy.org/eng/zcgx/sbgx/90ndzq/.

"Episode 56—Hyeonseo Lee." Korea and the World Podcast, January 19, 2016. http://www.koreaandtheworld.com/hyeonseo-lee/.

Erlanger, Steven. "Burmese Ban Top Opposition Candidate." *The New York Times*, January 18, 1990. http://www.nytimes.com/1990/01/18/world/burmese-ban-top-opposition-candidate.html.

Erlanger, Steven. "Clinton Approves New U.S. Sanctions Against Burmese." *New York Times*, April 22, 1997. http://www.nytimes.com/1997/04/22/world/clinton-approves-new-us-sanctions-against-burmese.html.

Eubank, David. "Under Attack: A Way of Life." Forced Migration Review, FMR Report 30, April 2008. http://www.fmreview.org/sites/fmr/files/FMRdownloads/en/FMRpdfs/FMR30/10-11.pdf.

Federal Register. "Notices, September 20, 2005." Page 55214. https://www.fincen.gov/statutes_regs/patriot/pdf/finding_banco.pdf.

"First U.S. Aid Plane Lands in Burma." *BBC*, May 12, 2008. http://news.bbc.co.uk/2/hi/asia-pacific/7395364.stm.
"A Former Political Prisoner's Take on Myanmar's Reforms." Interview with Bo Kyi. LinkAsia, Link TV, March 16, 2012. https://www.youtube.com/watch?v=MrXEvN1N7mc.
Global Witness Report. "Jade: Myanmar's 'Big State Secret.'" October 2016. https://www.globalwitness.org/en/campaigns/oil-gas-and-mining/myanmarjade/.
Global Witness Report. "Lords of Jade." December 3, 2015. https://www.globalwitness.org/en/reports/lords-jade/.
Green, Penny. "Countdown to Annihilation: Genocide in Myanmar." International State Crime Initiative, School of Law, Queen Mary University, London, October 2015. http://statecrime.org/data/2015/10/ISCI-Rohingya-Report-PUBLISHED-VERSION.pdf.
Heritage Foundation. "North Korea Human Rights Conference." Washington, D.C. April 2015. https://www.youtube.com/watch?v=C-2HbYHFjf4.
Hitchens, Christopher. "Worse Than 1984." *Slate*, May 2, 2005, http://www.slate.com/articles/news_and_politics/fighting_words/2005/05/worse_than_1984.html.
H.R. 757: North Korea Sanctions and Policy Enhancement Act of 2016, U.S. Congress. February 18, 2016. https://www.congress.gov/bill/114th-congress/house-bill/757.
Htun Khaing. "Shedding New Light on 88." Frontier Myanmar, August 8, 2016. http://frontiermyanmar.net/en/shedding-new-light-on-88.
Human Rights Documentation Unit. "Burma Human Rights Yearbook 1996." 1997.
Human Rights Watch. "Burma's Forgotten Prisoners." September 2009.
Human Rights Watch. "Human Rights in Burma (Myanmar)." 1990. https://www.hrw.org/reports/1990/WR90/ASIA.BOU-02.htm.
"Inter-Korean Trade Hits Record High in 2015 Despite Shaky Ties." Yonhap News, January 21, 2016. http://english.yonhapnews.co.kr/northkorea/2016/01/21/0401000000AEN20160121001500320.html.
Internal Displacement Monitoring Center. "Myanmar IDP Figure Analysis." http://www.internal-displacement.org/south-and-south-east-asia/myanmar/figures-analysis.
International Institute for Strategic Studies. "Disarmament Diplomacy with North Korea." IISS Strategic Dossier 2011, Chapter 4. https://www.iiss.org/en/publications/strategic%20dossiers/issues/north-korean-security-challenges-4a8d/nksc-06-chapter-4-ccb3.
"The Internet in Burma (1998–2009)." *Mizzima News*, December 24, 2009.
"Interview with Colonial Chit Myiang." *Burma Debate* 4, no. 3 (1997).
"Interview with We Se." From Burma to New York: The Stories of Burmese Refugees, Multimedia Project. http://fromburmatonewyork.com/.
Joint Kokang-Wa Humanitarian Needs Assessment Team. "Replacing Opium in Kokang and Wa Special Regions, Shan State, Myanmar." 2003.
"Juche Iron Production System Established." *KCNA*, October 7, 2010.
"Jung-Guk Nae Wa Ju-Min 100 Myeong-E-Ge Gyeong-Je Sa-Jeong-P-Ssa-Hoe Hyeon-Si-Re." 중국 내 北 주민 100명에게 경제 사정·사회 현실에 대해 인터뷰했더 ["We interviewed 100 northerners living in China about the economic situation and current society"]. *Choson Ilbo*, 朝鮮日報 July 8, 2014. http://thestory.chosun.com/site/data/html_dir/2014/07/08/2014070800866.html.
Kang, Ji-Min. "Neighborhood Watch: Inside North Korea's Secret Police System." NK News, February 26, 2014. https://www.nknews.org/2014/02/neighborhood-watch-inside-north-koreas-secret-service-system/.
Karen National Union Website. http://karennationalunion.net.
Karenni Independence through Education Website. "About the Karenni." http://www.karenni.org/about_the_karenni.php.
Kennard, Matt, and Claire Provost. "Burma's Bizarre Capital: A Super-Sized Slice of Post-Apocalypse Suburbia." *The Guardian*, March 19 2015. https://www.theguardian.com/cities/2015/mar/19/burmas-capital-naypyidaw-post-apocalypse-suburbia-highways-wifi.

Kessler, Glenn. "Message to U.S. Preceded Nuclear Declaration by North Korea." *Washington Post*, July 2, 2008. http://www.washingtonpost.com/wp-dyn/content/article/2008/07/01/AR2008070102847.html.

Kessler, Glenn. "New Data Found On North Korea's Nuclear Capacity." *Washington Post*, June 21, 2008. http://www.washingtonpost.com/wp-dyn/content/article/2008/06/20/AR2008062002499.html.

Kim Deok-hyun. "China's Imports of N. Korean Goods Fall 12.6 Pct. in May." Yonhap News, June 22, 2016. http://english.yonhapnews.co.kr/national/2016/06/22/26/0301000000AEN20160622010200315F.html.

Kim Jae Young. "Why Did We Never Complain? We Didn't Even Know How To." NK News, November 5, 2012. https://www.nknews.org/2012/11/why-did-we-never-complain-some-of-us-didnt-even-know-how-to/.

Kim Jeong-u.김정우. "Bukhan dae jungguk suchul 1wi pummok 'seoktan,' suip 1wihapseong Pilamentusa jikmul." 북한 대중국 수출 1위 품목 '석탄,' 수입 1위 '합성 필라멘트사 직물 ["North Korea's no. 1 export to China is coal; no. 1 import is 'synthetic filament-yarn textiles'"]. *Voice of America*, February 4, 2016.

Kim Seong Hwan. "30–40% of NK Thought to be Tuning into Pirate Radio: How Do We Reach More?" Daily NK, September 14, 2015. http://www.dailynk.com/english/read.php?cataId=nk00100&num=13460.

Kim Yoo-sung. "College Life in North Korea: It's Like the Military." NK News, February 10, 2016. https://www.nknews.org/2016/02/college-life-in-north-korea-its-like-the-military/.

Kwaak, Jeyup S. "North Korean Escapees Say They Perceive Solid Support for Dictator." *Wall Street Journal*, August 26, 2015. http://www.wsj.com/articles/north-korean-escapees-report-solid-support-for-dictator-kim-1440568866.

Kywa Zwa Moe. "Annan Criticizes Road Map." *The Irrawaddy*, November 12, 2003. http://www2.irrawaddy.com/article.php?art_id=1345.

Kyaw Zwa Moe. "From the Archive: The Heroic Medics of the 8888 Uprising." *The Irrawaddy*, September 19, 2016.

Lankov, Andrei. "Mathematics—a la North Korea." *Korea Times*, August 8, 2011. http://www.koreatimes.co.kr/www/news/nation/2011/08/113_93651.html.

Lee Seok Young. "Pyongyang Seeing Tighter Inspections." Daily NK, August 24, 2011. http://www.dailynk.com/english/read.php?cataId=nk01500&num=8094.

Letter to the Editor. "In Burma, 'Bloodless' Coup Began Violent Era." *New York Times*, August 13, 1988. http://www.nytimes.com/1988/08/13/opinion/l-in-burma-bloodless-coup-began-violent-era-570888.html.

Lintner, Bertil. "China Behind Myanmar's Course Shift." Asia Times, Oct. 19, 2011. http://www.atimes.com/atimes/Southeast_Asia/MJ19Ae03.html.

Lintner, Bertil. "Democracy as Practiced by the Burmese Generals: Myanmar: Today's Elections, First in 28 Years, Won't Empower an Oppressed People—But They Will Fatten the Treasury by Bringing Back Foreign Investors." *Los Angeles Times*, May 27, 1990, http://articles.latimes.com/1990-05-27/opinion/op-103_1_general-elections.

Longoria, Alvaro. *The Propaganda Game*. Documentary. Spain, 2015.

Lu Thit. "Do Not Make the Goal of Democracy Far Away from the People." The New Light of Myanmar, July 3, 2008. Translation at http://www.burmanet.org/news/2008/07/31/the-new-light-of-myanmar-do-not-make-the-goal-of-democracy-far-away-from-the-people-%E2%80%93-lu-thit/.

MacKinnon, Ian. "Burma to Let in All Cyclone Nargis Aid Workers." *The Guardian*, May 23, 2008. https://www.theguardian.com/world/2008/may/23/cyclonenargis.burma.

"Man Arrested for Allegedly Contacting Foreign Radio Stations." BBC Monitoring Media [London] Burma, February 15, 2002.

Mansky, Vitaly. *Under the Sun*. Documentary. Russia, 2015.

Min Zin. "Keeping the Pulse of Burmese Airwaves." *The Irrawaddy*, November 2002. http://www2.irrawaddy.com/article.php?art_id=2784.
Moe Maka Blog. "The Death of a Student—Ko Phone Maw—March 13th 1988 in Rangoon, Burma," Moe Maka, April 10, 2011, http://eng.moemaka.net/2011/04/the-death-of-a-student-ko-phone-maw-march-13th-1988-in-rangoon-burma/.
"My Hero Aung San." *The Guardian*, April 29, 2011.
"Myanmar Is Not Afraid of U.S. Sanctions: Suu Kyi." Eleven Myanmar, May 23, 2016. http://www.elevenmyanmar.com/politics/myanmar-not-afraid-us-sanctions-suu-kyi.
"Myanmar-Singapore Bilateral Trade Reaches $1.86 Bln." *Xinhua*, June 30, 2010. http://en.people.cn/90001/90778/90858/90863/7047513.html.
"Myanmar Trade, Exports and Imports." Economy Watch, March 17, 2010. http://www.economywatch.com/world_economy/myanmar/export-import.html.
"Myanmar's 2015 Landmark Elections Explained." BBC News, Dec. 3, 2015. http://www.bbc.com/news/world-asia-33547036.
Mydans, Seth. "Uprising in Burma: The Old Regime Under Siege." *The New York Times*, August 12, 1988. http://www.nytimes.com/1988/08/12/world/uprising-in-burma-the-old-regime-under-siege.html.
NAPSNet Special Reports. "The Mining Industry of North Korea." August 4, 2011. http://nautilus.org/napsnet/napsnet-special-reports/the-mining-industry-of-north-korea/.
Nay Htun Naing. "When the Promise of 1990 Election Was Nullified." *Eleven Media*, May 11, 2015. http://www.elevenmyanmar.com/opinion/when-promise-1990-election-was-nullified.
"Naypyitaw: A Home for Myanmar's Unexpected Democracy." Conference at East-West Center, Washington, D.C., September 6, 2013. http://publicinternationallawandpolicygroup.org/wp-content/uploads/2013/09/PILPG-Event-Review-Naypyitaw-A-Home-for-Myanmars-Unexpected-Democracy.pdf.
Nebehay, Stephanie. "Myanmar Set to Dodge Full U.N. Probe on Rohingya abuse," Reuters, March 9, 2017. http://uk.reuters.com/article/uk-myanmar-rohingya-un-idUKKBN16G03Q.
"1974 Constitution of the Socialist Republic of Burma." Article 157. https://www.ilo.org/dyn/natlex/docs/ELECTRONIC/74764/77203/F1514529724/MMR74764.pdf.
Noland, Marcus. "Analysis of UNSCR 2321 Sanctions on North Korea." Peterson Institute for International Affairs Blogs—Witness to Transformation, November 30, 2016. https://piie.com/blogs/north-korea-witness-transformation/analysis-unscr-2321-sanctions-north-korea.
"North Korea Amends the Constitution." IFES NK Briefs, no. 16–06–06, June 6, 2012.
Norwegian Refugee Council/Global IDP Project. "Profile of Internal Displacement: Myanmar." 2005. http://www.internal-displacement.org/assets/library/Asia/Myanmar/pdf/Myanmar-Burma-June-2005.pdf.
OECD. "Development Pathways Multi-dimensional Review of Myanmar, Volume 1." OECD, 2013. http://www.oecd.org/dev/multi-dimensional-review-of-myanmar.htm.
Oo, Hla. "Martyrs' Mausoleum Bombing Video (Rangoon—1983)." June 2011. http://hlaoo1980.blogspot.com/2011/06/martyrs-mausoleum-bombing-video-rangoon.html.
Oo, Hla. "1974 U Thant Uprising: A First Hand Account." New Mandala, July 23, 2008. http://asiapacific.anu.edu.au/newmandala/2008/07/23/1974-u-thant-uprising-a-first-hand-account/.
PBS Frontline "Interview with Madeline Albright." 2003. http://www.pbs.org/wgbh/pages/frontline/shows/kim/interviews/albright.html.
Pearson, James. "North Korea's Black Market Becoming the New Normal." Reuters, October 29, 2015. http://www.reuters.com/article/us-northkorea-change-insight-idUSKCN0SN00320151029.
Peck, Grant. "Arms Easy to Buy for Myanmar Junta." Associated Press, October 12, 2007.

http://www.washingtonpost.com/wp-dyn/content/article/2007/10/12/AR200710 1201310_pf.html.

Pidd, Helen. "Burma Ends Advance Press Censorship." *The Guardian*, August 20, 2012. http://www.theguardian.com/world/2012/aug/20/burma-ends-advance-press-censorship.

Poppe, Ludo. *Who Is The Drug King of the Golden Triangle?* Documentary. 1994. London: Journeyman Pictures. https://www.youtube.com/watch?v=ji2S_cGFPqc.

Preliminary Report of The Ad Hoc Commission on Depayin Massacre (Burma). July 4, 2003.

"Q&A: Protests in Burma." BBC, October 2, 2007. http://news.bbc.co.uk/2/hi/asia-pacific/7010202.stm.

"Report on Plenary Meeting of WPK Central Committee." KCNA, March 31, 2013.

"Response to Cyclone in Myanmar 'Unacceptably Slow'—Ban Ki-Moon." U.N. News Centre, May 12, 2008. http://www.un.org/apps/news/story.asp?NewsID=26634#.WEjEz WR96L1.

Revolutionary Council. Burmese Way to Socialism. April 28, 1962, http://www.ibiblio. org/obl/docs/The_Burmese_Way_to_Socialism.htm.

"Rohingya/Bengali: A Snapshot of Community in 1960s." The Network for International Protection of Refugees, August 2015. http://netipr.org/policy/downloads/snapshot-of-community-1960s.pdf.

ROK Ministry of Unification. "Major Agreements: The July 4 South-North Joint Communique." http://eng.unikorea.go.kr/content.do?cmsid=1889&mode=view&page= 8&cid=32113.

Russell, Clyde. "China Buys Record North Korean Coal as Sanctions Ignored: Russell." Reuters, September 26, 2016. http://www.reuters.com/article/us-column-russell-coal-china-idUSKCN11W0CO.

San Yamin Aung. "NLD Candidates Await Latest Appeal on Coco Islands Access." *The Irrawaddy*, October 12, 2015. http://www.irrawaddy.com/election/news/nld-candidates-await-latest-appeal-on-coco-islands-access.

Saw Yan Naing. "Information on Dead, Arrested, Missing Is Hard to Find." *The Irrawaddy*, October 2, 2007. http://www2.irrawaddy.com/article.php?art_id=8850&Submit= Submit.

Saw Yan Naing. "'Sandwich Reporting' Keeps the Censors Guessing." *The Irrawaddy*, August 12, 2010. http://www.burmanet.org/news/2010/08/12/irrawaddy-sandwich-reporting-keeps-the-censors-guessing-%E2%80%93-saw-yan-naing/.

Seol Song Ah. "In Russia, North Korean Laborers Risk Death for a Chance to Earn Cash." Daily NK, June 27, 2016. http://www.dailynk.com/english/read.php?cataId=nk 02500&num=14010.

["Seoul sea of fire statement"] "94년 서울 불바다 발언." March 19, 1994. https://www.youtube.com/watch?v=q6EnoB0f31s.

Sherman, Wendy. "Talking to the North Koreans." *New York Times*, March 7, 2001, http://www.nytimes.com/2001/03/07/opinion/talking-to-the-north-koreans.html.

"Signing of a Protocol Agreement for North Korea to Send a Number of Pilots to Fight the American Imperialists During the War of Destruction Against North Vietnam, September 30, 1966." History and Public Policy Program Digital Archive, Vietnam Ministry of Defense Central Archives, Central Military Party Committee Collection, File no. 433. Obtained and translated for NKIDP by Merle Pribbenow. http:// digitalarchive.wilsoncenter.org/document/113926.

"Singapore Denies Money Laundering Myanmar Leaders: TV." Reuters, October 5, 2007.

Solomon, Jay, and Neil King, Jr. "How U.S. Used a Bank to Punish North Korea." *Wall Street Journal*, April 12, 2007.

Spaeth, Anthony. "Setting Free 'the Lady.'" *Time*, July 24, 1995. http://content.time.com/ time/magazine/article/0,9171,983201,00.html.

Steinberg, David I. "Aung San Suu Kyi's Sanctions Conundrum." Nikkei Asian Review, April 25, 2016. http://asia.nikkei.com/Viewpoints/Viewpoints/David-I.-Steinberg-Aung-San-Suu-Kyi-s-sanctions-conundrum.

Stockholm International Peace Research Institute Trade Registers. http://armstrade.sipri.org/armstrade/page/trade_register.php.

"Summary: Karenni National Progressive Party." Myanmar Peace Monitor. http://www.mmpeacemonitor.org/stakeholders/armed-ethnic-groups/160-knpp.

Swe Win. "Exclusive—Abuse and Corruption Exposed in Myanmar's Prison Labour Camps." Reuters, September 1, 2016. http://uk.reuters.com/article/uk-myanmar-prisons-idUKKCN1175FQ.

Tan, Vivian. "U.S. Wraps Up Group Resettlement for Myanmar Refugees in Thailand." UNCHR. January 19, 2014. http://www.unhcr.org/en-us/news/latest/2014/1/52e90f8f6/wraps-group-resettlement-myanmar-refugees-thailand.html.

"Thailand: Burma Hits Refugees." *Off Our Backs* 26, no. 2 (February 1996).

Thant, Htoo. "Mobile Penetration Reaches Half the Country," *Myanmar Times*, June 2, 2015, http://www.mmtimes.com/index.php/business/technology/14815-mobile-penetration-reaches-half-the-country.html..

Times Staff and Wire Reports. "World in Brief: Myanmar: Opposition Gains, Standoff Continues." *Los Angeles Times*, May 31, 1990. http://articles.latimes.com/1990-05-31/news/mn-937_1_standoff-continues.

Trautwein, Catherine. "Myanmar Named Fourth-Fastest-Growing Mobile Market in the World by Ericsson." *Myanmar Times*, November 20, 2015. http://www.mmtimes.com/index.php/business/technology/17727-myanmar-named-fourth-fastest-growing-mobile-market-in-the-world-by-ericsson.html.

"Treasury Takes Actions to Further Restrict North Korea's Access to the U.S. Financial System." U.S. Treasury Press Release, June 1, 2016. https://www.treasury.gov/press-center/press-releases/Pages/jl0471.aspxSt.

2015 북한 대외무역 동향. *2015 Bukhan Daewae Muyeok Monghyang* ["2015 trends in North Korea external trade"]. KOTRA Report, 2016.

United Nations Committee for Development Policy. "List of Least Developed Countries." https://www.un.org/development/desa/dpad/least-developed-country-category.html.

United Nations Security Council Archive. "Security Council Condemns Nuclear Test by Democratic People's Republic of Korea, Unanimously Adopting Resolution 1718 (2006)." October 14, 2006.

United Nations Security Council Archive. "Security Council Strengthens Sanctions on Democratic People's Republic of Korea, in Response to 12 February Nuclear Test." March 7, 2013." http://www.un.org/press/en/2013/sc10934.doc.htm.

U.S. Department of State. "Joint Statement of the Fourth Round of the Six-Party Talks,Beijing, 19 September 2005," https://www.state.gov/p/eap/regional/c15455.htm.

U.S. Department of State. "State Department Cable 366371." Origin INR-10, Digital National Security Archive, December 28, 1983.

U.S. Government Accountability Office. Report to the Chairman, Committee on Foreign Relations, U.S. Senate. "North Korea Sanctions." May 2015.

U.S. Library of Congress. Congressional Research Service. CRS Insight: The Shutdown of the Joint North/South Korean Kaesong Industrial Complex, by Mark Manyin. IN10442. 2016. https://www.fas.org/sgp/crs/row/IN10442.pdf.

U.S. Library of Congress. Congressional Research Service. *U.S. Sanctions on Burma*, by Michael F. Martin. R41336. 2012. https://fas.org/sgp/crs/row/R41336.pdf.

U.S. Senate Committee on Foreign Relations Subcommittee on East Asian and Pacific Affairs. "Testimony by Veronika A. Martin (Advocate, Refugees Internat'l)." June 18, 2003. https://www.foreign.senate.gov/imo/media/doc/MartinTestimony030618.pdf.

"United Wa State Army." Myanmar Peace Monitor. http://www.mmpeacemonitor.org/component/content/article/57-stakeholders/169-uwsa.

University of Central Arkansas Political Science Website. "Burma/Karens (1948-Present) Timeline." http://uca.edu/politicalscience/dadm-project/asiapacific-region/burmakarens-1948-present/.

Vrieze, Paul. "Activists: Defamation Cases Surge in Myanmar." VOA, January 2, 2017. http://www.voanews.com/a/activists-say-defamation-cases-surge-in-myanmar/3659806.html.

Wa Lone. "Red Bridge Burns Bright for Student Activists." Myanmar Times, April 8, 2014. http://www.mmtimes.com/index.php/national-news/10110-red-bridge-burns-bright-for-student-activists.html.

Wai Moe. "Naypyidaw Orders New 'Four Cuts' Campaign." *The Irrawaddy*, March 4, 2011. http://www2.irrawaddy.com/article.php?art_id=20880.

Wai Moe. "The Opposition's Generation Gap." *The Irrawaddy*, June 25, 2004. http://www2.irrawaddy.com/opinion_story.php?art_id=3586.

World Bank International Tourism Data. 2016. http://data.worldbank.org/indicator/ST.INT.ARVL.

Yoon, Mina. "Who Do North Koreans Think Started the Korean War?" NKNews, January 8, 2014, https://www.nknews.org/2014/01/who-do-north-koreans-think-started-the-korean-war/.

Zain Al-Mahmood, Syed, and Alastair Gale. "North Korean with $1.4 Million in Gold Stopped in Bangladesh." *Wall Street Journal*, March 7, 2015.

Index

Albright, Madeline 66
Anderson, Benedict 88
Anglo-Burmese Wars 14
Anti-Fascist People's Freedom League (AFPFL) 27, 32, 38
Arakan *see* Rakhine
Aris, Michael 77, 81
Armistice, Korean 3, 13
Article 66(d) *see* 2013 Telecommunications Act
ASEAN *see* Association of Southeast Asian Nations
Association of Southeast Asian Nations 146, 185
Attlee, Clement 27
Aung Gyi 34, 39, 75, 79
Aung San 22, 23, 27, 30
Aung San Suu Kyi 1, 5, 22, 30, 133, 130, 187; and NLD 77, 79, 82, 137, 145–146; and reform process 182, 183; and sanctions 4, 139, 145–146, 149, 152–154
Australia 52, 154
Axis of Evil 2, 67

Ban Ki-moon 85
Banco Delta Asia 69, 156, 160, 161
BBC 78, 116,
Black Markets 46, 94, 119
Blue House Raid 50, 52
British Broadcasting Corporation see *BBC*
Buddhism in Burma/Myanmar 32, 95; as state religion 40, 91
Bush, George H.W. 58
Bush, George W. 2, 4, 9, 67, 69–70, 145–146, 156, 166
Burma Independence Army 22, 23–24
Burma Socialist Programme Party 45, 75, 92, 95
Burma Workers and Peasants Party 38

Cao de Benos, Alajandro 99, 108
Caretaker Government 39, 41
Carter, Jimmy 63, 67, 155

Central Institute of Civil Service 169
Cha, Victor 166
Chin 16, 32
China 2, 20, 23, 24, 26, 57, 58, 68, 85, 89, 98, 4, 174, 185, 190, 194; Cultural Revolution 36, 52; and Kachin 17, 43, 177, 178; and KMT 35; and Myanmar trade/economy 147, 150–152, 174, 189; and North Korea trade/economy 3–4, 99, 100, 110, 118, 119, 127, 158–159, 161, 162–164, 167; and nuclear weapons 60, 70–71; People's Liberation Army 26, 35; and reforms 55–56, 102; and refugees 172; relations with CPB and Wa 34, 36, 110, 173–174; and sanctions 142, 143, 146, 150, 154, 157, 158, 187
Chinese Minority in Burma 18, 36
Choe Sang-hun 122
Choson Dynasty 89, 98
Chosun University 121
Christianity: in Korea 12, 127; in Myanmar 15, 17, 91
Chun Doo-hwan 54, 123
Clinton, Bill 63, 65–68, 146, 193
Clinton, Hillary 6, 144
colonial infrastructure 13
Commission of Inquiry on Human Rights in the DPRK *see* United Nations—Commission of Inquiry
Committee to Protect Journalists (CPJ). 112–113
Communist Part of Burma 32–33, 34, 36, 92
Constitution: in Burma 40, 41, 80, 91–92, 112; in North Korea 72, 166; 2008 in Myanmar 8, 86, 124, 153, 177, 182–183
coup d'etat: in Burma 30, 37, 39, 41–42, 91–93; in South Korea 49
Cox, Robert 88
Cumings, Bruce 20, 26
currency reform 46, 74, 105
Cyclone Nargis 84–86, 122, 169, 183

235

Index

debt in Burma: personal 19; sovereign 46, 74, 105
defectors: from North Korea 101, 103–104, 114, 131; from the Tatmadaw 78
Democratic Voice of Burma 83, 116
Depayin Massacre 81–82, 146
Drezner, Daniel D. 141
DVDs, smuggled into North Korea 8, 126, 136

economic plans (multi-year) 48, 97
education 133–135
8888 Uprising see People's Democracy Movement and the 1988 Uprising
88 Generation 130, 135, 145
elections: in Korea 25; 1990 in Myanmar 1, 78–80, 81, 105, 112, 144, 154, 172, 183; other in Burma/Myanmar 1, 40, 91, 150, 153, 182–183; 2000 in U.S. 67–68
ethnic identity 15, 17, 18
European Union 139, 140, 144, 146, 151, 153, 187,

Facebook 7, 119; and defamation in Myanmar 8, 113–114, 188
famine 8, 36, 54, 56–57, 60, 90, 100, 108, 111, 128
Farrelly, Nicolas 180
Federalism: between the Koreas 53; in Burma/Myanmar 3, 40, 41, 169, 172
Four Cuts Doctrine 5, 169–172, 175, 177, 179, 186
Freedom of Information 1, 108, 116–123; in Myanmar 8; in North Korea 57
Freedom of Movement 109–111

General Bureau of Publications Guidance 111
Germany 46
Ghaddafi, Muammar 9, 72–73, 167

Harris, Paul 82
Hiroshima 13
Hussein, Saddam 72, 143, 167

India 14, 16, 37, 77, 151, 181, 185; migrants after independence 45, 92; migrants during colonial rule 18–19
inflation in Burma 31, 46, 74
Internally Displaced Person (IDPs) 110, 171, 172, 186
International Atomic Energy Agency 61–62, 63–64, 68–69, 70, 155
Internet 83, 116–119, 120
Iraq 2, 9, 143
Irrawaddy River 15, 85, 122
Islamists 33–34
Israel 64, 151, 165, 189

Jade: as exceedingly clever acronym 148; as export commodity 5, 147–148, 174
Japan 24, 27, 46, 60, 66, 69, 146, 154; colonization of Korea 12, 13, 19–21; invasion of Burma 19, 23–24
Japan–Korea Treaty of 1876 19
Jo Myong Rok 66
Joint Ventures in North Korea 56, 118, 120, 160, 164
journalism: foreign press 79, 81, 82, 84, 107, 121–123, 124; in Myanmar 112; in North Korea 111, 112
Juche 2, 47, 50, 51, 59, 90, 95, 96–97, 100, 102, 103, 104,

Kachin 16, 17, 28, 32, 40, 134; cooperation with British 21–22; Independence Organization/Army 40, 43, 177–178
Kaesong Industrial Park 4, 161–162, 164
Karen: 17, 23, 28, 32, 181; cooperation with British 15–16, 21, 22; insurgency 33, 36, 38, 42, 174, 176–177
Karen National Union 33
Karenni Insurgency 28, 36–37, 174–175
Kayah (Karenni) State 8, 109, 174–175, 181
Kaung Thet 83
Kenji Nagai, shooting of 84
Kerry, John 7
Khrushchev, Nikita 48
Kim Dae-jung 62, 66
Kim family 6, 55, 191
Kim Il Sung 25, 31, 48, 49, 50, 51, 52, 54, 56, 63, 134
Kim Jong Il 1, 51, 54, 56, 63, 70, 118, 165
Kim Jong Un 1, 71, 104, 128, 133, 158, 166, 191, 193
Kokang Army 174, 178–179
Korean Air Flight 858, 73
Korean Peninsula Energy Development Organization (KEDO) 64–65, 155–156
Korean War 25–26, 28, 47, 121; and Burmese politics 38
Korean Workers' Party 47 48, 125; Congress of 48
Kuomintang 28, 35–36

Laos 35, 42–43, 52
Larkin, Emma 122
Leap Day Deal 71
Least Developed Country 74
Lee Man-woo 53, 54

Malaya 18, 21; and counter-insurgency 170
Malaysia 52, 64
Mao Zedong: competition from Kim Il Sungism 52; support for in Burma 36, 43, 173
Maung Maung 39, 77

Mandalay 14, 33, 77, 180, 181
military affairs security *see* military intelligence
military-first politics *see* Songun
military intelligence 105, 112–113, 123, 124, 132, 136, 174
Ministry of People's Security 125
Ministry of State Security *see* State Security Department
Min Maung 42
missile program 30, 65, 71, 73, 155, 166; tests of 66, 71
Mitchell, Derek 145
Mon 17; and insurgency 37, 43–44, 176
Mongla Group 174
Monolithic System (North Korea) 51, 90, 96, 99–100, 104
Myanmar National Democractic Army *see* Kokang Army
Myanmar Post and Telecommunications (MPT) 117, 119

Nagasaki 13
Nargis *see* Cyclone Nargis
National Defence Committee (Burma) 39
National Democratic Alliance Army *see* Mongla Group
National Democratic Front 44, 172
National League for Democracy 1, 79, 80–82, 90, 105, 123, 129, 146, 149, 153, 183–184
National Narrative 87–88, 90; in Burma/Myanmar 91–95, 106; in North Korea 95–105,
Naypyidaw City 133, 179–182
Ne Win 31, 34, 38, 40, 45, 74, 75, 77, 95, 123, 128–129
1962 Printers and Publishers Registration Act (Burma) 112
Nuclear Program of North Korea 7, 61–73, 102, 165–167
nuclear test 4, 69, 71, 166
Non-proliferation Treaty 61–62, 64, 68, 155

Obama, Barack 6
Ooreedoo 120
opium 42–43, 110, 173–174
Orascom 120
Organization and Guidance Department 125
Orwell, George 107
Outposts of Tyranny 2

Pakistan 65, 155
Palaung Insurgency 42, 178–179
Panghsang 173
Panglong Agreement 27, 33, 37, 40
Pa-o Insurgency 37–38, 175

Park Chung-hee 49, 52, 53
Patriot Act 147
People's Democracy Movement and the 1988 Uprising 74–78, 84, 90, 105, 135, 144–145, 153
Phone Maw 74
Plutonium 61, 62, 70
Press Scrutiny and Registration Division (Myanmar) 112–113
prisons/prisoners: in Myanmar 4, 44, 79, 84, 124, 132–133, 145; in North Korea, 4, 124, 130–131, 193
propaganda 34 106, 108; in Myanmar 92, 116; in North Korea 21, 102, 104, 111, 135
Propaganda and Agitation Department (North Korea) 111
U.S.S. *Pueblo* 50–51, 52
Pyongyang City 12

radio 114–16, 111, 126, 136
Radio and TV Broadcasting Committee (North Korea) 111
Radio Free Asia 116
Rakhine 33–34
Rangoon Bombing 53–54, 73
Rangoon Institute of Technology 74
Rangoon University: destruction of Student Union 41, 94, 129; and political movements 30, 94, 129; under British rule 13
Rason (Rajin-Sonbong) 56
Reagan, Ronald 145
Republic of Korea: and economic growth 6, 52; and Japan 21; and Korean War 25–26; and Myanmar 53–54, 73, 151; and North Korea 6, 9, 28, 50, 53, 54–55, 161, 155, 165; and Sunshine Policy 66, 161; and United States 25, 52, 53, 62
Revolutionary Council 41, 42, 45, 92
Rhee Sungman 25, 49
Rice, Condoleezza 2, 69, 84
Roadmap to Democracy 8, 106, 182–183
Rodong Sinmun 51
Rohingya 8

Sadae 98
Saebyol chat app 119
Saffron Revolution 82, 86, 122, 132, 148, 169
Samzidat 112
San S. Po 16
sanctions 3, 7, 58, 138–143; on Myanmar 81, 144–154; on North Korea 62–63, 73, 154–167, 189
Sandwich Reporting 113
Sangha 89, 95
Saudi Arabia 58, 140
Saw Maung 77, 80
Sein Lwin 75–77

Shan 16, 17, 27, 181; and insurgency 28 35, 40, 42–43, 95, 174; and World War II 22
Shan State Army 42
Shan State Progress Party 42
Shwedagon Pagoda 77, 181
Singapore 145, 147
Sino-Japanese War (First) 20
Six-Party Talks 68–70, 71, 156
So Shwe Thaik 40
Songun 47
South, Ashley 177
South Africa 58, 140
South Korea *see* Republic of Korea
Soviet Union 13, 24–25, 28, 52, 56, 59, 62, 97, 96, 151, 192; and North Korea's nuclear program 60–62
Special Branch 124
special economic zones: in Burma/Myanmar 110; in North Korea 55, 66
Specially Designated National 144, 189
State Law and Order Restoration Council (SLORC) 77, 79–80, 145, 175, 177–178
State Peace and Development Council (SPDC) 81, 149, 175
State Security Department 124
statistics: North Korea stops publishing 4
Status of Forces Agreement 52
Steinberg, David 144, 149, 153
Sunshine Policy 66, 161

Taedonggang Beer 95, 99
Tatmadaw 5, 39, 57, 94, 168, 187; and ceasefires 173–179; and coup d'etats 30, 39, 41, 94; and economy 45–47; and four cuts *see* four cuts; and insurgent groups 5, 31–32, 38; and transition 8, 86, 106, 124, 153, 182–183, 188; and violence against civilians 74–78, 83–84, 105
Telenor 119
television 114–116, 132
textile industry: in Myanmar 122, 148; in North Korea 102, 110, 160
Thailand 28, 42–43
Thakin Soe 32
Thakin Than Tun 32
Thakin Tin U 38
Than Shwe 80, 85, 123, 130, 150, 154, 168–169, 180
Thibaw, King 14
Thompson, Robert 170
Tin Oo 79
tourism: in Myanmar 7
2008 Constitution of Myanmar 8

2013 Telecommunications Act 7, 80, 113–114, 187–188

U Nu 28, 34, 36–38, 40, 41, 80, 91–92
U Thant 94
Union Solidarity and Development Association (USDA) 81
United Nations: in Burma/Myanmar 35, 85; command in Korea 191; Commission of Inquiry, North Korea 131, 127, 187, 193; during the Korean War 25, 38; estimates of refugees 171; and Rohingya Crisis 186; Security Council Resolutions 69, 73, 155, 157, 160 187; UNICEF 119
United States of America: and the Agreed Framework 64; and alliance 6, 13, 53, 191–192, 194; and cyclone Nargis 85; and division of Korea 24–25, 26, 55; first nuclear crisis 64, 62–67; and Imperial Japan 20; and Korean War 26, 28; and nuclear weapons 26, 193; and sanctions 7, 69, 73, 140, 144, 145, 147, 149–150, 152–153, 156, 167; second nuclear crisis 67–73; and the Tatmadaw 189; and Vietnam 51
United States Treasury 69, 144, 156, 161–162, 189
United Wa State Army 110, 173–174
Uppatasanti Pagoda 181
Uranium 61, 65, 67–68, 70–71, 156
U.S.S.R. *see* Soviet Union

Vietnam War 50–52
Voice of America 115–116

Wa 110, 173–174
Ward or Village Tract Administration Law 126
Win Naing Oo 78

Yangban 20
Yangon University *see* Rangoon University: Yangban
Yi Seong Gye 89
Yongbyon Nuclear Site 68–69, 71
Young Pioneer Corps 134
Yunnan 18, 35, 36, 44

Zaw Min 76

www.ingramcontent.com/pod-product-compliance
Ingram Content Group UK Ltd.
Pitfield, Milton Keynes, MK11 3LW, UK
UKHW041940140426
5217IPUK00014B/578